FREE SATURDAYS

Betté Pratt

Copyright © 2020 by Betté Pratt.

ISBN: Softcover   978-1-950596-58-4

All rights reserved. No part of this book may be reproduced or transmitted in any form or by any means, electronic or mechanical, including photocopying, recording, or by any information storage and retrieval system without express written permission from the author, except in the case of brief quotations embodied in critical reviews and certain other non-commercial uses permitted by copyright law.

All Scripture is from the NIV Translation.

Printed in the United States of America.

To order additional copies of this book, contact:
Bookwhip
1-855-339-3589
www.bookwhip.com

ONE

Roger sighed, in two weeks he must think up something for a Thanksgiving service. He always hated the holiday, sure, he could go home to Mom and Dad and gorge himself on her traditional turkey, stuffing and the works, or he could crash his sister's festivities and watch football with his brother-in-law, but what was the point? Both places were far from Vansville, Georgia and they really celebrated Thanksgiving. He was happy for them, they had their spouses and stuff to do in a together sort of way, he guessed that was something to be thankful for.

He stood on the threshold of the building he called his church he'd just shaken hands with the last lady to leave to fix her husband's Sunday dinner. If he turned around he'd look into the sanctuary, or he could look out the door and see the hardware store across the street where grumpy old Brad hung his hat and did as little as possible to keep his store running. Of course, there was always the option that he could go home to the log house he'd had built, but what was there for him to lift his spirits? Milk the cow? Toss scratch to the chickens? Or feed the dog and cat? Mmm, that really sounded like a fun thing to do on this dark, dismal Sunday noon.

Not even a month ago he'd attended and stood up with his good friend, Ramon DeLord when he'd married the vivacious and beautiful Sandy Bernard. That happening had done two things for him; it had taken away his only confidant his age in town, because what newly married man wants to listen to the rantings of some bachelor when he'd rather be spending all his time with his new wife? The other thing it had done for him was put that vivacious, beautiful woman out of his reach and made him want one for himself. If he could find a lady even half what Sandy was he'd be an eternally happy man.

But Vansville didn't even sport one unmarried woman unless she was a widow and twice his age. He wasn't looking for a wife he had to coddle from now to her grave! Besides, Widow Isabel wouldn't look at him except to criticize what he did or how he looked. He still remembered how humiliated he felt when she'd lighted from Sandy's van and told him almost in so many words to get his tail home and put on something appropriate for the concert to be held in his church. Never mind that he wasn't involved at all and could sit in the audience.

He turned his head and looked into the sanctuary. He decided it was a fine looking place, besides, now it even sported an in-tune piano, thanks to Derek Casbah. The building was old, it had been built before the Depression the date on the Cornerstone was 1925. When he'd come to town and set up his office in the little back room, he'd unearthed an old book. Actually, it was papers bound together by two cardboard covers with a heavy ribbon tied at the back edge. It was well and beautifully written in long hand, even the words on the cover. The first author was the original Bradford Thomas, the present hardware store owner's grandfather.

He sighed again as he looked at the warm cherry wainscoting. He guessed what he called a church service wasn't anything close to what Pastor Bradford Thomas conducted so many years ago. The little church had started in his home in 1920. They'd outgrown his living room and bought the corner lot in 1922. All the members had banded together and done what they did best to make the church what it was today, except for the brand new ramp that he'd had his men build more than two months ago. The reason for that ramp had married his best friend. Not that he was alone in the world, but it sure felt like it.

He reached across the back wall and flipped off the lights, walked out onto the tiny covered entryway and closed the door behind him, making sure it was locked. He wouldn't be back for another seven days. Since he had two good legs, it wasn't snowing or raining, he walked down the five steps to the sidewalk. It was November the gray sky reminded him that winter would be here soon. He'd go home and think about what he'd say on Thanksgiving another day. Maybe between now and then he'd come up with something up-beat, maybe he'd find it in his heart not to be so depressed. He could only hope....

When he arrived at home, even before he opened the door of the Jeep, he knew the bovine welcoming committee was there. Cow had her head in the air, her mouth was open and even though he couldn't hear her, Roger knew she was raising a ruckus. He sighed and turned the ignition off, then he heard her loud, "Mooooo!"

Roger opened his door and stepped out. As he closed the door, he said, "Cow, what is it you want? I fed you this morning when I milked you. You've got grass to munch on, now get on out in the field and fill your belly with that green stuff."

Obviously, Cow didn't like Roger's suggestion, she stood still. "Moooo!"

"Yeah," he grumbled, "mooo-ve it out of here!"

"Mommy," the three and a half year old coming from her daycare said solemnly, "we gots free days off next week, Teacher said. Does next week got free Saturdays, Mommy?"

In the entry hall, Raylyn held Heidi's warm coat and the little girl pushed her arms into the sleeves, as Raylyn said, "No, Pumpkin, next week is Thanksgiving week. Thanksgiving is on Thursday and it's a holiday. Lots of people travel on that weekend to see family and friends so they have Friday off and then there's the real Saturday."

"Oh. Is we trabilin?"

Raylyn bent her knees so she was on the same eye level as Heidi. She smiled at her child and zipped the coat, then wrapped her arms around the child and said, "Yes, Honey, we're going to see Grandma Isabel. I don't think you remember her, but she's a special lady. You'll love her, I know and she already loves you."

"Can I take Dollie?"

"Of course you can, Pumpkin, it'll be a long ride and you'll probably take a nap on the way. Dollie'll think it's awful if you leave her home and she has to sleep by herself. Besides, you'd miss her too much, too."

Heidi looked sternly at her mommy, putting her hands on her hips. "Mommy, I doesn't take naps in the daytime. Not no more, you know that!" Raylyn would not remind her child that daycare insisted all their children lie down after lunch. Heidi's teacher always told Raylyn what a good nap she took each day.

They walked outside and Raylyn opened the back door of her compact for her daughter to climb in, then, as she helped her buckle her seatbelt, she said, "I know, but you see, we must get up very early, probably before it gets light outside, and start driving. We'll stop for gas a couple of times and get lunch. It may even be dark before we get to Grandma Isabel's. You may be so tired of all that driving you'll fall asleep."

"Mommy, I will not!" the child said, adamantly, kicking the back of the front seat hard enough that Raylyn was glad she wasn't sitting there yet.

Raylyn closed the backdoor, opened the front and slid behind the wheel. "Okay, we'll see what happens. Maybe we'll get there before dark."

"Even if we doesn't Mommy, I won't sleep."

Raylyn decided it wasn't worth fighting about. Yes, if she was excited enough Heidi'd be wide awake all twelve hours. Raylyn almost sighed out loud it would be an unending nightmare if all she had to do was sit back there with her dollie and her favorite books. She'd lose interest long before they left the state of Michigan.

"Mommy, is you gettin' me a new daddy some day?"

Raylyn gasped. *Where had that idea come from?* "Heidi! Why do you ask?"

"'Cause my friend Angel's gettin' a new daddy for Christmas. I be real good if I gots a daddy for Christmas."

Raylyn's knuckles turned white as she gripped the steering wheel in a death grip. "Heidi, honey, Mommy's not even seeing a man and you can't get a new daddy if your mommy's not dating a man. Honey, you know Daddy went to heaven when you were a baby, but he still loves you from there, you know."

"Mommy, my Sunday school teacher said it not the same."

Raylyn was still trying to cope with the senseless death of her husband. He hadn't had to enlist, but he'd wanted to defend his country against terrorism, he said. She sighed, "I know it isn't, Honey, but I haven't found a man I'd like to date and get married to. Can you be patient a while longer, please?"

Heidi sighed, "I try, Mommy." Her voice brightened, "But it be a long time till Christmas, I write a letter to Santa and ask him to send us a daddy!"

"I suppose. I guess it's worth a try, Honey."

Raylyn turned the corner onto her gravel driveway and pulled up to the closed garage door. She put the stick in park, then got out and muscled the door up. For a change, it stayed the first time and Raylyn hurried back to the running car. She pulled inside the garage and turned the key and at the same time heard the click of the seatbelt from the back seat. She and Heidi opened their doors at the same time.

When the car doors were shut and the garage door was grumbling down, Heidi asked, "Mommy, you gots paper for my letter to Santa?"

"Heidi, I have some paper, but you know Santa's at the North Pole. That's a very long ways away, he might not get it."

"Mommy," Heidi said, as if speaking to a slow learner, "Santa alays gets letters from good girls. You know that."

Raylyn sighed, oh to be young and innocent again! "Yes, pumpkin, I know."

She'd believed in Santa once, she'd even left cookies and milk by the Christmas tree when she was only a year older than Heidi, but that seemed like a lifetime ago. That was before her dad had died of a gun shot and her mom had to work twelve hour days to put food on the table for her brothers still at home. It was also before Dan had been killed in an ambush in the Middle East two years ago. In fact, she almost hated to think about Christmas, she'd only gone through the motions for Heidi last year. Just getting through Thanksgiving seemed like a hurdle that might be too high. That was one reason she was going to Vansville, Georgia to visit Gramma Isabel. She guessed she did have a few things to be thankful for, really, but right now she wasn't sure what they were.

The house smelled good when Raylyn opened the garage door into the kitchen. She had taken the fifteen minutes to start her crock pot with her special recipe for beef and noodles this morning. Thursdays were always hard to get a decent supper because she didn't go to work before ten, so there were always chores she left for Thursday morning and there was choir practice at the church at seven thirty. As soon as she and Heidi had their coats, hats and mittens off, Raylyn pulled plates from the cabinet.

"Heidi, go wash your hands in the bathroom quickly, then come help me set the table so we can eat real soon."

Heidi made a face, but said, "Yes, Mommy."

When she came back, Raylyn had the plates on the table, napkins and silverware on the placemats. Heidi pushed her special stool up to the counter then climbed up to get the plastic glasses from the high cupboard. As she handed Raylyn the glasses, she asked, "Heidi, why'd you make a face when I told you to wash up?"

Heidi hadn't dried her hands too well they still dripped water on the all-weather carpet. "Mommy, Teacher had me wash up afor you came. I wasn't dirty."

"At this time of year you can't get your hands too clean."

"Well, 'course you can!" Heidi huffed, as she jumped from the counter. "Mommy, Teacher alays rubs stuff on her hands afer she washes hers. She says it keeps her skin from drying up! It'd fall off, right?"

The pretty young woman smiled at her daughter. "Honey, that doesn't mean they'd fall off, or anything. Having dry skin only makes them feel bad. People don't like to touch somebody's hands if they have dry skin."

"I don't wanna get dry skin. Mommy, I hungry, we gonna eat now?"

"As soon as I pour your milk, Honey."

"Mommy, you doesn't drink milk, how come?"

Did three year olds always ask so many questions? Did I ask as many when I was her age? Raylyn answered, "I'm not that crazy about milk, Sweety. I drank a lot when I was a little girl growing up just like you do and when you were growing in my tummy I drank lots, but I grew up and I'm not carrying a baby now, so I drink tea instead."

"Oh, 'K."

The little girl gave her mommy a big smile and climbed up on the special chair that let her reach the table comfortably. Of course, it wasn't a *high* chair three and a half year olds didn't do *high* chairs. Importantly, she shook out the huge napkin beside her place, laid it on her lap and said, "Mommy, if you gots me a daddy, you could get me a baby sister. Angel's gonna get a baby sister when she gets a new daddy."

Raylyn nearly choked on the mouthful of tea she'd sipped from her too full glass. Quickly she set the glass down on the counter and covered her mouth before she sprayed tea all over the counter and the floor. Convulsively, she swallowed the mouthful and dragged in her breath. "Honey, I need to find the daddy first," she gasped. "It might happen that this daddy that you want so badly won't have any children."

Unconcerned that her mommy had nearly choked on her drink, Heidi waved her hand and said, "Santa make sure you get him, don't worry."

Raylyn brought her tea to the table and slid into her seat. Heidi said, "Mommy, I wanna pray for supper."

Raylyn took Heidi's hand and said, "Okay, but not too long, we only have a few minutes before we must leave for church for choir practice."

Heidi's head fell to her chest. She pulled her hand from Raylyn's, clasped her hands in front of her forehead and said, "Dear God, thank You for tis food that Mommy fixded tis morning. I real glad You didn't let it burn or get real hot to catch our house on fire, we gots to live here, You know. Bless Mommy in choir tonight help her sing good, so Pastor Leonard lets her sing at Christmas. And dear God, make Mommy start seein' a man so I can have a daddy for Christmas, Amen."

Raylyn was shaking her head as she opened her eyes and raised her head. She knew that once her daughter got something in her brain that she wouldn't let go of it. This one about a daddy might be in circulation for a long time. Raylyn had no idea where it had come from, well maybe from daycare, but since she didn't know any single Christian men, it might be around for a very long time.

They were barely finished loading the dishwasher with supper dishes when Heidi said, "Hurry, Mommy, we not be late for choir practus."

That night as Raylyn tucked Heidi into bed, the little girl said, sleepily, "Mommy, I 'cited to trabil for Tankgibin'!"

"Yes, so am I. Now get to sleep, morning comes soon."

"'Night, Mommy." The child's eyes were already closed. She hugged her dollie and turned on her side. A long sigh left her lips as Raylyn turned out the light.

"'Night, Sweetheart," Raylyn whispered. Since she'd had a full day at work, Raylyn wasn't far behind Heidi. In fact, she took a long soak in the tub then crawled into bed.

The phone rang and as soon as Roger answered, the voice didn't identify himself, only said, "Since you worked on that ramp and did such a good job over Labor Day, how'd you like to come help paint our new bedroom suite?"

Roger leaned against the counter and crossed his ankles. "Listen, friend, putting stain on some boards so they don't rot doesn't make me a qualified painter to cover your walls. Besides, what's the matter with the artist who lives at your house?"

"Sure it does! It's not like you're going to get a brush or put any detail on anything. You get a roller that covers a foot at a time. You can go up and down or side to side, any old way you want. Besides, my wife's cooking spaghetti and you're invited to stay for supper. Now, just turn me down! Besides, this is man's work, that artist's brushes are much too small."

"Hmm, well, I think I could spare some time this afternoon and evening. When do we start this task?"

"Any time you get here."

Roger looked at his watch. "It'll take more'n four hours to paint one room?"

"I thought I said bedroom *suite*. That's more'n one room, Man."

"Ahhh, I'll be there soon."

"Good, we'll be watching for you."

"Mmm, figured as much," he grumbled.

Roger replaced the receiver on the wall receptacle then collapsed on his chair at the table. Why did he tell the man he'd come over?

He'd tried to stay away from town any time he was sure that light blue van was around. The lady who drove it drove him crazy! He wished she had a twin somewhere, even one in a wheelchair, he didn't care! Now he'd committed himself to go to the house where she lived, of all things! He sighed he must be a glutton for punishment. She was not only beautiful and vivacious, but every time she saw him she tried to foist her religion on him! He had enough religion, wasn't he the man the church people in town asked to come run their church and paid him to give his talk each Sunday?

He looked at his watch again. He'd been moping for fifteen minutes, he'd better get on the move or his phone would be ringing again. Now that the man was married and had left the trail for the winter, everything he put his hand to had to be done yesterday. This was Georgia! People took their time in the south, didn't they? Not that he was a native, or anything, but he still liked the slower pace. He stood up and stretched, then reached for his coat and shrugged into it and wrapped his scarf around his neck. He grabbed his keys that hung by the back door and sauntered out. Curly, his mutt greeted him with his tongue hanging and his tail wagging.

"Curly, I'm going to help some guy paint his house. It's that house with the beautiful woman, you know. Why don't you find us some females?" Watching the lazy dog collapse on the porch, Roger sighed, "Maybe that's too hard a task for you. Never mind."

Roger pulled open the Jeep door and slumped behind the wheel. As he started up, Curly lumbered to his feet, wagged his tail once, then flopped back down and rested his chin on his paws. Roger started the car and shook his head, as the dog closed his eyes. A dog's life couldn't be that hard that he needed a nap in the middle of the day. Just as he pulled the stick down into drive, Linus, his cat, came along and climbed up on Curly's back. After giving the dog's back a good needing, he slumped down on top of him, then put his head down on his paws and closed his eyes. Disgusted, Roger turned the wheel and left.

Roger drove down his long, rutted driveway onto the county road and headed into Vansville. Ramon and Sandy lived on the far side of the town, so Roger had to drive through, passing the hardware store, across from his church, the post office and the grocery store.

He wondered if he should stop and buy something, some little thing to take to the newlyweds, since this was the first time he'd be in their home since the wedding last month.

He shrugged and pulled to the curb, shut off his Jeep and headed inside. "Hello!" came a voice from the back of the store.

"Hi, yourself, Alex, how's it going?"

When Roger reached the counter, Alex gave the young man a genuine smile and said, "It's doin' fine, young fella. Had my favorite customer in today. She always makes the day worth waking up to."

"Who's that?"

"Why, Sandy, of course!"

Of course, Roger thought sourly. "I'm on my way to their house to help Ramon paint and then eat some of Sandy's famous spaghetti. Since I haven't been to the house since they were married, I thought I'd stop in and take a little something."

Nodding, Alex said, "Mighty fine idea there, young man. What'll it be? You know I have a lot of good stuff here."

Roger turned slowly around and looked down the aisles of the small store. At first, he didn't see anything of interest then he saw the refrigerator section. "How about some of those poseys you're keeping cold in that refrigerator?"

"Sure! You go pick out what you want and I'll wrap them up and cover 'em good. Hot house plants don't like this real cold weather, you know." As Roger opened the door of the refrigerator to get his bouquet he wondered how cold was 'real' cold, he'd never stand a chance in refrigerator cold. However, he didn't comment, what was the point? He guessed the store keeper knew more about keeping flowers than he did.

Roger left with his flowers, wishing he was going to some single woman's house with his bouquet. He shook his head. When had he become so lonely for a woman? It wasn't hard to remember, he'd been fine until he'd met Sandy Bernard at Isabel's cabin while she practiced for the concert at his church. At that moment he'd morphed into a discontented single man. He drove slowly trying to remember, he hadn't had a date since he came to Vansville! Maybe he should go to some of the ministerial meetings in Blairsville maybe he'd meet a woman.

He pulled onto Ramon's driveway that was free of cars. Straight ahead was what used to be Ramon's office, but now sported a double garage door. He did a double take, the last time he'd been here there'd been one normal size door where people walked in and out and two windows, now there was a garage door? As he shut off the engine he contemplated that. It made sense, the room was at the same level as the driveway and it was big enough to make a double garage out of it. The whole time Sandy had been working as Ramon's receptionist she'd had to park on the blacktop, making sure there was enough room so she could lower her lift to the ground and wheel herself off without another car too close. Goodness knows she'd gotten soaked many times going from that office to her van in those weeks.

"Good thinking," he mumbled. "Give the guy credit."

He climbed out of his Jeep, bringing the flowers with him then stood on the parking lot wondering where he should go to get in. A shiver went up his back, November air was penetrating. Before he'd taken one step the door down the walk opened and Sandy's smiling face appeared. "Come on, Roger, it's cold, surely you aren't old and senile and set in your ways so much that you can't walk to this door instead of trying to go in our garage."

Roger grinned at the beautiful young woman. "You talked me into it, Sandy. I'm on my way." As he reached her, he said, "What's this Ramon's talking about, a bedroom suite? He's changed his office into a garage? Man! Will wonders never cease!"

She grinned back at him. "It's all in whom you marry, Roger."

Mmm, yeah, I'm sure that's true, he thought. He walked up and handed her the covered package that was obviously flowers. "Here, I thought I'd better bring a house warming gift."

Sandy took the paper wrapped flowers and backed up so that Roger could come in, then began ripping off the paper. When the flowers appeared, she exclaimed, "This is perfectly super of you, Roger! Ramon!" she called, "Your slave is here, but he brought flowers for me."

Roger looked at the bubbly woman in front of him and said, "Don't you have a sister - a twin sister - you could invite to come for Thanksgiving?"

"Roger, I have no twin sister. I have a sister who's in nursing school. For being six years younger than me, she acts like she's at least ten years older, maybe even fifteen. She has eyes for no one she will make one whale of a *single* nurse. Besides, she's determined that she's to go to Africa or India as a missionary. She's determined to work among the poor and needy, she'll find her fill in both those places, I'm sure."

As Ramon rounded the corner into the living room, Roger said, not loud enough for either Sandy or Ramon to hear, "Such a pity."

Ramon slapped his friend on the back and exclaimed, "Good to see you, Man! You've kept out of sight for a long time."

"Yes, well, you've been busy since I last saw you."

Ramon grabbed Roger's hand and pumped it vigorously. "Not that busy! I took out a mortgage on the house and had the garage and the addition enclosed professionally. With cold weather just around the corner, Sandy had to be able to get in and out of the van where it's warm and dry, so we had that done first."

Sandy followed the men as they walked to the new suite. As Roger looked around at the large room, Sandy chuckled and said, "I'm good with a brush, you know, but Ramon says it's too small to do much good on the walls in this new part. I keep threatening to put an eagle or a vulture at the head of his side of the bed, but he says I can't reach high enough for him to see it over top of the headboard."

His eyes twinkling, Roger nodded and said, "Since you don't come to my church, I could take down some of the ramp and build you a scaffold so you could paint your picture higher up on the wall. There's a man in my church who's good with lighting, he could install some of those little lights in the bird's eyes that'd make it look like it's coming after him at night. I'd be glad to find out about that."

"Listen, Man," Ramon grumbled. "whose side are you on, anyway?"

Sandy chuckled. "I'd better leave you two painters to your work. I'll get my spaghetti sauce going in a few minutes. Shall I bring you fellas some tea?"

"That's a good idea, Love, why don't you do that?"

When the chair motor faded, Roger grumbled, "You are so lucky!"

"Oh, I know! I thank God every day for her."

Later, after eating until he could hold no more spaghetti, Roger groaned as he stood up from the table. "What a meal! Sandy, you out-did yourself again! Man, how do you keep your figure with this kind of cooking all the time?"

Ramon didn't blush, not with his dark complexion, but he was clearly embarrassed. "Well, ahh, I walk a lot and I've been working on that suite a lot, too. I get a lot of that up and down movement, you know."

Hearing the discomfort in Ramon's voice, Sandy quickly changed the subject and said, "So, Roger how'd you like to have a concert as payment for working so hard this afternoon? Maybe it'd relax you enough so you can fall asleep when you get home."

Rubbing his full belly, Roger exclaimed, "Sandy, that dinner was payment enough! But I'll never turn down your concert. Especially since you won't come to my church and play on my newly tuned piano."

Leading the way into the living room, Sandy wasn't smiling when she said, "Roger, you preach the gospel and we'll gladly come to your church."

"Sandy, I tell 'em what they want to hear."

Picking up the black pouch from the music ledge, Sandy looked at Roger without a hint of a smile and said, "Roger, ever since Adam and Eve in the Garden of Eden the Devil has been telling people what they *want* to hear. God's Word tells them what they *need* to hear that will change their lives and when they die allow them to spend eternity in heaven." She slipped the pouch over the back of her chair and moved a slight bit so she was at the right distance to play.

"Yeah, I think you've told me that before."

Raising her hands over the keys, she turned her head and said, "It hasn't made a difference yet, has it?"

Before he could answer, Sandy turned her head back to the piano. Only seconds later beautiful music started flowing from her fingers and filled the room, but for several minutes the sound was lost on him, as he contemplated what Sandy had said and asked. He'd been to seminary, for crying out loud! She was a self taught woman. What did she know about preaching, or what to say from a pulpit?

Music flowed around him and finally he relaxed in the easy chair next to the couch where Ramon lounged. Both men raised their feet and put them on the coffee table. Ramon had closed his eyes already when Roger tuned in to the beautiful music it was something he'd never heard before. As the tones flowed around him he couldn't help but feel a little jealous of Ramon, the man could hear music like this any time he wanted.

He let out a long sigh and had just closed his eyes to absorb the music more fully when, without an interruption, the music changed to something familiar, something he hadn't listened to in many years, but he remembered from his childhood. By the third chord, the words were sliding through his mind.

> "On a hill far away stood an old rugged cross.
> The emblem of suffering and shame,
> And I love that old cross where the dearest and best
> For a world of lost sinners was slain.
> So I'll cherish the old rugged cross
> Till my trophies at last I lay down,
> I will cling to the old rugged cross,
> And exchange it some day for a crown."

He opened his eyes and looked at the young woman who had raised her hands from the keyboard and was now turned enough to look at him. As the music died away, she asked, "Roger, when was the last time you told your audience about that old rugged cross and the One who died on it to take away the sins of the world?"

Those blue eyes bored into him and Roger's gut clenched, the huge helping of spaghetti turned into an enormous rock of cold granite. His feet hit the floor and he was out of the chair in an instant. Without a smile or a backward glance at either Ramon or Sandy, he rushed to the front door, grabbed his coat and before he had it all the way on, he had the door open. Only second's later it slammed behind him, but not before he heard the familiar strains of 'Amazing Grace' coming from the living room. Roger ran to his Jeep, yanked the door open and climbed behind the wheel. A scant minute later he was spinning his tires out of the parking lot, turning on two wheels onto the street. He roared through town as if the demons of hell were chasing him, indeed, probably Someone was chasing him.

As the front door slammed, Sandy continued to play the old hymn until the end of the verse, but Ramon left the couch and came up behind her. Putting his hands on her shoulders, he said, softly, "Perhaps you were a little hard on him, Sweetheart?"

Still leaning on the little black pouch, so the chord lingered, she raised her hands and tilted her head back to look up at him. A sad smile graced her lips, as she said, "Honey, remember I told you the responsibility of those souls he's leading falls on him? No, I don't think I was too hard on him at all."

Much to Raylyn's surprise, her boss came to her office Wednesday noon and said, "Raylyn, shut 'er down, wrap it up and get out of here! I know you're planning a long drive for Thanksgiving. What if you started this afternoon and finished up tomorrow, wouldn't that be a help with your little one?"

"Maxine! I never thought of doing that, but it'd be great! I just sent my final draft to the printer. I'll take a minute to wash my coffee cup and I'll be out of here. Thanks so very much!"

The older lady smiled and patted Raylyn's shoulder. "No problem, girl, at Thanksgiving I love to make someone's day. Have a good trip and don't show until first thing on Tuesday."

"Maxine!" Raylyn jumped from her chair and hugged the other lady. "Terrific! I can go to church with Grandma Isabel! That'll be such a treat. Thanks!"

"Oh, you're welcome."

Smiling, the older lady left Raylyn's office and disappeared down the hall. Raylyn grabbed her mug and raced after her, but turned toward the kitchenette to wash her mug. It was twelve fifteen when Raylyn grabbed her purse from the bottom drawer and her shoe bag from under her desk and her coat from her coat tree and rushed to the door of her office. She pulled it closed behind her and left the office area of the hospital.

Raylyn's foot was heavy as she left the big parking garage and headed for the daycare where Heidi was. She took a deep breath and raised her foot from the gas pedal a fraction. There was no need to get a ticket for speeding and be delayed. She still had a few last minute things she needed to throw into their luggage before she could be on the road. Even though she was so excited and couldn't imagine stuffing something in her stomach, she knew she and Heidi needed to eat lunch before they left. A drive-thru didn't work with a little one in the back seat.

Raylyn parked on the street in front of the daycare. Quickly, she went to the door and pushed it open. Young happy voices greeted her, even though she couldn't see any of the children from where she stood. There were so many, she couldn't distinguish Heidi's voice from all the rest. She made her way toward the voices, her heart banging more quickly in her chest the closer she came to them. She could start the trip this afternoon and maybe even get to Vansville yet today! Well, long after dark, actually.

She walked into the big room as Clair, the cook, set a large covered pan on a serving table and started to lift the lid. At that minute, Heidi saw her mommy. She opened her arms wide and screamed, "Mommy! You comed early!"

Raylyn grabbed the child, hugged her and said, "Yes, Pumpkin, my boss gave me off. You get your coat and I'll tell Teacher I'm taking you now."

"'K!"

Raylyn turned as Heidi ran toward the coatroom. Before Raylyn found the director, Heidi was back beside her with one arm in her coat, the wrong arm, of course. Martha Murray came up to them and said, "I heard Heidi, so I came. You're able to leave already? No more work this afternoon? That's great!"

"That's right, Marty! Maxine gave me this afternoon off and I don't have to be back to work until Tuesday, so Heidi won't be back until then." Raylyn pulled Heidi's hood up over her hair and stood up. "Marty, have a great Thanksgiving! I'll see you."

The director smiled at Raylyn. "Of course, Raylyn, you do the same and drive carefully. It's a long ways. Don't try to drive when you're too exhausted to know where you are. That never works well for us girls."

"I have CDs galore that'll keep me awake. Besides, I'm so excited to see my grandma! It's been a couple of years since I have."

They waved and Marty said, "See you next week, Heidi."

Heidi waved. "'K, Ms. Marty!"

Free Saturdays

Heidi followed Raylyn out the door. She skipped along beside her mommy and bounced from one foot to the other as Raylyn opened the back door. Heidi scrambled inside into her seat, grabbed the shoulder strap of the seatbelt and pulled it over her while Raylyn took the buckle to snap it in place. Raylyn was excited, too, she pushed the back door closed and opened the front door almost in the same instant. Seconds later she merged with traffic anxious to get home.

After a quick lunch, gathering Heidi's toys and books that she insisted had to go and zipping the two pull-behind suitcases, Raylyn hurried everything out to her car in the garage. Loading the things in the warmer place was much more to her liking than taking them out the front door and crossing the lawn to the trunk in below freezing weather.

When Heidi was safely buckled into the back seat with her dollie and books close around her, Raylyn raised the garage door and started up. It hadn't been raining when they came home from the daycare, but as she stepped out to lower the garage door, she felt a fine mist on her cheeks and her heart sank. She lived in Michigan and knew how to drive in winter, but driving on icy streets never had been a favorite past time.

As she waited for the garage door to hit the ground so she could lock it, she murmured, "Father, God, keep us safe. You know I don't like to drive when the roads are wet and the bank thermometer said it was twenty-nine degrees. It must have just started misting, so the roads will be slippery really soon. Take us safely all the way to Vansville, Georgia. Thank You, in Jesus' Name, amen."

With hands that weren't quite steady, Raylyn slid back into her car. A little voice from the back said, "Mommy, it raining."

"I know, Sweety, Mommy must drive very carefully. Since it started since we came home from the daycare, I hope we can drive out of it pretty soon. Can you be really quiet and read your book while Mommy drives for a while?"

"'Course, Mommy, I be real good."

Raylyn looked at her daughter in the rearview mirror and smiled at her. "Thanks, Honey, I really appreciate that."

"Yes, Mommy."

Raylyn put the stick in reverse and backed slowly out onto the street. She had good tires, Dan had made sure she knew how to tell when she needed new ones and she'd had these put on only a few months ago. She'd had the car serviced not long ago, when she'd decided to make the long trip to Georgia at this time of year. As she pulled the stick down another two notches into drive, she swallowed a sigh. Didn't the company she worked for have an office in the south? That would do two things; get her away from the memories and the freezing weather.

When she finally reached the bypass, the rain hadn't stopped, but the roads were so heavily traveled that they were wet, not slippery. When she realized that, she quickly accelerated until she reached the speed limit. Other cars zipped by her, but she decided not to join them. She'd heard on the radio on the way from work to the daycare that many more policemen would be patrolling the roads this weekend. She was sure that would be true all the way. Why put a damper on the weekend by getting a ticket that she didn't have money to pay for anyway?

When she finally left the bypass and was driving on the interstate south, she looked in the rearview mirror again. It had been so quiet in the back seat she wanted to thank Heidi for being such a good girl. However, she smiled and kept silent Heidi was sound asleep, her dollie snug in her arms and her head on the pillow Raylyn had brought.

"Thank You, Lord," she murmured, and drove on.

She was right, the rain stopped a few miles south of the bypass, but the clouds were dark and heavy. She knew, just by looking at them, that they could start dumping moisture on her at any time. Still, she determined not to speed, but to go with the flow. The farther she went from the city, the faster the traffic went.

She'd looked at her dash clock when she left her driveway. It would be easy to remember, she'd done it all, left work, picked up Heidi, come home and fed them, then packed the car in just over an hour. Her clock read two thirty. It had taken an hour to get on the interstate. According to her calculations, it would take twelve hours from now to get to Vansville, Georgia. What she hadn't decided since she'd started so early in the day was whether to drive straight through and get to her grandma's house at two or three in the morning or stop and try to find a motel room. On Thanksgiving weekend that might prove to be an impossibility. She'd known for a long time that Thanksgiving weekend was the most traveled holiday. She sighed she was joining thousands of travelers. She drove until she was cramped, but she wanted Heidi to sleep as long as she would. It would be so much easier on her if she slept rather than watch the road or get bored with her toys for such a long trip.

Several hours later, Raylyn saw Heidi become restless and her eyes opened sleepily. Her gas gauge registered nearly empty, so she pulled off at the next exit, happy for the break herself.

"Mommy, it stop raining!"

"Yes, I'm really glad. Do you need to go potty?"

"Oh, yes! Right now!"

Raylyn pulled up to the building, she could get gas after they went to the restroom, but Heidi had to go when she had to go. Raylyn grabbed her keys from the ignition and opened her door as Heidi opened hers. They rushed inside together and found the restroom. Raylyn was very glad there was no line she and Heidi were the only ones in the room.

When they left the restroom, Raylyn found some decent snacks and purchased them, then took them to the car. She backed into an empty gas slot and started the gas, then helped Heidi to open several of the snacks. At least she could start to eat before she had to be belted in. When she finished pumping the gas, she helped Heidi into her seatbelt and spread out her food close by. Heidi was happily munching when Raylyn climbed behind the wheel, arranged her own snacks and headed back to the interstate.

Of course, the day before Thanksgiving was not the shortest day of the year, but with the dark clouds, dusk came early. They'd eaten some good snacks and her car went a very long ways on a tankful of gas. Their normal supper time came and went and Raylyn kept driving, thankful that Heidi didn't know how to tell time yet. When Heidi said she had to go potty again was time enough to stop.

At her usual time to go to bed, Heidi had to go potty, so Raylyn pulled off at the next exit. It was dark, but the station was well lighted. This time, the gas pumps weren't crowded, so she pulled into a slot then took Heidi inside. They bought some snacks again, these were mostly for Raylyn, but there was one that Heidi liked a lot. Raylyn opened it for her before she started pumping her gas and Heidi had finished before the gas shut off. Raylyn made Heidi as comfortable as possible inside her seatbelt and hoped the child would soon fall asleep. Raylyn wasn't tired she determined to drive as far as she could tonight. The earlier she arrived in Vansville tomorrow, the better she liked it.

Raylyn opened her snacks and left the station, then drove back onto the interstate. It was eight o'clock by her dash clock. If she calculated right, she had between six and seven hours to drive. She'd gotten up at six to get them both out of the house by seven thirty this morning. She was realistic enough to know that she'd probably not make it tonight, but she was pretty sure that the longer she drove the less her chance of getting a motel room anywhere along the interstate. One of those rock and hard place situations.

Heidi fell asleep almost as soon as the car settled into the rhythm of the road. Raylyn could hear her breathing and was glad. Raylyn reached to the visor over her head and pulled out her favorite CD, then pushed it into the player on the dash. Her favorite Christian artist began singing her favorite songs and she hummed along. If she'd been by herself, she'd have sung the songs, but with Heidi asleep, she hummed quietly. It was after midnight and she was still wide awake. By now, the clouds had moved off and the moon was shining. Of course, the roads were bare and she was glad.

Vansville was a little town, quite a ways from the interstate. Blairsville wasn't even close to the interstate and it was much larger than Vansville. Raylyn turned off at the right exit and as soon as she found the right highway she knew she was in trouble. There had been lots of traffic on the interstate, with headlights shining into her car, now she was on a two lane road and cars were few and far between, especially at this hour. She yawned, fatigue set in only moments later. With Heidi asleep in the back seat, she knew she couldn't turn her CD player up to top volume to keep her awake. Maybe she'd stop at the pull-off and take a nap for a little bit.

TWO

Roger sat in his office behind the sanctuary Wednesday before Thanksgiving trying to get some thoughts together. The people of the church wanted a service in the morning while their turkeys roasted and he tried to come up with something to say. He'd put it off and put it off, hoping to get some inspiration. So far, the only inspiration was the words of the hymn that had bombarded him while Sandy played the music that evening last week. That night he'd fled to his hillside home and had only come to town on Sunday to lead the worship service at the church. He'd sat on the platform during the praise team's songs, but he hadn't felt like participating. He'd read his prepared reading and then shook hands at the back of the church as his regulars filed out. He'd smiled, but it felt pasted on and his face was tired as he went home afterward.

As he sat behind his desk now, he pulled his large book from which he took most of his readings in front of him. He opened to the table of contents and looked for 'Thanksgiving.' There were readings listed, but as he read them he remembered using all three on previous Thanksgivings and none of them appealed to him. At the top of the page there was a number next to the word 'Thanksgiving'. That drew his eyes to the bottom of the page. The note said, "See also Psalms 100 & 136." He hadn't read the Old Testament in a long time, maybe he could think up a word or two to add to the Psalm.

Roger looked around for a Bible, but after searching for fifteen minutes he realized that the only one in the church was the big pulpit Bible that sat Sunday after Sunday on the table below the pulpit. He didn't even have one of his own in the church! He left his office, went into the auditorium and walked to the table. He was ashamed when he picked it up and turned with it that dust flew off around him from the pages that were open. There was so much that it made him sneeze. After he blew off the remaining dust, he took the heavy Book back to his office, turned to the book of Psalms and found 100.

He began to read:

"Shout for joy to the LORD, all the earth.
Serve the LORD with gladness, come before him with joyful songs.
Know that the LORD is God.
It is he who made us, and we are his; we are his people,
the sheep of his pasture.
Enter his gates with thanksgiving and his courts with praise;
Give thanks to him and praise his name.
For the LORD is good and his love endures forever;
His faithfulness continues through all generations."

He sat down at his desk, laid the open Bible down in front of him and folded his hands over it. He bowed his head and tears welled up in his eyes. Brokenly, he finally said, "Well, God, I guess I've been away for a long, long time and I don't have much to be thankful for myself, but these words say Your Love endures forever and Your faithfulness continues through all generations. I guess that means from my great-grandfather all the way to me. I guess You meant for me to find these words today so I can use them tomorrow for these people who'll come to hear what I have to say to them. Thanks."

He raised his head and wiped his eyes, pulled a piece of paper on top of the page opposite Psalm 100 and picked up a pen. For the next fifteen minutes he couldn't write fast enough to keep up with his thoughts. He filled the page and put a period after the last word. His hand was cramped. He was finished and he knew, even without rereading, that what he would say would be the best he'd ever used from any pulpit. At long last, his heart was at peace.

When Raylyn left the interstate for the highway to Blairsville, she'd fought sleep until she'd gone through the city then looked for the pull-off. At the small parking area, she drifted in and managed to put the lever into park. Her eyes drifted closed immediately, she couldn't have held them open another instant. Twenty minutes later, the sound of a car going by was enough to wake her. After her nap she pulled back on the road and kept on. This close, she knew she had to make it, even if they had to sleep in her car the rest of the night. Raylyn drove on, but soon the streetlights of Vansville appeared. She was exhausted, but she saw the light on her grandma's porch and sighed in relief. She turned onto the gravel parking lot and pulled up in front of the small house. It was three o'clock in the morning.

She looked from the porch light down the sides of the house, but couldn't see a light inside and wondered if she should go to the door, but Grandma Isabel had left the light on, so the door might be unlocked. She wouldn't lose anything if she tried the door and found it locked, but she yearned for a decent bed, so she opened her door and grabbed her purse. The dome light made Heidi stir and soon her eyes opened.

"Mommy, is we done trabilin?" the child asked, sleepily.

"Yes, Sweety, grab your dollie while I get our luggage. Grandma Isabel left the light on, so I think maybe we can get inside. We'll see what happens then."

"'K, Mommy," Heidi said around a yawn.

Heidi's seatbelt clicked as she grabbed her dollie and as many books as her arms would hold. Her door opened as Raylyn went to the trunk and pulled the lid up. Heidi was out of the car as Raylyn lifted the two suitcases from the trunk. When everything was closed up, Heidi held her dollie and books close and walked beside Raylyn as she walked up the walk to the steps that led to Isabel's porch. The two suitcases bumped up the steps behind them, even though Raylyn tried to be as quiet as possible, she was too tired to carry the heavy bags.

The minute they stepped onto the porch the door flew open, startling both Raylyn and Heidi. The lady with salt and pepper hair had a huge smile on her face and her arms wide open. She exclaimed, "I had a feeling you'd come tonight! Get in here now! It's much too cold to stand out there one more minute."

Heidi didn't wait for her mommy, she rushed over the threshold, but Raylyn pulled the suitcases inside and Isabel gave the door a shove. Obediently it closed. Letting go of the luggage handles, Raylyn exclaimed, "Grandma Isabel, it's so good to see you!" She threw herself into her grandma's arms and felt the warmth immediately. After an instant she pulled back and said, "Grandma, remember Heidi?"

Isabel squatted down immediately. Pulling the little girl close, she looked at the child lovingly and said, "Of course I remember Heidi! She's getting so big and she's so pretty, just like you, Child!" Releasing her, Isabel stood up. "Come on, I know you're exhausted, I've made up the beds in my guest room and turned down the covers. All you have to do is find your night clothes and fall into bed. I won't even tempt you with any food, just the bed."

"Grandma, that's terrific! We are tired." Raylyn couldn't help the sigh that escaped, as she reached for the handles of their luggage.

Isabel helped Raylyn with their coats, then started down the short hall and said, over her shoulder, "Of course you are! We'll talk in the morning. The church on the corner is having a Thanksgiving service at eleven, so sleep as late as you want," Isabel went in a room to flick a switch for the bedside lamp.

"Thanks, Grandma," Raylyn sighed, as she looked at the inviting bed. "Grandma, this is super! Thanks so much!"

Seconds later, while Raylyn found both hers and Heidi's pajamas, Isabel padded across the hall to her room. Heidi's eyes were nearly shut as she crawled into the bed, pulled her dollie close and sighed as Raylyn pulled the covers over her, kissed her forehead, but she was already asleep. Raylyn turned to the other bed and soon she fell asleep in the comfortable bed. Even though Isabel wasn't a very good sleeper, she fell asleep in minutes, glad that her precious granddaughter and great-grand-daughter had arrived safely. She would love and pamper them for as long as they could stay. Only moments after her guests arrival, the house was dark and quiet.

At dawn, Roger heard his cow moo between the house and the shed that passed for his barn. It sounded like she was right under his window, but of course, that couldn't be, there was a fence outside the barn the wide driveway came between the fence and the house. He groaned, but bounded out of bed. He knew that having farm animals meant rising early was a way of life. He shrugged into his farm clothes and headed for the back door as the cow mooed again.

He grabbed his heavy coat from the hook and pushed his arms into the sleeves, as he buttoned it with one hand, he lifted his hat from another hook and slapped it on his head, then he grabbed the handle of the milk pail, swung it off the shelf and grumbled, "I'm coming, Cow, kindly give it a rest! Good thing the neighbors aren't close."

He stepped off the porch onto the top step and nearly sat on his rear. It had started to mist and what he'd thought was dampness when he looked out was really a thin glaze of ice. More carefully, he finished the trip to the shed and opened the door so Cow could make her way into her stall. Roger filled the feed pail with her feed and dumped it into the trough, then went around to get his pail and his stool to start milking.

As the milk made pinging noises in the pail, Roger wondered who would come to the service today. He'd heard rumors that the big church in Blairsville wasn't having a service, because the minister's mother had had a stroke a few days ago, so the man and his family had left for Atlanta to be with the rest of his family. He wondered if any of those who lived here and went there would come to his church for the service. More specifically, would Ramon and Sandy be coming? That thought sent shivers up his spine. It would be the first time he'd see them since he'd fled from their house. As soon as he milked the last drop, he let the cow out into the pasture and filled his feed pail with scratch grain for his chickens. He opened the coop door, then went in and shut it behind him. After scattering the grain, he shooed the hens from their nests and gathered the four eggs. Maybe he'd have scrambled eggs for breakfast.

He wondered what he'd do the rest of the day. Maybe he'd clean his gun and go hunting. A rabbit might taste good for a solitary Thanksgiving dinner. Before he left the chicken coop the rooster strutted up to him, ignoring the grain on the floor and started pecking on his work boots. Maybe he'd make a good Thanksgiving dinner! When Roger walked back inside his house, he heard talking, so he set his two pails on the counter, rushed to his phone and picked up the receiver. He recognized the voice, so he said, "Hey, talk to me now that I'm inside!"

"Hey, friend, I guess you noticed there's ice everywhere."

Roger chuckled and said, "Yeah, I almost had a bruise on my sitdown on the way to the barn to milk. So what's up?"

"Ah, yes, forgot you got that ornery cow you gotta milk in the morning. I guess you heard there's no service at our church in Blairsville. Anyway, we're planning on picking Isabel and her company up and coming to hear you. Do you want Sandy to play, or do you have someone else?"

Making sure his wayward heart beat normally, he said, "Sure! That'd be great! Nobody's played that piano since she did."

"Okay, see you at eleven. You got someplace to go for dinner?"

"Well, yeah, back here for a hotdog."

"Eat your hotdog, old man, but come on over at three for a real dinner. Isabel and her company will be here, too."

Remembering the last time they'd met at his church, he asked, "Are you sure she and I can coexist under the same roof?"

Ramon chuckled, remembering what Roger referred to. "I think her grand-daughter and great grand-daughter can mellow her."

"If you say so I'll chance it. Thanks for the invite."

"Sure, we'll see you later."

Roger quickly strained his milk and refrigerated it. He'd left his short message at his office, so he didn't have to look for it here. As he took his shower and washed his hair, he wondered what Isabel and Sandy would think. It was definitely not something he'd normally say from his lectern. He hadn't really thought about a program, in fact he hadn't even thought about any music. He realized that was really foolish, especially when several of his praise team had told him already that they'd be out of town. He sighed, Sandy would save his hide and after he'd run out of their house without even a 'thank you for dinner,' he was surprised she'd volunteer to play for his service. He shook his head. She was a conundrum. He was a glutton for punishment. Why did he keep putting himself into her path? He shook his head, *who knew?*

Linus walked circles around his ankles and finally Roger put his fork down on the plate. As he stood up, he said, "So you're hungry, too? Don't you get enough mice?" Of course, the cat didn't answer, he put his tail in the air and walked sedately to his dish, then looked up at Roger with an expectant air. The servant, of course, went to the pantry and brought back the large bag of cat food and dumped some into the dish. Linus didn't even look at Roger, just stuck his head in the dish and started crunching on the hard pieces of food.

Raylyn pulled her brain reluctantly from the fog and realized a cold, little hand was stroking her face. She opened one eye and looked into the smiling face of her wide-awake daughter. "Mommy, I smell sompin real good. Mommy, you gots to get up! You be sleeping way long tis morning."

There was a clock on the stand between the beds and Raylyn glanced at it. It told her it was eight thirty. It couldn't be that late! She never slept past seven thirty even on Saturdays! She groaned, after all, she'd only fallen asleep sometime after three. Slowly and reluctantly she pushed the covers off her shoulders. The cool air in the room helped wake her a bit more. She sighed and said, "I'm awake, Sweety. Have you been to the bathroom?"

"Yes, Mommy. Gamaw show me where. I show you."

Raylyn pushed the covers slowly off the rest of her body and swung her legs off the side of the bed. After sitting up for a few seconds, she took Heidi's hand and stood up, took a step off the rug and the jolt of the cold hardwood floor did the job of waking her the rest of the way. She let Heidi lead the way to the door and down the hall. "So what woke you up, Sweety?"

"Daylight, Mommy."

Raylyn groaned again. Of course the daylight! Heidi had slept a lot in the car, all the time after dark last night, no wonder she'd gotten awake at her usual time. Heidi left her at the bathroom door. Raylyn watched as the little girl, in her princess jammies, skipped on down the hall and into Isabel's kitchen. She knew that was fine, she could hear Isabel puttering around. When she'd disappeared, Raylyn closed the door and turned on the shower to warm up. A shower and clean hair sounded good for the first order of the day. After she and

Heidi were dressed, they wandered to the kitchen where Isabel was bustling around.

Without turning from the stove, she said, "Is my company hungry for cinnamon buns?"

Raylyn slid onto a chair and said, "Grandma, how could anybody resist that delicious smell? It fills up the house and smells wonderful! If I remember, you make the best cinnamon buns from scratch."

"What's scratch?" Heidi asked, innocently, scowling first at Raylyn then at Isabel.

"Sweety, what I mean is Grandma makes them from the beginning and bakes them in her oven, not like Mommy does and buys them from the store."

"Oh. Are they good that way?"

"Pumpkin, you've never tasted better!"

Heidi nodded. "They smell yummy!"

After Isabel brought a pan full of steaming buns, three mugs, one of hot chocolate and two of coffee to the table, Raylyn said, "So what happens today, Grandma?"

"Ramon and his wife…"

Raylyn's eyes turned to saucers. "What! What did you say? Gramma, did you say… Ramon's married?"

"Yes, Sandy came to Vansville for an interview to be his receptionist. She got the job and won his heart in short order. Anyway, they're stopping by for us at quarter till eleven, maybe a little before that, depends if she plays or not. Since there's no service at our church in Blairsville, we'll go hear Roger read his reading on Thanksgiving. At three we'll get ourselves over to their place for dinner."

"Who's Roger?" Heidi asked.

"He's the man who calls himself the preacher at the church in town."

After stuffing a mouthful of the delicious bun into her mouth, Raylyn asked, "Why do you talk like that about a pastor, Grandma?"

Isabel licked off all five of her fingers on her left hand, wiped it with her napkin then placed it over Raylyn's hand. After her mouth was empty enough to answer, she said, "My dear, Roger Clemens hardly deserves the title of 'pastor,' he's a young man, now I don't have anything against him for that, but instead of the good old hymns, he's got some sort of band that plays stuff so loud you can hear it through the closed door across the street at the gas station. His 'talks' or 'readings' leave you empty, without any substance at all."

"Oh?"

Isabel picked up her cup and looked at her grand-daughter over the rim and said, "Yes. Sandy, Ramon's wife, is sure he's not even a believer himself."

"Wow!"

Right on time, there was a horn blast outside. Isabel, Raylyn and Heidi all had their coats and hats on, so they went out the door. At the end of their walk sat a new, light blue van. Heidi stopped dead on the steps and stared. The big passenger door was open already and a big metal shelf was in the process of going down to the ground, but she couldn't see anyone who was making it happen. Raylyn took Heidi's hand. She didn't say anything, she was stunned, too. However, Isabel was walking down the walk toward the van, so Raylyn followed her.

When the lift was on the ground, Isabel stepped on and said, "Come on, you two. Get on here with me so Ramon can take us up."

Tentatively, Heidi put one foot on the metal lift then only after Raylyn had stepped on did she bring her other foot up. Immediately, the lip came up behind her and the lift started to rise. Heidi looked up at her mommy it was easy to see the terror in her eyes. "Mommy, what's going on?" she whispered.

From inside the van a cheery voice said, "Hi, I'm Sandy, you must be Heidi! Isabel told me all about you. I'm glad you can ride in my van."

Isabel stepped off and so Raylyn and Heidi also stepped off. As soon as they were inside the van the lift started to close. Heidi didn't leave the spot, just turned around so she could watch the metal come toward her. When it stopped, the van door began moving. When it finally closed, Heidi looked away and for the first time saw the big man holding a box in his hand.

"Who are you?" Heidi demanded.

"I'm Ramon and that's my wife, Sandy. Do you like our special van?"

When the door finally clicked shut, she said, "I dunno. How come it does that?"

Before Ramon could answer, Sandy said, from the driver's seat, "Heidi, could you come here a minute?"

Heidi looked at the closed door one last time, then turned to stare at Ramon and the box in his hand, then finally made the final turn and looked at the woman behind the wheel. She scowled when she saw the wheelchair. "How come you got a chair like that? Teacher gots a van I ride in sometime, but her chair don't got wheels." Heidi looked at the other seat up front and said, "She gots two seats just like that one."

Sandy smiled at the little girl and held out her arm. Heidi moved cautiously toward her, but Sandy didn't say anything until Heidi was right beside her. Sandy put her arm around the child, then picked up her hands and placed them on the arm of her chair. She said in a voice meant only for Heidi's ears, but the others could hear, "Heidi, my legs don't work like yours or your mommy's so they had to make my van special just for me. You see, when I drive I can't use my feet, I have to do everything with my hands."

Heidi looked at the lady's hands, then at the steering wheel, and finally up to Sandy's smiling face. Heidi's eyes turned huge. "Wow! You gots busy hands!"

Sandy chuckled. "That's right! You go back there and sit with your mommy. We'll be at the church in a couple of minutes then you can ride back down on the lift again. Okay?"

"Oh, yeah!" Heidi broke away from Sandy and scampered across the open space to climb up next to the window beside her mommy.

Isabel watched the little scene between her friend and her great-grand-daughter. There was never anyone better with children than Sandy. She knew of no one who was afraid of the lady in the wheelchair. She had every child for miles around coming to her door for piano lessons and they all loved their time with their teacher. She'd never ask, but she wondered if Sandy could have children of her own.

Would being paralyzed from the waist down deny her that? Isabel shook her head imperceptibly and sighed, Sandy deserved children of her own. The van moved from her lot and soon stopped at the curb in front of the church. There was one other car there, it was a Jeep.

Roger could hardly shave his face. He'd showered and washed his hair, but he knew he must shave in front of the mirror over the sink, because his hands were trembling. He didn't really understand his nervousness because he'd given many talks in his church before and of course, there had been many in front of his fellow seminarians. He'd even had a few Sundays while he was a student where he'd been a substitute at a nearby church, but this time he knew it would be very different. First of all, Sandy and Ramon would be there to hear him and secondly, this was the first time ever he'd given a talk that was his own. It hit him, he was a college graduate with an advanced degree and he was nervous about giving a speech?

When he finished shaving he was glad he'd done this before breakfast, because there'd be plenty of time for all the nicks to stop bleeding before he showed up at church at ten thirty. He ate his usual meal of fresh eggs and bacon and then went to his closet to see what he had to wear that wouldn't cause Isabel to send him back for more appropriate dress. He realized that woman had him cowed. He found a white dress shirt and dark slacks, he didn't own a full suit. As he threaded his belt through the loops on his slacks, he looked at his tie rack. It was sorely lacking, he hadn't worn a tie in five years and even then only for graduation from seminary.

He tucked the shirt in his slacks, pulled on dark socks and dark dress shoes, then looked for a mirror to do his tie. He definitely needed a mirror, five years was a long time to remember how to tie a tie and of course, he didn't have one of those ready-made jobs. With the tie around his neck, under his collar, he went to every room in the house. He couldn't believe it! His was definitely a bachelor's pad the only mirror in his house was the little one on his medicine cabinet in the bathroom. He couldn't see how he looked if all he could see was from the crown of his head down two inches below his shoulders! He sighed, he ought to purchase a mirror, but then he remembered he was paying for the pile of lumber at the church that Sandy would use for the second time today to get herself inside. He shook his head bachelorhood was not his cup of tea.

While he stood in front of the mirror, he put off tying his tie and instead pulled off the little pieces of tissue he'd used to blot all the nicks on his face. He'd only shaved two days ago, without a nick. What a total wreck he was today! Now he didn't have white spots on his face, but the dark, dried blood spots were very prominent. He took his washcloth and gingerly wiped at the blood, hoping that none of them would start bleeding again. That would take the cake! Finally, he made the knot in his tie to his satisfaction.

At last he was ready to venture out to his Jeep and head into town to the church. He pulled on his suede jacket and pulled the leather gloves from the pockets. The mist had stopped and the sun shone weakly, but it was cold, so the ground was still covered with a thin skiff of ice. He remembered almost too late that his dress shoes had smooth soles. He caught himself in time to keep from going down again. This morning, his old dog didn't even bother to leave his house to greet him. Linus had stayed in the house when he opened the door. He sighed it seemed only humans were stupid enough to get out in the elements today.

As he turned from the country road to the highway through town, he realized he'd better get a quick attitude change between here and the church. After all, it was Thanksgiving. "Okay, here it comes! Smile, Clemens, you'll be on candid camera!" Somehow, that didn't do the trick. He cleared his throat, but couldn't think of any words for another pep talk.

He drove into town to the church and parked in his usual place. He'd planned to be the first and he was. He hurried inside and found the bag of icemelt and went back out with it. He sprinkled all the steps and the walk then remembered the reason for the long ramp was coming and she'd probably have trouble making it up the ramp with any ice on it at all, so he went over to the head of the ramp and started down, sprinkling his salt liberally as he went. With barely anything left in the bag, he went back inside to take the bag to his office. He dropped the bag and reached for the zipper pull on his jacket.

He was barely in his office when the front door opened and a child's voice said, "Mommy, it be dark in here! How come nobody turned on the lights? Doesn't nobody got lights like at home?"

"Of course, Heidi, they have lights in Vansville, but this isn't a huge church like the one we go to at home. I'm sure someone will be here soon to turn on the lights. We'll wait here inside the door for them."

Roger shrugged out of his coat and hung it on the hook inside the office door. He'd never heard those voices before. One was definitely a child, but the other was a young woman. His heart kicked up a notch, Isabel and her company must have arrived, along with Sandy and Ramon. He'd hardly pushed the bag of salt under his coat and grabbed his speech when he heard their voices added to the first two.

He walked out into the auditorium with a smile on his face, but in the dim light his eyes fastened on the new lady and wouldn't look away. The lady was the most beautiful creature he'd ever laid eyes on. Her face was lovely, even in the near darkness and her figure had not an ounce of extra fat. She wasn't overly tall, he figured she'd fit perfectly into the circle of his arm. *Clemens, get a grip, she has a child, therefore, there's a husband somewhere.* He swallowed, then swallowed again and finally croaked out, "Hello, I'm Roger Clemens, the preacher."

Ramon stepped around the corner into the auditorium and flipped the light switch, as he said, "Say, what's the deal, man? Aren't you planning on folks seeing when they come inside or is this an outdoor meeting?"

Roger dragged his eyes from Raylyn and said, "Well, yeah, I only got inside after salting the walks and the ramp."

Sandy smiled as she wheeled herself forward and said, "Thank you, Roger! I'd dreaded trying to get up that ramp with this ice, but it was great with your salt. Thanks for doing that for me. It meant you had to get here extra early. I guess we aren't very good hosts! We didn't let Isabel introduce her guests."

Isabel silently looked Roger up and down and then said, matter-of-factly, "Humph! Found you a tie, did you? I'm right proud of you, Roger Clemens, you almost look the part. Roger, meet my grand-daughter and great-grand-daughter from Michigan. They've come for the long weekend. This is Raylyn and Heidi Keys."

Roger wondered where the absent Mr. Keys was, or was she an unwed mother? Maybe there were church-going women with children who'd never been married, but he didn't know any. Finally his heart rate settled and he swallowed the cotton in his mouth then chanced another look at Raylyn. He stuck out his hand said, "I'm pleased to meet you. Welcome."

Raylyn took Roger's hand, but released it after one shake. "Yes," was all she could say.

Heidi held out her hand to Roger and said, "You don't sound like us!"

Roger took the little girl's hand and shook it. Not looking at the young woman, he was able to say, "It's probably because I'm from Montana. We don't talk like you people from the Midwest." He smiled at the little girl and continued, "Of course, you don't sound much like the natives around here either."

Heidi didn't understand that, she'd only heard one native, so she said, "Gamaw Isbel says you gots a talk we gotta hear."

Raylyn instantly dropped her eyes and her voice, placed her hand on the child's shoulder and whispered to Heidi, "Sweety, that's not nice. You don't talk like that to our pastor!"

"But she said…"

"Shhhh…"

Before anyone could say anything else, Sandy said, "Roger, would it be okay if I started playing something while people come?"

"Of course, that'd be great! Help yourself!" He chuckled. "I'm sure you know where the piano is, Sandy."

Giving him a broad smile, she set her control and wheeled herself across the back and up the side to the piano. "Have anything picked out you want played especially for Thanksgiving?"

"Ah, no, I thought you could do whatever you do best and be the star, after me, of course." He grinned as she looked across the seats toward him.

Sandy laughed, as he'd hoped she would. "Okay, I'll get right on that."

Roger could see she didn't have her little black pouch in her hand or on her lap, so he asked, "Does Ramon have your sustainer?"

"No, when I play hymns I don't really need it. It's when I'm playing that hard stuff that I can't hold the sounds with my fingers."

Roger didn't have to be humiliated any longer by a three year old, others started coming in the door, so Roger moved away from the little group and Ramon ushered Isabel and Raylyn up the middle aisle, then led them into the second seat. Sandy began softly playing hymns and the auditorium began to fill up with towns people. Roger pasted on his regular 'ministerial smile' and stuck out his hand to greet those coming in. However, he found his eyes wandering to the middle seat of the second row frequently. From the back of the church all he could see of the attractive young woman was her auburn curls that touched her shoulders and her shoulders covered with the sweater in delicate pink that she wore.

After he realized for the third time where his eyes had wandered, he admonished himself, *Clemens, stop your roving eyes! She probably left her very busy husband at home to do office work. Who'd want to meet your wife's grandmother, anyway?*

Roger faced the back of the auditorium and greeted the people coming in. After that third time, he concentrated on not looking toward the front, so when his watch buzzed for the hour and he turned around he was shocked to see that nearly every seat was taken. He swallowed and realized that his palms were sweating. From the back he looked around at the people, they were all from Vansville, but many of them didn't come here on Sundays.

In a panic, he shifted from one foot to the other and searched his mind, trying to remember what he'd done with his one page talk. He remembered taking his coat off and hanging it up, then grabbing the paper from his desk. He'd come through the door into the auditorium and all coherent thought had left his mind when he'd seen the woman standing beside Isabel. What could he have done with his paper? He had to have it he'd never given a speech without some kind of help and prompts before.

He felt his pants pockets, no crumpled up paper in the front pockets. His wallet and a white handkerchief were the only things in his back pockets. Finally, he felt his shirt pocket and something crackled. He looked down to see a nicely folded piece of paper and pulled it out. When had he folded that paper so neatly and stuck it there?

Pushing the paper back in his pocket, he walked down the center aisle and climbed the three steps to the platform. He'd done this every Sunday for five years, but today, his legs felt like water. He nearly lunged for the lectern then held on to keep his sweaty hands from shaking. The music stopped and all eyes looked at him expectantly.

God in heaven, his heart cried out, *what am I doing here?*

As Sandy quietly backed her chair to beside Ramon, Roger pasted on his best smile and looked at the audience, but not at the middle seat on the second row. "Good morning, folks, welcome to Vansville Church on this cold Thanksgiving Day. Thanks to Sandy DeLord for supplying our music. It's been great, Sandy! Most of you know we have our praise team supply our music on Sundays, but to a man, or woman, they told me they'd be out of town." He smiled again and said, "Now, you tell me how one can properly give thanks to God without music!"

After the chuckling quieted, Roger nodded and said, "Just as I thought, it's almost impossible. Since our praise team usually leads our singing and we project the words on the wall up here, we don't have any song books, but since we have such an accomplished pianist, I thought perhaps we could sing some favorites before we have prayer and our lesson for the day." Was he ad-libbing it or what! Maybe babbling was a better word.

Sandy moved back to the piano as several hands went up immediately and Roger acknowledged each one. When he had five selections, he said, "I'll take one more."

A little hand went up, but a voice accompanied it and said, "I wanna sing 'Jesus Loves Me,' Mr. Roger."

Roger dared to look toward the source of the little voice. Heidi sat on her mommy's lap waving her hand wildly. Roger almost lost his train of thought again, seeing the face that was right beside the little one, but after a second's hesitation, he said, "I think that would be a good one to start with. Could you play it for us, Sandy, and we'll join you, then we'll sing the others."

After they had sung the six requests, Roger picked up his Bible that he had dusted off and brought from home. He opened it and said, "If you have your Bible, would you turn with me to Psalm 100. Follow along as I read:

'Shout for joy to the LORD, all the earth,
Serve the LORD with gladness, come before him with joyful songs.
Know that the Lord is God.
It is he who made us, and we are his; we are his people,
the sheep of his pasture.
Enter his gates with thanksgiving and his courts with praise;
Give thanks to him and praise his name.
For the LORD is good and his love endures forever;
His faithfulness continues through all generations.'"

Roger slid his Bible to the side but left it open and said, "Let's pray."

Sandy sat in her chair and said the words in her heart from memory as Roger read them, her heart sang as the young man read Scripture from the Bible. From what she had heard from others in town Roger never even brought a Bible to the lectern with him and here he was, not only holding the precious Book in his hands, but he was reading from it. *Yes!* she thought, *Praise the LORD!* Thanksgiving was in order!

Roger opened his eyes, but kept his hand on the Bible, then reached for his pocket and said, "I sat here in the quietness the other day and after reading this passage from the Bible it seemed as if my head was so full I had to grab a pen and paper and write down some thoughts. Perhaps they won't mean as much to you as they did to me, but I hope they do."

Roger smoothed out the paper in front of him, but then his eyes looked out at the people before him. From then on, he hardly looked at the paper, but spoke from his heart. Just before noon he seemed to run out of words. He looked down at his paper and what he had said made more sense than the words on his paper, so he folded it and put it on the page of his still open Bible. He closed the Book and laid his hand on it. Amazed at himself, he had spoken for half an hour and never used a note!

"Friends, let's pray. God in heaven, we wish to thank You for this Thanksgiving Day that we have had to share together and with

You. Bless each person who is here and may they have a day full of happiness. We pray in Jesus' Name, amen." He raised his head and looked at those in front of him. "You're dismissed. Have a great day!"

Quickly, Sandy wheeled herself to the piano and played two verses of a familiar hymn, as Roger left the platform and made his way to the back. People stood up and followed him down the aisle. Soon, the only ones that were left were the five people who had come first. Sandy stopped playing and joined those at the back.

She was the last in line and said, "Roger, you spoke powerfully today! I wish you'd been making a recording."

He took her hand and held it. As he looked at her, he said, "Sandy, something happened to me the day I decided to prepare for this service. Believe me, I had nothing to do with the words that came from my mouth today, God put them there as they came out. I have no idea what I said."

Sandy smiled at the young man. "Roger, I've been praying for you ever since you ran from our house last week. I had a feeling that God was out to snag you for Himself. Praise God for what He can do!" She pulled her hand from his and put it on the control of her chair. As she began to move, she said, "We'll see you at three sharp or even before if you're not busy. Come prepared for a great meal!"

"Thanks, Sandy."

Heidi held tightly to her mommy's hand, but she turned around and gave the young minister a bright smile. She waved and said, "Bye, Mr. Roger, you done good. I glad we sang 'Jesus Loves Me'!"

For the life of him he couldn't remember her name! Was that awful, or what! She was the first child who'd been in his service, ever, if he recalled right. He smiled. "Thanks for asking that we sing it, it belonged in our service."

Raylyn never looked back and Roger was glad, wasn't he? He heard the furnace running, they wouldn't need it on until Sunday morning, so he turned and stepped back inside. He closed the door, then went to the thermostat and turned it back, then made his way to his office for his coat. He sat at his desk in the quietness for several minutes marveling at what had happened in the service. Finally, he shrugged into his coat and turned out the light. His mind was in a whirl as he made his way through the sanctuary and out the front door.

Raylyn sat between Isabel and Heidi on the way back to Isabel's house. Across the space she asked Sandy, "What did Mr. Clemens mean when he asked you about your sustainer? You played beautifully, Sandy."

"Thanks, Raylyn. The reason he asked about my sustainer is that I usually carry a small black pouch that fits over the back of my chair. Since my foot can't work the sustaining pedal on a piano, my brother and I concocted this pouch with wires that hook to the piano. I move my shoulder to operate the pouch. When I play something as uncomplicated as hymns I don't need it, I can hold down the keys with my fingers."

"You play beautifully! We have a professor of piano who is the regular pianist at our church and you play just as well."

Sandy looked into her rearview mirror and said, "Surely you must be exaggerating! I've only had a few years of lessons, but I do love to play."

"Don't you listen to her!" Isabel exclaimed. "That girl gave us a two hour concert two months ago all from memory. It wasn't hymns, either. You could have heard a pin drop while she played and everybody wanted her to go on and on. Now she has children coming every day for lessons."

"Wow! Cun I take peony lessons, Mommy?"

"Sweety, not from Miss Sandy, we live too far away."

Heidi shook her head. "It weren't far, Mommy."

Raylyn shook her head. "Sweety, you slept a lot while we came."

"Mommy, I don't sleep during the day! You know that!"

"Pumpkin, you were asleep when I drove during the night."

"Oh. Oh, yeah."

"So you want us at your house at three?" Isabel asked.

"Unless you want to come earlier. I thought we'd eat at three. Now you don't need to bring anything, you know."

"Listen here, young lady, I will!" Isabel exclaimed. "You don't have candied sweet potatoes on your menu?"

"No, that's something I don't have, but don't you bring anything else!"

"We'll see," Isabel answered, mysteriously.

Inside Isabel's house Heidi said, "I like Miss Sandy. How come she don't walk?"

"Honey," Isabel answered, "when she was born, one of the workers in the hospital nursery's hands slipped. Sandy fell a little, but it was enough that she hit the sharp edge of the changing table and it broke something in her back. She's never walked."

Raylyn gasped, "Oh, my! Nothing could be done?"

"No, it was her spinal cord that was severed."

"She's a wonderful lady!"

"That she is! She's Vansville's artist in residence, believe me. She not only is a very accomplished pianist, but her paintings are gathering national fame." Isabel nodded toward a portrait prominently hanging on her living room wall and added, "She used to live in my first cabin. One day she sat me down and in an afternoon she whipped that up and gave it to me." With a sly look in her eyes, she asked, "So what do you think of the man in the pulpit today?"

Isabel watched as a delicate pink that nearly matched her sweater crept onto Raylyn's cheeks. Raylyn licked her lips and said, "Grandma, I thought you said he didn't have much to say, just read some words off a paper. He was really good and he hardly looked at his notes."

"Yes, that he was. I wanted to give him the benefit of the doubt when he first came five years ago. First of all, I couldn't stand that loud noise he calls his 'praise team' but he read his talk and it had nothing to say, especially about our Lord. I looked at some of the people who regularly come here I could see they were dumbfounded."

"What he had to say was very good."

Nodding sagely, Heidi said, "Yeah, him was good."

After a quiet moment, Heidi sitting on the couch beside her mommy and playing with her dollie, looked up at Isabel and said, "I think he outta be my new daddy!"

"Heidi!" Raylyn exclaimed, "Don't even think that!"

"Why not, Mommy? He gots no wife nor nothin'. You mailded my letter to Santa and now we comed here and found him. I even prayed to Jesus, too."

Raylyn's cheeks were not just pink now, they were flaming, but Isabel was chuckling. "Heidi, you may have something there."

Raylyn cleared her throat and gasped, "Grandma Isabel, we live a thousand miles away!"

Isabel waved her hand at her grand-daughter. "Sandy lived in Philadelphia and had never been outside of Pennsylvania in July. Ramon was not a believer in our Lord, but He brought Sandy here to our little town and He put some fine Christian people on the hikes Ramon led this past summer. Sandy would never have married a non-believer and Ramon almost didn't hire her as his receptionist, but God had plans for them. My dear child, don't sell Him short. From what I heard today, God has been working in Roger's heart and you can always find work in the field you love. If you feel something for him, and I think you do, leave it with Jesus."

Raylyn's head was slowly going back and forth, but the words, "Oh, my!" were all that came from her mouth.

Heidi, however, had no problem. "Yes! Yes, Mommy, yes!"

THREE

Roger stood on the tiny stoop of the church and looked up and down the street. Nothing moved except a few stray flakes floating down from the clouds that obscured the sun since his service began. He tucked his Bible under his arm to zip up his coat, trotted to the Jeep, slid behind the wheel, put the machine in gear and hurried out of town. Not that a church pastor would speed, of course. He had almost three hours before Thanksgiving dinner at DeLord's. That thought hit him between the eyes, he wouldn't be the only one there; Ramon said that Isabel and her company were coming! Was it impolite to cancel at the last minute? He swallowed, that company included the beautiful woman who had him tongue-tied whenever he looked at her.

He pulled into his spot at home and cut the engine. Much to his surprise, since it hadn't really warmed up much, his old dog met him as he stepped from the vehicle. Absently, he reached down and scratched his ears. The mutt turned his eyes up and looked adoringly at his master. He had short hair and was shivering, but he wagged his tail, as he walked beside his master. "So, what are you doing out of your house, old man? I can tell you know it's cold and there's snow in the air, but you're standing out here shivering." Roger snapped his fingers, reached down and scratched the old dog's ears again and said, "Ah, I know. It's been a while since I sprang for a bone and you think it's about time I did. Well, let me see what I can find. Come on, I gotta search the fridge."

Roger went inside, left his coat and gloves on then opened his refrigerator. There sat the leg bone he'd cut most of the meat off of, but left some purposely and wrapped in saran. He'd saved it from his last pot of beef stew. He carried it out the back door, but as soon as the dog saw the bone in Roger's hands his tail started wagging his whole body and his tongue made a big swipe of his lips. The dog immediately took the bone offered and collapsed on the porch.

Roger chuckled at the old dog and sat down in the old chair - the old sit-upon, it could hardly be called a chair any more - he kept on the back porch and said, "Say, Curly, remember I told you to find us some females? Don't bother for me. Maybe I can do my own search." Then he remembered that the beautiful woman had a child, so that pretty much ensured a husband. "Well, maybe not," he added.

He let out a long sigh and said to the dog who just chewed contentedly on his bone, "This new lady came to my church this morning, Curly. She's got the most awesome auburn curls you've ever seen and…and well, I guess a 'man of the cloth' isn't supposed to notice such things, but every ounce is exactly where it's supposed to be and the curves…" His words trailed off and he sighed again. "But she's got a kid, Curly that means she's married, right?"

The cold was seeping into his bones and sent a cold shiver up his back. It was near the end of November, after all. He looked beyond the porch and noticed that the snow was doing more than flaking and the cold wind had picked up. After a gust of wind whipped around him, he put his hands on his knees and pushed himself to his feet. The dog was still gnawing on his bone and didn't stop just because his master stopped talking and went to the door. Roger opened the door and stepped inside, there was no sense to being cold. Why waste the nice warmth put out by his well stoked wood stove? He shrugged out of his coat and hung it on the peg next to the door, then went in the living room to check his wood box and the stove. Both were in good shape, but he'd have to add wood before he left this afternoon.

He went to the phone and picked it up, he'd call and make up something so he didn't have to be in her company this afternoon, but what could he say? Ramon and Sandy both knew he didn't have family in the area, he'd as good as told Ramon he had no plans. Sawing down a tree and splitting wood for his stove held no appeal this time of year. Besides, his woodshed was full. He sighed and dropped the receiver back onto the receptacle. He had no reason not to go for dinner. He'd just have to avoid the woman. *Piece of cake!*

Raylyn looked at the little person sitting beside her and swallowed hard. Heidi's eyes were dancing and her smile stretched across her entire face. She was clapping and bouncing on the couch, making the other end of the cushion pop up. Raylyn couldn't remember the last time the child had been this excited. Raylyn, on the other hand, was shaking her head hard, her hands covered her mouth and her blue eyes were round, with a horrified look in them.

"Heidi!" she exclaimed. "I hardly know the man! We only met there at the church, we didn't say but a few words to each other. You have no idea!"

Being the devil's advocate, Isabel said, "If it helps any, Ramon and Sandy have invited him to have dinner with us."

"Grandma Isabel!" Raylyn licked her lips. Her mouth went dry and a big wad of cotton covered her vocal cords.

Isabel looked at her, there was no smile, but her eyes were twinkling. "Yes, dear?"

Raylyn cleared her throat and looked from one to the other, before she could say, "Grandma, you and Heidi must be a buffer!"

"Why?"

"Because...."

"Because? That's your only reason?" Isabel asked.

Raylyn's only answer was to jump up and race down the hall to her room. Isabel and Heidi still sat in their places. After they heard the door close, Heidi looked at the older lady and solemnly asked, "Why'd Mommy run off?"

Isabel smiled and crooked her finger at the little girl. Heidi slid off the couch to climb trustingly onto the old lady's lap. She turned so she could look at the old lady. "Gamaw, what's wrong wif Mommy? Doesn't you think I need a daddy? You know I need a daddy! My friend at school's getting a daddy for Christmas. Gamaw,

I send a letter to Santa to get us a daddy, and…and I pray to Jesus, too."

"Yes, sweetheart, I think you need a daddy, but your mommy… Have you ever been scared, little one?"

"Sure! Mommy and me gots scared when them guys comed to our house and told Mommy Daddy'd gone to heaven."

Isabel shook her head and picked up one of Heidi's hands. "How about the first day you went to preschool, were you scared then? When you saw Mommy walk out the door?"

Nodding vigorously, Heidi exclaimed, "Oh, yeah! I real scared! Mommy say she didn't want to leave me, but she had to. I real scared till she comed back."

"Well, it's kind of like that. Mommy's a bit scared right now."

"Oh, yeah, sure," Heidi said, but Isabel wasn't convinced she understood.

Raylyn sat on the bed and stared at nothing in particular. It was a small room, but warm with the cherry wainscoting and the lovely homemade area rugs. It was big enough for the two twin beds, a nightstand and one dresser, all in cherry. The bed covers were beautiful quilts made locally. Next to the dresser was the door to the closet. There was one window with a raised blind to take the best advantage for the spectacular view of the mountains that circled Vansville, but Raylyn didn't see any of it. What she saw were the two men at her door two years ago.

They'd come quietly and knocked on her door. When she went, she noticed they were both dressed in military uniform and they'd jostled each other, filling her small doorway. Neither of them was smiling and she knew, without them saying a word, why they had come. The pain, the likes of which she'd never felt before, had started even before they'd asked to come in. Numbly, she'd nodded and stepped back.

Heidi was barely a year old and could only move around by holding onto things, but somehow she'd followed her mommy to the door. Raylyn could still feel the tiny hands clutching her pantleg. She remembered reaching down and picking the child up, hugging her to her chest fiercely, hoping to ward off what she knew was coming. Heidi, bless her tiny soul, had wrapped her arms around Raylyn's neck, put her head into her neck and held on. Somehow the little body warmed her enough that she didn't collapse in front of the men.

Barely inside the door, one man smiled kindly at her, took her arm and said, "Could we sit down, Mrs. Keys?"

She followed her barely audible "Yes." by turning into her living room and collapsing into the closest chair. The men followed her and sat facing her.

The older man came quickly to the point. "Mrs. Keys, we hate to be the barer of such bad news, but your husband, Daniel, was killed in that last sniper attack that the terrorists launched on the Embassy yesterday…."

She hadn't heard anything else. Dan was dead, senselessly, he had died. He hadn't needed to go to war, he was the only son and he'd been working in his dad's company as a vice president. He was supposed to fill his dad's shoes in a few years. He was a reservist, but his unit had been called. But he was dead a terrorist sniper's bullet had brought him down.

His dad's dreams, her dreams had been shattered. His parents had no son, she had no husband and most importantly, their baby had no daddy. When the men finished talking she'd seen them out the door, closed it behind her and slid down the door to the floor, still holding her precious daughter on her shoulder.

She didn't know how long she'd sat, tears sliding down her cheeks, wetting the back of her child and dripping onto her slacks. Only a few minutes later the phone started ringing, it rang until the answering machine picked up, but it only sounded in the recesses of her mind. She hadn't answered it and she'd only moved when someone started pounding on her door and pushed against it, making it open and pushing her across the floor. It had been her in-laws. By now, as she sat on the bed in Isabel's guest room, tears were streaming down her cheeks.

She shook her head. *How can she even think about another daddy? How can I replace the only man I've ever loved?* As if the weight of the whole world was upon her shoulders, Raylyn bent over, her arms resting on her knees and her forehead resting on her wrists. Tears gushed from her eyes, dripping onto her legs, soaking her slacks. Her sobs were nearly silent, but they wracked her body, sending shudders from her shoulders to her toes.

That's how Isabel found her. She knocked, but got no answer, but she could hear the faint sounds of Raylyn's sobs. She'd left Heidi reading one of her books to her dollie and come down the hall when Raylyn hadn't come out right away. Isabel shook her head and came to Raylyn immediately. Silently, she sat beside her and put her arm around the hurting girl's shoulders. With her other hand she stroked her hair, pushing it behind her ear.

When Raylyn's sobs finally subsided enough that she could make sound, she whispered brokenly, "Grandma, how-w c-could I d-do that to D-Dan?"

"Do what, Dear?"

"Well… well, go out with another man and maybe get married again."

Isabel tugged on Raylyn's shoulders until she sat up and leaned against Isabel's chest. After several seconds, Raylyn's arms crept around Isabel. It felt wonderful to rest in her loving, caring arms. After several minutes of being quiet in each other's arms, Isabel said, "My dear, you wouldn't be doing anything to Daniel. There will always be a place in your heart that will be very special for him; where you will hold his memory and all the happy times you had, not only as a couple in love, but as a family with your new baby. No one, nothing can take that from you. Perhaps he never had the chance to tell you, but I know he wouldn't want you to mourn for him or refuse to move on to another relationship for the rest of your life."

"But Grandma, you never remarried after Grandpa died."

Isabel hugged her grand-daughter, placing a kiss on Raylyn's forehead. Raylyn's head was on her chest, so close she could hear Isabel's steady heart beating. Finally, Isabel said, "My darling child, I'm old. My beloved Harvard was my mainstay for fifty years. He died three years ago and I've lived my life with him. We had our love and blessings. If I had lost him when I was twenty-five or so like you, he'd have wanted me to find someone else to love, just like Dan would want the same for you."

A great shudder wracked her body then she asked, "So you think it's all right?"

"Of course I think it's all right! God never meant for a woman to raise her children alone. He meant for a man to take a woman as his wife and the two of them to live together and build a family together. Remember, illness, suffering and death only came into the world after Adam and Eve had sinned. Remember, the first human death only happened when Cain became angry with Abel and that was because Cain had displeased God with a wrong sacrifice and Abel had pleased God with his. Wars come about because sinful people let hatred rule their lives and govern their minds. God knew there would be sin, but it wasn't His desire."

They sat for several quiet minutes before Raylyn said, "But I still love Dan, Grandma."

"Honey, Daniel was your first love. You loved him soon after you met in college. Your love grew until you both felt the desire to share your lives, so you married; you had a child, whom you both loved. Dan went to war because he wanted to keep this country safe for you and Heidi and for many others to live. He gave his life for that and that love you had for him didn't die when he did, but it can't grow, it can't flourish, because he's no longer here.

"That love that you have is like a tree that's been cut down, but new sprouts, new growth springs up from that stump. That tree will never be the same, but there is still life in those roots that causes new growth, perhaps even a new trunk to come from it, different limbs. Your love for Daniel was cut down, he was taken away from you, but there is still love there.

"It's still spring time in your life a new love can spring up, can capture your heart and can grow into a very wonderful thing. Honey, it can give you a new man to love, who can love you and can be a loving daddy to your delightful daughter. Don't turn your back on something that God may be urging you to accept."

Raylyn nodded and pulled in a great puff of breath. "I understand, Grandma. Thank you so much for coming in just now. I would never have thought of it as something like that. I think I'd kind of forgotten that God still is in control. We are here on this earth for God's glory." Her voice dropped, as she continued, "I guess

Dan had fulfilled God's purpose for him here on earth and God took him home."

"Yes, my dear, I believe that with all my heart." Isabel looked at the clock on the nightstand. "I think my great-grand-daughter might think it's time for a snack."

Raylyn also looked at the clock. A tiny smile turned up the corners of her mouth. "Yes, I think you may be right, Grandma. She can always eat."

Isabel patted Raylyn's arm and said, "Dear, you go wash your face and put a little powder on it. It won't do much good for her to see that you've been crying. I'll give Heidi a snack while I heat some water and make us some herb tea. How's that?"

"That sounds super, Grandma!"

They stood up and Isabel reached for the doorknob, but before her hand even touched it, the door opened and a little person stood in the opening. Concern immediately put lines on the little face. "Mommy, what's wrong? You be crying?"

"Yes, Sweety, I was crying, but Grandma Isabel and I talked and I'm not crying any more. I'm on my way to the bathroom to wash it all away. Grandma Isabel said she'd get you a snack. How about that?"

Heidi grabbed Isabel's hand and a smile burst across her face. "I love snacks, Gamaw! We go to the kitchen for snacks?"

Isabel took the little hand and smiled at the child. "Good! Let's go find something to put in that little tummy to keep it from growling until we get where dinner's going to be. And you know what? I need to fix those candied sweet potatoes I promised Sandy. You can help me. Will you help me?"

Dragging on Isabel's hand, Heidi exclaimed, "Goody! I help Mommy a lot with stuff."

"Well, let's let Mommy wash her face while we go to the kitchen."

"'K, Gamaw, I ready!"

Just yesterday, Roger had gotten a care package in the mail from Billings, Montana. His mom knew he usually spent Thanksgiving in Georgia, because it was during the week and much too far to come for a few days. However, she knew her son had a large sweet tooth, so several times a year she sent some things she knew he liked and one of those times had always been Thanksgiving. About one thirty Roger's stomach reminded him that he'd eaten his eggs and bacon soon after he'd milked and long before he'd gone to the church for the service. He opened the pantry door and pulled out the huge tin that had come yesterday, pried off the lid and grabbed three of the sugar cookies that his mom had cut into the shape of turkeys and decorated.

As the first mouthful melted in his mouth, he said, "Mmm, none better!"

He put the lid back on and set the tin in the pantry again. Right next to it in the cool room sat something else his mom had sent, a huge pecan pie that he knew she'd made. He looked at it and his mouth watered, but he brought it into the kitchen and set it on the counter. It would taste even better sharing it with friends.

He was turning to leave the kitchen when Linus walked sedately by. His tail was like a flag and his nose was definitely in the air. Without stopping beside Roger he went to the back door and said, loudly, "Meow-w-w-w!"

"Oh, so now you want to go out? You think it's warmed up enough for you? Of course, your friend and body warmer is out there." Roger went to the door and opened it. When Linus hesitated, Roger's foot came up to his rear and gave him a nudge. "No chickening out now, fella, you're out of here! There's Curly, go keep each other warm."

With nothing much else to do around the place, he hadn't changed his clothes from the church service. He wondered what he should wear to Ramon's house. After all, it was Thanksgiving dinner that they'd invited him to. At his sister's he'd be out of place if he wore anything but jeans and a T-shirt, but at his parents, he'd be expected to wear slacks and a button-down shirt, just as he had on. He cleared his throat there was also a lovely young lady who was coming for the meal. Of course, he didn't want to impress her, not at all.

"But she's married, with a child," he grumbled. "Where could Mr. Keys be?" he wondered as he moved to his desk in his den. Seeing he was alone in the house, there wasn't an answer coming in a voice he could understand.

He left home with his pie about two o'clock. He wanted to find out what he could about Isabel's lovely grand-daughter. If somehow there was no husband, he'd like to know about it. After all, hadn't God Himself said, "It is not good for the man to be alone. I will make a helper suitable for him."? (Genesis 2:18) There was no harm in finding out about her, he rationalized. What better place than at the home of the people who'd invited him and them for dinner?

As he drove through town toward Ramon's house, he noticed that there were two cars parked in front of Isabel's place. It was too far away for him to see where the second car's license plate was from, but it was definitely not from Georgia. He let out the air he hadn't known he was holding. He'd have Ramon and Sandy to himself for at least a few minutes. All the businesses in town were dark and closed as he went by. Not like Billings, at least something, a gas station or a convenience store would be open on Thanksgiving there. He pulled in next to the house and cut the engine. Grabbing his pie, he hurried to the front door and knocked.

"Come on in!" the cheery voice called.

Roger opened the door to a most delicious smell. Immediately his nose went in the air and his stomach growled, he rubbed it with his free hand even before he saw anyone. Ramon came up and said, "What have you got?"

"Mom sent a care package that came yesterday. She makes the best pies and she sent me this one. I thought we could share it."

Without taking his eyes from the pie, Ramon took Roger's jacket and said, "Man! Let's go in the office and halve it! The turkey hasn't come out of the oven yet."

While he was speaking, however, they heard the sound that Sandy's wheelchair made and she appeared at the door. "What are you two schemers trying to get away with?"

Innocently, Roger shook his head. "It was all his idea I brought this pecan pie to share with everyone for dessert."

Sandy gave Ramon a disgusted look "Might know who'd try to run off with the goods."

Ramon shrugged. "You can't say I didn't try."

Sandy took the pie from Roger and smiled at the two friends. "Since you were headed for the office, why don't you go on in there until I call for some help with the turkey. I know you two guys have lots of man talk to catch up on. I mean, you two used to be best buddies, at least that's what I've been told." She looked pointedly at Roger and said, "You, my friend, have been keeping yourself in hiding."

Neither of them denied her statement and as Sandy headed back to the kitchen, Ramon urged Roger toward the office. Leaving the door open so they could hear when Sandy called, they both fell into chairs away from the desk. Ramon grinned at his friend and asked, "Bored? You came early."

The two men sat down in the gallery of Sandy's paintings and put their feet on the desk. During the hiking season this was the hub of activity, but during the winter nothing much happened. Roger looked around at all the beautiful pictures, some from every season. After a few minutes, he said, "No, wasn't bored. Tell me what you know about that lovely new package that came to my church today, with a child but no husband, by the way."

Ramon shrugged. "Not much. Isabel doesn't talk to me much, but she does to Sandy. All I know is what Sandy's told me. She's an assistant administrator in a large hospital in Grand Rapids, Michigan."

Roger raised his eyebrows. "Pretty high power! What's her husband do? Is he so busy he couldn't come with her for four days?"

Shaking his head, Ramon said, "There is no husband. His reserve unit was called up to fight in the war against terrorism. He was caught in sniper fire. He died two years ago."

"That's the pits!" Roger exclaimed.

"Yeah, it is, but maybe she'd look at you, Man! You're not a half bad critter to look at, you know." Ramon's eyes twinkled as he looked at his handsome friend.

"Well, thanks a lot!" A tinge of pink crept up his Scandinavian skin

Ramon shrugged. "You got a hot somebody hidden away that nobody knows about? I mean, I guess you could."

"No, I haven't and you know it! There hasn't been one cotton-pickin' single woman in this town since I came except last summer and you gobbled her up."

Ramon shrugged, unrepentant. "That's the breaks of the game, Man!"

"Yeah, I know."

A cheery voice called, "I need some help here in the kitchen. Can you guys tear yourselves away from your meaningful male conversation to help me?"

"On our way, Love," Ramon called back.

The two friends left the office and moved down the hall toward the tantalizing smells. "So what's to do?" Ramon walked over to his smiling wife and bent over. He put his hand on her shoulder, then lowered his lips to hers and gave her a long kiss. "Mmm, none better, Love. I do believe your kisses get better all the time."

She was holding a large carving knife by the point. After their kiss, she put the handle into Ramon's hard chest. "You can carve the turkey. You, strong friend, can carry those big bowls to the table in the dining room." As she turned to show Roger which bowls she meant, she said, "Put them down the middle of the table, on either side of the centerpiece. The platter with the turkey goes in front of Ramon's chair at this end, but everything else can go anywhere. People can pass things around. There should be one extra place for Isabel's sweet potatoes. Roger, I know that's something you can handle."

Roger smiled at the lovely young woman. "Gotcha! I'll get that table loaded as quick as I can. These smells are making me starved."

As Roger came back from taking his first load, he asked, "So how come it's Isabel and her company and me? What about Millie and Derek? Don't they rate as family?"

"What about them?" Ramon answered. "Derek and I don't get along too well and Mom's still got glass in her craw because of Sandy. We put a call in to Philadelphia, but Colleen still thinks Sandy should be home, never mind that she's married now. Charlie has to do his mail route tomorrow and Saturday because too many others asked off for this weekend. Marcy doesn't get off at all for the holiday and she's working nights. Ed's got his girlfriend and well... you know. We're planning a trip up there for several days at Christmas, so we didn't push it."

"Where's your family, Roger?" Sandy asked.

"Dad's the ranch foreman on a huge spread outside Billings, Montana and Sis is married to a high-powered lawyer in St Louis, Missouri. I always have an open invitation to go either place for Thanksgiving, but it always seems like such a long ways to go for so short a time. I'm going to Billings for almost two weeks with Christmas in the middle. My sister and her husband also come. We gather there every year for Christmas."

"Christmas is on Sunday, what'll your church do?"

"The doors'll stay closed."

"That's too bad. Vansville can't celebrate the true reason of Christmas," Sandy said.

Roger shrugged. "Yeah, that's true, but that's the way it is. I've never held a service in the church on Christmas Eve or Christmas Day because I leave. No one else has ever volunteered to do something."

Isabel's kitchen smelled good. She always cooked her sweet potatoes, never took them from a can. Soon after she came from Raylyn's room, she had a large pan cooking on the stove. While they cooked, she stirred up some blueberries with Heidi adding sugar and butter for her. She also insisted that the sweet potatoes always tasted better after they were cooked if they were baked with the butter and sugar to melt and saturate the pieces of potato. While they baked on one side of her oven, she baked her blueberry cobbler on the other side. It smelled good enough to make anyone's mouth water.

Isabel had let Heidi cut up the chunks of butter into both pans and had given her free reign with the brown sugar also. Both dishes were well covered with both butter and brown sugar. Raylyn only sat and watched, the older and younger person wouldn't let her lift a finger. She smiled, loving the way Isabel and Heidi related to each other.

Isabel looked at the clock and turned off the oven. "Well, little one, we'll leave these things in the oven until we're ready to leave, then we'll put them in my insulated carrier to take along. You and your mommy run along and get ready to go. We only have about fifteen minutes before we should leave."

"'K, Gamaw!" She gave Raylyn a huge smile. "Come on, Mommy!"

Raylyn slid out of the seat, saying, "I'm coming, Pumpkin."

In their room, Heidi asked, "Is we seein' the lady in that chair with wheels?"

"Yes, Sweety. We're going as guests to Ms Sandy and Mr. Ramon's house."

"Gamaw said somebody else comed."

"Yes, Pastor Roger will be there, too."

"Oh, yes, him! Good! Mommy, you gotta tell him he's my new daddy."

"Heidi!" Raylyn gasped. "I'll do no such thing! Pastor Roger and I only met this morning. I'm not about to tell him that! He may already have a girl friend."

"Nuh-uh, Mommy. I knowed he don't."

Shaking her head emphatically, Raylyn said, "It doesn't matter, I'm not telling him any such thing. And you, young lady, will not tell him that, either!"

"Aw, Mommy, how do I get a daddy for Christmas?"

Raylyn cleared her throat. "Heidi, I never promised you that! I told you you must be patient and wait for Mommy to find the right man."

"But I waited!" she pouted.

"Sweety, it was only a few days ago you wrote your letter to Santa."

"It was long time! 'Sides, he gotta work fast, Santa only leaves the nor'pole once a year, so he gotta brung him for Christmas."

"I know, but remember Jesus is with us always. He may not hurry quite so fast."

Heidi had finished dressing, so she put her hands on her hips and gave her mommy a scowl. "Mommy, you're just makin' 'scuses. Jesus can work even faster'n Santa if He want."

Raylyn sighed, turning to the mirror to try to rescue the job she'd done for church earlier. How do you counteract such reasoning? "I know that, Sweety. Jesus can do anything, I know. We'll have to wait and see what happens. Mommy's not going to be the one to say and neither are you, do you understand?"

Copying the sigh, Heidi said, "Yes, Mommy, I 'stand."

When the two came from the guest room, Isabel picked up her insulated bag and said, "I'm ready to go! Get your coats, it's snowing out, so it's plenty cold. We'll be there even before the car warms up."

"'K, Gamaw! Can we makes a snowman?"

"I doubt it, little one."

"I like snow!"

Heidi clamored into the seat behind Raylyn, for the short distance between the two places Raylyn wouldn't worry about Heidi's carseat. Isabel put her insulated bag on the seat beside Heidi. When all the doors were closed and the seatbelts fastened, Isabel backed around Raylyn's car and headed away from her little house. She drove through town, passed the closed businesses and turned onto the paved driveway of the last house before the open road.

"Ah, Roger's here already!" Isabel exclaimed. "I bet the old bachelor's been trying to pilfer some of Sandy's turkey before we get there."

"Gamaw, he not old! He be just right to be my new daddy."

Nobody opened the doors before Isabel shut off the engine. Seriously, Isabel looked at the little girl in the rearview mirror. "Little one, that's something that your mommy and Roger have to decide. You and I must keep our mouths shut about that."

Heidi's head dropped and she mumbled into her chest, "I know. Mommy say that, too."

Raylyn gave Isabel a grateful smile.

Everyone in the house heard the four doors close on the car stopped on the parking lot. As Ramon stood up to get the door, he said, "That must mean she's bringing food, too. Bless her, she's a dear."

"Of course she is!" Sandy exclaimed. "The woman's eighty years old, she shouldn't be doing so much!"

"She loves to cook, Sweetheart, let her."

Sandy was right behind Ramon as he opened the door. "Isabel, what's in your bag?" Sandy asked. "Mmm, it smells super!"

"Just candied sweet potatoes and blueberry cobbler."

The little voice spoke up, "I help Gamaw, I done the sugar and butter. An' we stuck the pans in the oven, too."

"Oh, wow!" Sandy exclaimed as she held out her hands for Isabel's bag. "Heidi, want to come help me find a place for these?"

"Oh, yes! Where's Mr. Roger?"

"He's in there. Come on, hop up by my feet and I'll give you a ride!"

Heidi's eyes grew to saucers. She looked from Sandy's face to the footrest and back again. "Oh, wow! Can I?"

"Of course!" Conspiratorially, she added, "We'll get there real fast this way."

Heidi stepped up on Sandy's footrest and they took off.

Raylyn stood watching the pair, a smile spread across her face. Sandy turned her chair nearly on a dime and headed for the kitchen with Heidi standing on the edge of the footrest and holding on to the armrest without the controls. As Ramon took all three coats, Isabel whispered to Raylyn, "Isn't she something?"

"She's wonderful!" Raylyn exclaimed.

After the pair had disappeared into the kitchen and Ramon returned from depositing the coats in the nearest room, he led them into the living room where Roger was. The young man hadn't been playing entirely fair he'd been standing at the window that looked out on the walk from the parking lot to the front door. Even though the drapes had been drawn back, he'd stood back far enough that he was not obvious from outside, but he had a good view of the trio as they came up the walk. Of course, he hadn't really looked at Isabel or even Heidi much, but he'd zeroed in on Raylyn. Now he sat in a comfortable chair.

"I guess everyone's been introduced before, so let's sit down until Sandy calls us for dinner. Everything's ready, it shouldn't be but a minute," Ramon said.

A cheery voice called, "Ramon, Honey, could you ask about drinks?"

"Sure, Sweetheart!"

Ramon quickly gathered the information then left the room, which left a very uncomfortable pair of young adults and an old lady. Isabel turned to Roger, who nearly groaned internally. "So, young man, what do you do with your time six days a week?"

Roger sat back against the seat and said, "Isabel, I have a tiny farm. I own six acres outside of town. I graze my cow on the grass on the field behind my house and small barn. I have chickens, an old dog and a cat. My six acres is all that's cleared on the hillside, but the man who owns the rest of the land wants it cleared and made into farmland. He's given me all the trees as payment, so I spend lots of time cutting trees into firewood. In the evenings I'm writing a book I hope to have published soon."

Nodding, Isabel said, "Sounds like you're quite industrious, I wasn't aware of all of that." Nodding to her grand-daughter, she continued, "Raylyn's an assistant administrator of a hospital in Grand Rapids for several years. She's really busy she can't come see me very often."

"I see." He looked at Raylyn and asked, "Do you see much blood and gore?"

"Oh, no," she was perfectly at ease talking about her work. Ever since she'd taken the job she'd loved every minute of it. "No, not at all. In fact, I see way too many papers and computer screens to my liking."

Roger chuckled. "I hear that!"

"Come on, everybody!" Ramon's voice boomed. "Dinner's served."

The three in the living room stood and Roger moved immediately to Raylyn's side. He didn't touch her, but she could feel his warmth close beside her. It sent her heart pounding in her chest so hard she was sure he could hear it. They followed Isabel through the archway into the room dominated by the big table covered with a white tablecloth and nearly groaning with large dishes of food. There had been covers on them when Roger brought them in, but Ramon had removed those covers and the colors of the many dishes dominated the table.

As soon as they'd crossed under the arch, Heidi skipped over and took Isabel's hand. Her little face was beaming with a smile as she led her toward a seat on the left side of the table. When they reached the chair, Heidi touched it and said, "Gamaw, you sit there and I sit next." She pointed to the end chair and said, "Mr. Roger, you sit in that seat and Mommy you sit over there. Ms Sandy goes in the empty place and Mr. Ramon gots the big chair up there where the turkey sits."

Roger looked down at the little girl who was the image of her mommy. "Have you got it all figured out, Heidi?"

"Uh-huh, but Ms Sandy help me. See, there be only two of you guys so you gotta sit at the little parts of the table, it's 'quired."

Keeping a straight face, Roger looked down at the pretty little child and nodded sagely. "Ah, so that's how it goes."

"'Course! And 'sides, I sit here, 'cause I got milk and nobody else does."

"I saw Ms. Sandy gave you a ride on her chair."

Heidi's curls bobbed up and down as she nodded and clapped her hands. She exclaimed, "Oh, yes, it be fun! We ride fast!"

"I know! I watched you."

Before Raylyn could pull out her own chair, Roger slipped behind her and pulled it out for her. Very solicitously he held the chair and helped her pull it in to the table. He was rewarded by a smile as she looked up at him over her shoulder. His eyes twinkled as he smiled back at her. Ramon couldn't do that for Sandy, so he went to Isabel's chair and pulled it out for her. He smiled at her as he did.

"Young man," she said, "I'm not used to all this attention!"

"It's okay, Isabel, you deserve it, you gave my sweetheart a place to live until I got slowed down enough to marry her."

"Yes, God had to knock you senseless before you figured it out!"

Ramon chuckled. "No, Isabel, I'd figured it out before, but I couldn't be sure until then that the other half of the equation had it figured out. When I woke up flat on my back and she was there, then I knew for sure we were both on the same page. It was all downhill from there."

Roger grinned. "Yeah, I'd say. I don't remember did you even get home from the hospital before you proposed?"

Sandy reached out and took Raylyn's hand. As she took Ramon's, she said, "Let's hold hands while we say grace." Ramon reached over for Isabel's. That prompted Raylyn to tentatively lay her other hand on the table. Roger didn't hesitate, he picked it up and immediately his thumb began making circles on the back of her hand. She shifted in her chair and took a quick glance at Roger, but he had looked away as he reached for Heidi's hand. When they were holding hands around the table, Sandy said, "Roger, would you say the blessing?"

"Since it's your first Thanksgiving and we're in your home, I think it'd be appropriate for the head of your house to say it." He didn't add out loud, but to himself he said, *Besides, my mind's a blank holding onto this lovely hand.*

Ramon didn't hesitate he grinned, but closed his eyes immediately and said, "Our Father, we want to thank You for this day. We've been in church and heard some good preaching and now we're gathered around this table for a feast. On this Thanksgiving Day we want to give You our thanks for all Your blessings, including this food. Bless also the hands that have prepared it. In Jesus Name, amen."

"Amen," Roger added, quietly.

Roger was reluctant to let go of the hand he held in his right hand. He definitely felt a connection with this woman. He didn't want to flatter himself, but he thought that perhaps she felt it too. For the first time in his entire life he wished he was left handed so he could eat and hold her hand at the same time. He felt a tug and reluctantly he let the hand go, but he'd have been content to hold it all night. His gaze went to her face and she smiled tentatively at him. It definitely sent a shard of awareness through his whole body and he smiled back.

The little hand on his other side slid from his and before he'd stopped looking at the lovely woman to his right, two little hands were clapping. Heidi was on her knees looking at all the dishes of food on the table. "Oh, this be great! We gots so much food and it's so yummy!" Looking directly at Roger, she asked, "Does a daddy usually put the food on a little girl's plate?"

There was a moment of stunned silence, broken a second later by a gasp from Raylyn, as the full impact of what her daughter had said hit her. However, it left her speechless. Roger felt like he'd been hit in the solar plexus with a sledge hammer, but after grabbing a breath to fill his empty lungs, he stammered, "Well-ll, Heidi, perhaps he does. Will you need some help?"

"Uh-huh. Mommy usually does, but she sit over there."

That'd be one way out of playing daddy. He gave the child a smile and said, "Maybe you'd better give her your plate."

Shaking her head, Heidi said, "No, it be you. See, when you gets a big dish you puts a little on here, then a big on yours."

Nodding, Roger said, "I see. I'll remember. It may help me someday when I get to be a little girl's daddy."

Heidi opened her mouth, but there was movement across from her as Raylyn shook her head and next to her as Isabel put her hand on the child's back. Heidi closed her mouth, then nodded and said, "That be good, Mr. Roger."

Ramon chuckled as he picked up the turkey platter, then looking across the table at his friend, he said, "Not forward or anything."

Roger didn't look at his friend, but at the lady to his right. The high color on her cheeks kicked him in the chest and made him desperately want to go back to holding her hand, or perhaps even kissing her....instead he said, "Oh, no, not one bit!"

Raylyn felt like crawling in a hole and pulling in the sod. She ducked her head and looked at her plate. Her hands in her lap worried her napkin as she wadded it up into a tight ball, while the pink worked its way up her neck to her cheeks, burning as it went. Roger's brain just about emptied as he saw that pink on those lovely cheeks, but he swallowed and brought his mind back. He chuckled at her non-verbal response and picked up a bowl of dressing that sat in front of him.

As he took the spoon, he muttered, "Now, let's see, a little goes on this plate and a lot goes on this one. After I do that I pass it on."

Laughing and clapping her hands as Roger handed the bowl to Isabel, Heidi exclaimed, "That be just right, Mr. Roger!"

As the food was passed, Isabel decided not to let Heidi monopolize the conversation. She didn't know the child well, because she'd only seen her one other time as an infant, but now she seemed to have endless energy and nearly the same amount of words, so she asked, "Roger, where'd you get your message today? I've heard from my friend, Geraldine that you usually read something from some book you have, but you didn't today."

Roger took a deep breath and shook his head, before he said, "Isabel, I have no idea where that message came from today! A few days ago I went to my office planning to find something to use for this service. When I found I'd already used all the readings and helps in my book, I looked up that Psalm and read it through. One of the verses really inspired me and I wrote down my thoughts, but when

I reached the lectern this morning, words started flowing from my mouth. I didn't seem to have any control over what I said. I never even said what I'd written down, either. The words stopped and what I'd written didn't seem appropriate."

Sandy was grinning, but before she could say anything, Isabel nodded and said, "Young man, that's called the prompting of the Holy Spirit. The Spirit knew there was someone in that service who needed to hear what you said. He put those words in your mouth. I must say, your message was very appropriate and well received, from what I heard people saying at the close."

"Thanks, Isabel," Roger said, humbly.

FOUR

Glancing momentarily at Sandy across the table from her, but then quickly back to Roger, Isebel said, "You know, I had a wonderful idea pop into my head! Just now, in fact."

"Oh, really? What's that? I'm a bit leary of these ideas you have."

Isabel picked up a roll from the basket in front of her, then passed the basket on to Ramon and said, "I know you and Ramon and Sandy will be gone for Christmas, but I think for the Sunday before Christmas there ought to be another concert at your church, a Christmas concert. I am very sure there is one here who could fill two hours with some heavenly Christmas piano music without any difficulty. Don't you agree, Roger?"

Roger had been watching Sandy's face during most of Isabel's speech. Her mouth had opened, but there hadn't been an opportunity for her to squeeze a word in. Still not giving Sandy a chance to speak, he nodded and said, "Isabel, I agree one hundred percent! What a magnificent idea!" Then before Sandy could answer either of them, Roger said, "Sandy, you'd have no trouble whipping something like that up in two weeks, would you?"

After a pause, Sandy looked at him with her eyebrows raised and asked, "Roger Clemens, do they teach you how to pleasantly twist somebody's arm at that seminary where you trained?"

Looking as innocent as possible, Roger exclaimed, "Sandy! Why would you say that? Pleasantly twist…?"

"Because my friend that is exactly what you're trying to do right now with my arm! If you twist too hard I won't be able to use it to play, you know."

Heidi's head was going back and forth. A scowl marred the little girl's forehead. A three year old was a literal child. Pointing from Roger to Sandy, she said, "Ms Sandy, Mr. Roger is here, you be there. He not twist your arm. He too far away."

Sandy looked at the little girl and said, "Heidi, you'll learn as you grow up that some people's words feel like their hands are doing the work instead of their lips. Mr. Roger's words felt like he was twisting my arm."

"Oh, 'K, but I hope he don't twist it too hard, you play real pretty tis morning. I like it a lot. I wish we live close so you could teach me how to play the peony like you."

Sandy brought her hand to her lips and sent a kiss to the little girl. "Thanks, Sweetheart, I appreciate that. I wish you lived closer, too. I'd love to have you be one of my students." She looked at Roger and said, "And would this be in place of your noise-making praise group?"

Getting into the spirit of the moment, Roger took a mouthful of cranberry sauce, but didn't answer her directly, instead he said, "Why don't we make it a matinee, like say, at two o'clock in the afternoon? Or maybe three. If we had an intermission as we had last time and you played a little over or there was an encore at the end, when I announce it this Sunday I could ask the ladies to bring some snack food for afterward." Without looking at Sandy he said to Ramon, "What do you say? You'd be the MC, of course and we'd have a really fine way to put our village into the Christmas spirit."

Ramon waved his hand while Roger finished. "Hey, wait a minute! I made it through that last one, but I had about a month to digest it. You're springing this with only two weeks! I know Sandy can come up with a two hour concert, but me - you know mom said I stutter."

Giggling, Sandy's hand covered Ramon's. "Honey, you didn't stutter once when you were there on the platform. You did the best job, I was really proud of you and I told you that."

He turned his hand over and threaded his fingers with hers then he squeezed hers. "Love, you know I might with so little time to rehearse." He snapped his fingers. "Maybe Roger ought to be the MC."

Sandy shook her head and squeezed his hand again. "If you're not the MC then the answer to Roger's question is absolutely no. Do *you* want to disappoint the people of this fair town like that?"

Roger threw his head back and laughed. It was a full laugh, one that drew others into it. After a minute, he looked at their two hands still holding each other and said, "And who's twisting whose arm now?" After another chuckle, he said, "Do I perceive that we'll have a concert on the Sunday before Christmas?"

Heidi nodded and said, "Oh, yes, Mr. Roger. I think you twisteded Ms Sandy's arm just right. And, umm, Ms. Sandy twisteded Mr. Ramon's arm good, too. It be in your church?"

Roger looked at the child's happy face and said, "You think so?"

"Uh-huh."

"So, what day next week can I come by and get your list so I can put together a program? Oh, and a picture, of course."

Sandy sighed, "Roger, you are something else! I'll need to think about it and get out my books. How about next Thursday?"

"That'll be great! And a picture, of course."

Sandy sighed, "I heard you."

Ramon's eyes twinkled as he looked at Sandy and asked, "Will you have something by Mr. Chop in, Sweetheart?"

"Mr. Chop in!" Heidi exclaimed. "Mr. Ramon, you and Ms Sandy know somebody call Mr. Chop in?"

Ramon chuckled, but Sandy smiled at the little girl. "No, Sweety, that's a little joke Ramon and I have from the last concert. One of the men who wrote one of the songs I played before, his name is Mr. Chopin, but on a paper it looks like Chop-in. Ramon was being silly, he knows how to say it right." Turning to Roger, she gave him a big smile and said, "You'll have that ramp well salted, won't you?"

"You know I will! If you're going to play, it'll be perfect for you." He raised his hand, as if swearing an oath. "I promise."

"Thank you." Sandy turned toward Raylyn and said, "You know, we're totally ignoring you! Raylyn, do you and Heidi have family in Grand Rapids?"

Raylyn had been perfectly happy watching the interchange between the others at the table. Once Isabel made her suggestion, she was also quiet. It was very obvious that the newlyweds really loved each other and that they had a good relationship with Roger. It was obvious that Sandy was a most talented woman and she wasn't afraid to use it. Working in a hospital setting, Raylyn knew that Sandy was very remarkable, a lady with a severe handicap, but with a sunny disposition and never a word of bitterness or cynicism.

On top of that, she'd been watching Roger. The only ministers she'd ever known were those in the churches she'd attended, both as a child and now as an adult. None of them had been young like Roger, except for the youth pastor in her present church. The ones she'd known herself had been married with children who were teen aged or older. In fact, her present pastor had grandchildren who lived close by and went to his church. She'd never eaten a meal in their homes or known them well enough to enjoy their company except at a rare fellowship gathering at the church. This young man was like anyone else she'd ever known who was her age.

She was completely caught off guard by Sandy's question. She looked at Sandy for a second, trying to remember if she'd heard the question. She gave an inner shrug, no harm in making a stab at what she thought Sandy had asked. "Um, family? Well, I have a great-aunt who lives in an assisted care facility. She's the only one who lives there in Grand Rapids. We don't see her much she doesn't know us when we do go. About four years ago my dad was killed in the line of duty while he was on patrol in one of the seedier sections of Detroit. Mom still lives in one of the bedroom communities near Detroit. Grandma Isabel is her mother, but she doesn't do much outside her home now that Dad's gone."

"That's too bad! He was a policeman?"

"Yes, and a very good one. He was about to get a promotion to detective when he was killed." She looked at Sandy and asked, "You folks have a lovely home and this meal is fantastic! What do you folks do?"

"Ramon owns his own hiking service. It's very popular, as you can imagine, with Vansville sitting squarely in the foothills of the Appalachians. Starting in the early spring, all summer and late into the fall he leads groups on hikes around the area and has another man working with him. I'm his receptionist, answer the phone and do the bookings for the service. Of course this is the off season."

"Listen to her!" Ramon said, disgustedly. He shook his head then kissed her hand. "Sandy might have come as my receptionist, but she's way more than that! Isabel and I learned that soon after she came. Sandy's an artist of the highest caliber; her gallery in Philadelphia is constantly sold out. She can't keep up with their demand. Locals have commissioned many pieces and we've sold lots of her paintings right from here." He nodded down the hall. "We call our office her gallery. She's also an accomplished pianist. I'm sure you figured that out and has a scad of students who come each week for lessons."

"Yes, I enjoyed her playing." She turned to Sandy and said, "I wish I could be here that Sunday, I'd love to hear what you'll play for Christmas."

"That's an excellent idea!" Roger exclaimed. "We'll make a recording."

"Then I'll really stutter," Ramon groaned. "If I see a mike, I know for a fact I'll stutter."

Disgusted, Sandy exclaimed, "You won't either! You lead groups of hikers all those months each year. You don't know those people and most of these people know you. Why should you stutter in front of people you know and not with strangers?"

"I don't know, but I'm a lot more nervous up there than on a trail."

Sandy patted his hand and smiled lovingly at him. "You'll do fine, Honey! Raylyn, what do you do as a hospital administrator?"

Wishing the conversation could go on around her, Raylyn said, "My degree is in business administration, so I oversee all the accounts generated by the patients we have at the hospital in Grand Rapids, which means I have five financial counselors under me. They all have to clear their decisions with me."

"Wow! I bet that keeps you hopping!"

"It does, but I'm glad to say I've always been able to leave my work at the hospital and I don't have to work much overtime."

"With Heidi, I'm sure you're glad of that."

"I am. The only thing, I hate leaving her at day care for so long every week."

"As a single mom, I'm sure that's true."

Sandy looked around at the empty plates and rubbed her own tummy. "How about we move to the living room for more conversation and save dessert for a little. We surely can't do justice to all that's still in the kitchen after all this!"

"What's still in the kitchen besides Grandma's cobbler?" Raylyn gasped.

"Roger brought a pecan pie his mom sent him and Sandy's made an apple pie and some sugar cookies for some little person."

"For me?" Two little eyes lit up.

"Yes, for you! Want to help me take things to the kitchen, you can have one then, okay?"

Clapping her hands, Heidi slid from her chair and ran to Sandy's side. "'K, Ms Sandy! I help you now!"

"Be very careful, Sweety!" Raylyn exclaimed, knowing how the child could become careless when she was excited.

"I be real careful, Mommy!"

Raylyn also stood, but Sandy immediately said, "Oh, no, Ramon and I and our helper can take these things out, you folks go on in the living room. We'll be along in a few minutes. We only need to load the dishwasher."

Isabel also stood and pushed her chair up to the table. "I have to use your restroom. It's down the hall a bit, isn't it?"

"Yes, there on the right, Isabel."

Raylyn looked up at Roger who was standing silently beside her, but not touching her, of course. She had to swallow when she saw the look in his eyes, that were a dark blue, but looking intently at her. He was a very handsome man. His outdoor work kept him well toned. He didn't have facial hair and his blond hair was trimmed to perfection. She wondered if that was because this was a small town and people who lived in a small town had a certain image they expected from their pastor or if that was his preference.

Because he took her breath away, she hesitantly said, "Um, I guess that means we're to go in the other room and find a seat."

Smiling at the lovely lady, he held out his hand toward the living room and said, "Yes, I think that's what it means. After you, my lady."

Raylyn walked in front of him, but not so far that he couldn't put his hand on the small of her back as they headed into the next room. With his hand there she could hardly put one jello-kneed leg in front of the other, so she headed for the closest seat. She surprised Roger by sitting on the couch. Gratefully, he sat down beside her and leaned back, still with his hand on her back. "Are you busy tomorrow?"

"I have no idea what Grandma Isabel has planned."

"We'll find out when she joins us. If she has no plans for you and Heidi, would you and she like to come to my farm for, say, the afternoon and start it off with some hot soup and finish it off with some hot chocolate?"

"Heidi would love that! We live close to downtown Grand Rapids and she's only seen cows and chickens on a field trip her daycare took."

"How about you, pretty lady, would you like to come?" his words were meant only for her ears and they were so close to her ear that they moved strands of her hair.

"I...I think it'd be great," she whispered back, unable to make the words any stronger. She couldn't help it her heart was fluttering wildly in her chest. She was sure he could hear it.

Roger saw movement and knew Isabel was close to entering the living room, so he moved and leaned back against the couch, putting his arm across the top behind Raylyn, who was still sitting forward a little. Isabel noticed how closely Raylyn and Roger sat beside each other, but she made no comment. As soon as she sat in the chair close by, he asked, "Isabel, what are your plans for Raylyn and Heidi tomorrow?"

Letting a shudder run down her back, she said, "It won't be shopping, that's for sure! Blairsville is something else the day after Thanksgiving."

Slowly letting herself lean back and therefore allowing her head to find Roger's arm, Raylyn said, "I think that's true anywhere, Grandma. If I were at home tomorrow, I'd stay home for that very reason. I hate to shop with the crowds. Roger has asked if Heidi and I could go to his farm for the afternoon."

Nodding, she said, "I don't see why not."

A whirlwind came into the living room, followed by a smiling, handsome young man. When the chair stopped, a little girl jumped off and came over to the couch. She didn't climb onto the empty cushion beside Roger, or ask him to lift her up onto it. She turned her back to it and jumped back, high enough to land squarely on the seat beside him. Raylyn didn't act as if she was afraid Heidi wouldn't land where she was supposed to, either. It appeared she had done it many times before.

The instant she was seated, she clapped her hands and exclaimed, "Mr. Ramon and me talk Ms Sandy into playin' Twinkle, Twinkle Little Star. She gonna do it now. Mr. Roger, you and Mommy gotta listen real good."

"Oh, we will!" Roger promised. He knew what they were in for.

She looked up at him as Sandy threaded her way to the piano and attached her black pouch to her chair. "How come you're sittin' next to Mommy like that?"

By now, Roger had pulled his hand from the back of the couch. "We were the only ones who came in here at first and I had something to ask her." He looked at Raylyn and when she nodded, he asked, "Would you like to come with your mommy to my farm tomorrow to see my cow and chickens?"

She clapped her hands and nearly yelled, "Oh, yea! For all day?"

"How about for lunch first?"

"Yup!" She bounced on the seat. "That be great, Mr. Roger. I see one cow afore in my life." She saw Sandy push the black pouch onto the back of her chair, and asked, "Ms. Sandy, what you do that for?"

"Heidi, remember this morning I told you my legs didn't work so I had to do everything with my hands when I drive?" When the child nodded, Sandy continued, "Well, most people use their feet on those pedals down there when they play the piano. Since I can't do that, my brother and I rigged up this thing that I use instead of my feet. It does the same thing somebody's foot would do on those silver things down there."

Heidi's mind was ever active. She heard Sandy say, 'brother', so she said, wistfully, "Oh. I wish I had a sister."

"Maybe you will someday, Sweety," Sandy answered and smiled at her. Those words sent a huge knife into Raylyn's heart. Heidi deserved a brother or sister and also a daddy, but was she ready to give her one?

Sandy put her hands on the keys and said to Heidi, "Would you like to sing the song along with me as I play this first part?"

Her curls bobbing as Heidi jumped off the couch, she said, "Oh, yes! I like that song a lot, Mommy and me singed it sometime."

Sandy started playing and the child's clear voice joined the lovely rich voice of the pianist. The simple tune filled the room as the two sang. They finished the verse and Sandy nodded to Heidi, but then her fingers went on to play Mozart's masterful rendition of the piece that inspired someone to pen the childhood poem to go with it. Heidi stood and watched Sandy's fingers fly over the keys. After a few minutes when she knew there would be lots more, Heidi turned and came back to sit on the couch beside Roger, this time she climbed slowly onto the cushion and turn around then plop on the cushion, she was enthralled with the music.

"Wow!" she whispered and Roger nodded, but didn't say anything. Raylyn couldn't remember when Heidi had been so still and quiet.

When Sandy raised her hands from the keys, Heidi was the first to clap. Everyone else joined her, but then she exclaimed, "Ms Sandy, that be so-o-o good! I not know about that other part of Twinkle, Twinkle."

Sandy smiled and said, "Thank you, Heidi. It's one of my favorites, too."

"Could you teach me to play that?"

"I think so, come on over." Sandy held out her hand to the child. When Heidi was beside her, Sandy moved her chair away from the piano and reached for the child. "Come on up here." Sandy turned to the others in the room and said, "You folks go on with your conversations, we'll be busy for a few minutes."

However, Raylyn was totally enchanted with Sandy and watched as she put Heidi on her lap, then pulled herself back close to the piano. Oblivious to the rest of the adults, Sandy took Heidi's hands and placed them on the piano keys, then began pressing the fingers down so that the notes sounded and played the tune. When they finished the verse, Heidi's face was beaming and she raised her hands to clap.

Still from Sandy's lap, she turned and said, "Mommy, did you hear that? I played Twinkle, Twinkle Little Star!"

"I heard you, Sweety. Maybe you could try it again."

"Oh, Ms. Sandy, can I?"

"Of course. Would you like to try it without my hands?"

Nodding, she said, "But you help me if I forget?"

"Sure I will!"

"'K." Heidi never looked at her mommy, but lifted her hands to the keys. She concentrated so hard that she caught her tongue between her teeth and one curl slipped across her cheek. Heidi began and very slowly pushed down all the right keys until she'd played the tune. "I did it!" she exclaimed.

Sandy smiled and started clapping. "Yes, you did great, Heidi! You're a very smart girl because you did it the very first time. Lots of my students can't do it the very first time they try, but you did!"

"Oh, it be fun! I like to sing, too. We singed a lot in my Sunday school class. Teacher singed us a new song every time and then we sing. Sometime we singed four or two more. You sing good, too, Ms Sandy."

When the others stopped clapping, Sandy pulled the black pouch from her chair. Sandy looked at Raylyn and said to Heidi, "You know, I think I have something you'd like, you and your mommy. Want to come see? It's in the other room."

"Oh, yes!"

Raylyn looked at the other three in the room, but none of them gave her any clue, so she stood up and followed as Sandy, keeping Heidi on her lap, went down the hall toward the last room. Roger followed closely behind Raylyn, with Isabel and Ramon coming along behind. Sandy pushed the half opened door into Ramon's office wide and switched on the light, then wheeled herself into the room.

Raylyn gasped as she looked at all the beautiful pictures. "Oh, my! Look at all these beautiful paintings! You did them all, Sandy?"

Sandy nodded, but she said, "Now, I have to tell you. That one up there is Ramon's. These four belong together and they're so big I don't think you'd want them, but any one of the others that you like you can have."

Heidi flung her arms around Sandy's neck and exclaimed, "Really? Oh, Ms. Sandy these be so pretty! Mommy which one shall we get?"

"Are you sure?" Raylyn gasped. "You want us to take one? But you could sell any of them for a lot of money!"

"Of course, I'm sure! Heidi was such a big help in the kitchen and she played that piece exactly right the very first time and you're her mommy... Pick one."

Raylyn held out her hand and said, "Come on, Heidi, let's look at each one. There are so many to choose from."

"Yes!" the child exclaimed.

Heidi finally found one that was a beautiful winter scene, but tucked down in a lower corner, but very obvious, sat a snowman with a big black hat on his head, charcoal eyes and smile and a big carrot for a nose. He had a colorful red plaid scarf around his neck that looked like it was blowing in the breeze, there were red mittens on the ends of the stick arms and there were black shoes peeking out under his large round snow bottom. Of course, that's what caught Heidi's attention, but the snow covered mountains were magnificent.

Looking up at the picture, then pulling her hands from Raylyn's she clapped and exclaimed, "Mommy! Frosty, the snowman! Can we have this one, Ms. Sandy?"

"Of course, Ramon will take it down for you."

Heidi spun around and with a smile from ear to ear, she ran back to Sandy with her arms wide open. "Oh, Ms. Sandy, thank you, thank you! Mommy and me hang it real special at our house when we gets home."

"I'm glad, Sweety, I'm glad you found one you like." After hugging the little girl, she said, "I think our dinner's settled enough, let's go have dessert."

"'K, that cookie be really good, Ms. Sandy. I like dessert lots and I help Gamaw make that berry stuff, you know."

They ate dessert along with some extra good coffee and another glass of milk for Heidi. After everything was cleared away, they played a game even Heidi could play. Long after dark, Raylyn was feeling the effects of her not-so-long sleep the night before and Heidi's eyes were drooping, even though she was trying so hard to stay awake. She loved Ms. Sandy and had had the best time of her life. The joy of the day helped Raylyn forget her own sorrow.

Raylyn watched Heidi yawn for the fourth time and said, "I think I have a sleepy child who needs to go to bed. We didn't get here until three this morning, so I'm a little weary myself. We've had the best time, Ramon and Sandy! Heidi and I won't forget this Thanksgiving in a very long time, I promise you that."

After another yawn, Heidi said, "I had fun, Ms. Sandy!"

"I'm glad, Heidi. I hoped you would. I'm glad you came."

"Oh, yes! Mr. Roger, too."

"Yes, Ms. Heidi," Roger said, "I had a great time, too."

Soon Isabel took her empty dishes and her insulated carrying bag and mother and daughter out the door. It had stopped snowing and the clouds had moved off. The sky was now peppered with stars and a half moon shown silently down on them. It was silent in the little town and with everything closed for the holiday; there was no glow in the sky. Since the clouds cleared, it had turned quite a bit colder. Raylyn had to open the back door of Isabel's car for Heidi, but she climbed in by herself. Raylyn had to fasten her seatbelt and even though it was only a couple of blocks back to Isabel's place, Heidi was asleep before they arrived.

As Isabel pushed the gear stick into park, Raylyn said, "Grandma, how can she be such a wonderful person with such a handicap?"

"She is wonderful, isn't she? She was raised in a dedicated Christian home. From what she's told me, her dad and brother and sister have always treated her like any normal person and expected her to do as much as she could." She shook her head. "Of course, her mom has always been a wet blanket, but she's overcome that obstacle even. She is a wonderful Christian herself. Believe me, she's been an inspiration to everyone in this town. That concert she gave around Labor Day was the turning point. She's sold so many paintings and done a huge mural for a rich couple here in town and talk about piano students! I don't see how she'll have time to be Ramon's receptionist next year. I love her and hardly think of her as handicapped. I wish she was my grand-daughter just like you are."

"She's so good with Heidi!"

"Yes, she loves children. It's very obvious. I don't know if it's possible, but she deserves some of her own."

"Yes, she does."

After Isabel, Raylyn and a very sleepy Heidi left, Roger followed Ramon and Sandy to their kitchen. He felt a bit in the way until he sat down at their kitchen table and watched as Ramon rinsed the dessert dishes and handed them to Sandy to load into the dishwasher. It was only then he realized that Sandy couldn't reach into the sink it was too high for her to reach something on the bottom. Ramon worked on the pans while Sandy finished putting things away. They worked really well together.

When there was a lull in the noise, Roger said, "Thank you, you two for inviting me today. It's been a great time."

Chuckling, Ramon said, "I think there was a minute or two there that you were at a loss for words."

"Yeah, well, I've never had a three year old propose to me for her and her mom."

Sandy chuckled. "I think she was about to tell you more, but her other two relatives put the squash on it."

"Mmm, it had me worried for a minute there."

"So what do you think?" Ramon asked.

"About what?"

"About Raylyn!"

Roger shrugged and wet his lips. "She's beautiful, she's intelligent, she's a church goer, what's not to like?"

"So you're not interested since she lives a thousand miles away."

Shaking his head, Roger stretched out his legs under the table and said, "I never said I wasn't interested. It's true I can't pick up and move. I'd have to resign from the church and help them find someone else. I'd have to sell my farm and that might take some time. I don't feel like I'm too mobile right now, no."

"Suppose she moved here?"

"Why would she do that?"

Ramon shrugged. "It's obvious the child wants a daddy."

Roger pointed his thumb at his chest. "You think I'm daddy material?"

"You did all right with her today. She didn't seem to have a problem relating to you right from the start."

"Yes, you did, Roger," Sandy said. "Don't sell yourself short."

Trying not to let anything show on his face, Roger tried for nonchalance and said, "Well, nothing's been said. If the bridge comes up, maybe it'll get crossed and maybe it won't. We'll have to see."

Roger glanced up at the kitchen clock. "I guess I'd better go. Cow is probably prancing back and forth by the back door."

As he found his coat, Sandy asked, "Do you sell your milk, Roger?"

Shrugging into the jacket, he said, "I don't have a pasteurizer, so most of it I feed to my other animals."

"I'd pay you for a gallon a week."

He scowled. "Without being pasteurized?"

"Uh-huh."

"If you're sure. I have a gallon in the fridge right now, I milked it this morning. I'll bring it by in the morning. Would that be okay?"

"Great, how much do you want for it?"

He shrugged. "Would two dollars be too much? I have no idea what I should charge. It can't be what you'd pay in the store for regular milk."

"Of course, that's fine. You know I'll be here."

"Great! I'll see you then."

Roger zipped his coat, said goodbye again and went out into the cold night to his Jeep. He took his time driving home. The streets of the little town were dark and quiet the few streetlights didn't do much to light anything beyond the sidewalks. Several houses were dark, it wasn't late; so he figured those people were out of town. Of course, Thanksgiving was the most traveled holiday in the country. When he reached home there was a set of yellow eyes waiting by the back door and just as he'd predicted, Cow was prancing back and forth on the other side of the fence and began mooing as soon as she saw his lights.

He shut off the Jeep and made his way to the door. In between Cow's unhappy moos, Linus was purring loudly. He was sure he'd have some food waiting on the other side of that door. Roger opened the door the cat darted inside and was at his dish even before Roger had the door closed, the light on and his coat off. He hurried to his room and shed his good clothes, replacing them with his barn clothes so he could go milk. He sighed he hoped that soon Cow would go dry. Milking during the winter wasn't something he was looking forward to. Shrugging into his old coat, he grabbed up the milk pail and headed back out the door.

"Okay, okay! Give it a rest, Cow! I'm coming. Relief is only a few squirts away."

Later that night, Roger went to bed and looked out the window at the stars. Even through his regular sized window it seemed there were dozens. The sky was so clear and nearly black. He thought perhaps he could see forever. He couldn't see the moon, but it put a sparkling glow on the tops of the trees he could see through his window. It was a night to remember.

When he finally closed his eyes he saw a lovely face wreathed with beautiful auburn curls. He couldn't help but remember sitting close to her on the couch after dinner. She didn't seem to be hung up on the fact that he was a church man. Something else he hadn't thought about until now, no one had mentioned her dead husband. She hadn't acted as if he was still a big factor in her life, but who could tell? Then he remembered she'd leaned back and allowed her head to rest on his arm. That memory made his heart speed up. Her hair had been so soft and silky and smelled like spring.

As he lay there, his thoughts full of the lovely young woman, he murmured, "God in heaven, Raylyn would make a wonderful wife for me. You know how lonely I've been ever since Sandy came to town and I realized that my best friend had captured her. I know You could work something out, if You wanted to. I could sure hope that You would." He sighed, "We both know she lives a thousand miles away and that she's got a high power job, but that's no problem for You, either, Lord."

A verse from his childhood Sunday school teacher crossed his mind. "'...*we know that in all things God works for the good of those who love him...*'" (Rom. 8:28) Those words somehow reassured him as sleep pulled him in, but all night long his dreams were centered around a very lovely woman and her pretty little girl. Two people he'd spent all afternoon and evening with and whom he'd asked to come spend the next afternoon with him. Could he hope something could come of it? He sighed, this was a big bed and that side was cold and empty.

He woke up early to his four legged alarm clock outside his window. He sighed, as his feet hit the floor. Chores never went away. As he dressed and headed for the kitchen, he muttered, "Man! I only milked that beast less than eight hours ago! Can't she figure out that a man wants to sleep in once in a while?" He turned on his coffee maker then shrugged into his old coat, picked up the pail and headed out the door. He did his regular routine, fed the cow, milked her then turned her out. He cleaned the stall so there were no smelly remains and headed for the barrel with the scratch grain for the chickens. He filled the pail then let himself into their coop. He was about to roust the hens from their nests when he caught himself. Heidi had only seen live chickens once. Possibly she'd never seen a hen sitting on her eggs. Instead of pushing all the hens out onto the floor, he reached under two of his best layers and pulled out two eggs for his breakfast, then took his empty pail and left the coop. He fixed his breakfast, then rummaged in his freezer for some beef cubes to use for the soup he'd have for lunch.

Ramon's question came back to him. There was no question what he thought about the beautiful woman! If she'd have him, he'd move heaven and earth to make her his bride and her child his child. However, as he'd told them, he had obligations here. These people had called him to this church. He knew he hadn't been a good pastor, just as Sandy said, he hadn't told anyone about the old rugged cross in - he couldn't remember how long. He couldn't remember where, but he knew there was Scripture that told him as a pastor he was responsible for the souls of those he pastored. It sent a chill up his spine. That would change as of this week!

If he handed in his resignation, he felt obligated to help them find a replacement and what would he do in a big city like Grand Rapids? He shuddered to think, he'd never been a pastor of a large congregation; he didn't think he was that good, either. Not only that, he had this small farm and he certainly wasn't well off enough to keep it while moving to Michigan. He would have to sell it and who was interested in buying a small parcel of six acres? It was too small a plot for any cash crop and too far from town to be a good buy for a business man with a family. One thing in his favor, though, he'd had enough foresight to build more than a bachelor needed. It was a three bedroom house with two baths. Still, it would be hard to sell.

Who was he kidding? How could he be sure, since Raylyn said they lived close to downtown Grand Rapids, that she'd want to live this far out in the country? Maybe she didn't like the country smells, perhaps the weeds or pollen made her allergic. How about Heidi, would she adjust to being a country girl? With his salary, she'd probably want to work to keep up her lifestyle. He sighed, well he could provide babysitting if she did find a job around here.

He put the meat chunks in his crock pot and turned it on. "All, hypothetical," he grunted. "What am I worrying about? She may be mourning her dead husband still for all I know."

Something scratched at his back door. He looked Linus was curled up on his favorite rug between the kitchen and the living room. The noise came again. It had to be the old dog. He didn't have a bone, so he went to the pantry and pulled a large scoop of dogfood from the bag then went to the back door with it.

When he opened it the old dog looked up at him and his long tongue swiped his lips. "So you think it's breakfast time? Well, there's no bone today, so here's some kibble." As he emptied the scoop over the dog dish, he said, "I guess you'll have to find your own female, Curly, I've invited a young lady to spend the afternoon here. So, eat your heart out, Old man!"

It took Raylyn quite a while to fall asleep, even though she was very tired. Wednesday had been a very long day and the night very short on sleep. Thursday hadn't been physically strenuous, but Heidi had done her best to make it a bit stressful. Actually, she couldn't remember when she and Heidi had had such an exciting day. She shook her head, probably not since Dan had died. When her dad was killed, her mom had become the next thing to a recluse, but it hadn't affected her quite so much, as she'd already moved from her childhood home. Her mom went to church, but it was a huge city church and she sat nearly on the back row and didn't socialize before services. She didn't invite friends over, she just hurried out of church after each service so no one would ask her to join them to do anything. Raylyn had to invite themselves over to ever see her mom. She realized as she stared out the window at the cold winter scene that she'd started down that same road herself since Dan had been killed.

Not that she let her mom or her sister-in-law make her decisions, but she wondered what her mom would think if she became involved with Roger. Of course it was almost a moot point, she lived and worked in Grand Rapids and truly loved her job and Roger was a pastor in a small town in Georgia. She'd never known of a romantic relationship that truly lasted when the parties involved were a thousand miles apart. Perhaps military families did, but even they suffered. Of course nothing like that had been mentioned today.

Still she thought about the man. He was her age, he was the most handsome man she'd ever met and he had a great way about him. She'd liked his message this morning, which surprised her, because Isabel had said he didn't have much to say from the pulpit. He'd seemed surprised at his own words when they'd talked about it over dinner. She'd really like to go to his church on Sunday and see if what he'd done today was an anomaly or if he would be saying something relevant from Scripture. She was sure he'd be an excellent preacher if he used Scripture to speak to today's problems. What would Isabel say about going to his church instead of the big one she obviously loved in Blairsville? Finally, her eyes closed and sleep claimed her.

During the night, she woke with a start something had brought her back from a sound sleep. She lay under the warm covers and looked toward the window, across the bed that held the tiny lump of her daughter. The child was sound asleep obviously what ever woke her didn't bother Heidi. She smiled, it wasn't traffic, Isabel's house sat back a good ways from the street and besides there was no traffic in this tiny town. Still, she was so used to city traffic day and night, she knew it wasn't that. Moments later she heard a mournful howl and realized that had been what she'd heard, a wolf was calling to his mate or his pack and the night was so clear and still the sound had carried clearly from the hills that were quite a few miles out of town. No wonder she'd gotten awake, she'd never heard a wolf call before.

Roger said he lived on a small farm. She wondered if that wolf was closer to his place and if he'd heard it. She closed her eyes and saw clearly Roger's eyes, the color of the sky straight overhead on a perfectly clear day at noon. His hair was short, but not so short that she'd missed the waves of the longer hairs. He'd worn a white shirt in the pulpit and obviously hadn't changed to come to dinner, but the blue tie had set off his blue eyes and his ripe wheat colored hair. She could tell instantly that he wasn't a sit-behind-a-desk preacher; he didn't have to work out in a gym. His muscles, those in his arms, chest and legs were toned from his farm work and logging. Even the dress, button-down shirt couldn't hide them. He would be any woman's dream. Could he be hers? She stifled that thought and turned over. What could ever come of it? She was only here for the long weekend she might not see him after today.

She was about to fall back to asleep when the wolf's howl split the silence again. She knew this was a tiny town, but she hadn't been that aware that it was so close to wilderness. Wolves didn't come so close to civilization any more. Of course, she'd heard what Sandy said Ramon did for a living, but maybe it didn't register how remote this area of Georgia was. Why not? The Appalachian Trail started in Georgia and went north. She'd crossed it once and the area had been very remote and wild. Finally, sleep claimed her, but she slept with her dreams the rest of the night. They were dreams of a very handsome, in shape, young man with blond hair and blue eyes, who just happened to be the pastor of the only church in town.

It seemed only minutes later when that cold little hand was brushing her face again. "Mommy, wake up, come on!"

"Sweety," she murmured, "do you have to have such cold hands to wake me?"

"Mommy, do you gotta sleep so long? We 'posed to go to Mr. Roger's farm today. You needs to get up!"

To protect herself, Raylyn took the little cold hand and pulled it under the covers. "Pumpkin, it can't be lunch time yet. We aren't to go to Mr. Roger's place until it's time for lunch. Remember he said we'd start our time there with hot soup for lunch."

Heidi sighed, "Mommy, it be Saturday yet?"

"No, Sweety, it's Friday. Tomorrow's Saturday. Remember, I told you."

"Yeah, Teacher said we gots free days bacation this week. But you said they not be Saturday. I member you say that."

"That's right, Sweety, yesterday was Thursday, but it was a special day because it was Thanksgiving. Today's Friday, but we still have the day off because lots of people go away like we did for the long weekend. Then tomorrow's finally Saturday and Sunday we go to church."

"We's goin' to Mr. Roger's church." It was not a question.

Wanting to make it very clear right from the start, Raylyn said, "We came to see Grandma Isabel, Heidi. We'll go wherever she goes."

Mutinously, Heidi stamped her foot and said, "Mommy, she better go to Mr. Roger's church!" The little girl turned on her heel, yanked her hand from her mommy's and went to the door. "I tell her we go to Mr. Roger's church on Sunday. It be 'portant!" Before Raylyn had her wits about her, Heidi turned the knob and pulled the door open. Raylyn sighed as the door snicked shut behind the little girl.

She turned over and looked at the clock on the bedside table. It was seven o'clock and she hadn't heard any noise on the other side of the door. Only moments later she heard a banging across the hall and her heart climbed into her throat. "Heidi, no!" Raylyn's voice whispered loudly, but the child didn't hear her.

FIVE

Heidi was so intent on telling Isabel about going to Roger's church she was waking the lady up! Raylyn threw back the covers and scrambled from the warm bed. Goosebumps skidded down her back as her feet hit the cold floor, but she hardly noticed as she ran around the bed intent on grabbing her child before she'd roused Isabel. She yanked the door open just as Isabel's door opened across the hall and Raylyn's heart fell to her toes.

Heidi never turned to look at her mommy instead she looked up into the sleepy face of the old lady and said, "Gamaw, we go to Mr. Roger's church on Sunday!"

"Heidi! You mustn't talk to Grandma that way!" Raylyn said, reaching for Heidi's arm.

Ignoring Raylyn, Isabel pulled her robe around her and crouched down in front of Heidi. "Why do you say that, little one?"

Heidi, dressed in her Princess PJs, put her hands on her hips and with as much authority as any three and a half year old can project, she said, "Gamaw, Mr. Roger be my daddy some day. I know it! We go to his church on Sunday." Raylyn sucked in her breath, even so, cotton wadded up in her throat.

Taking the child's hand, Isabel stood up and took two steps back into her room, leaving the door open with Raylyn standing, immobile in the hallway looking in. She sat in the chair and pulled Heidi to her side. Holding her around the waist, she said, "Little one, what happened at Roger's church yesterday isn't what usually happens at that church. They never have Sunday school like I know you have at your church and I don't know of any children who go there. We didn't see any other children there yesterday. As far as I know, there aren't even any rooms they could use for Sunday school. Nobody plays music like Ms Sandy did yesterday."

"Why not?" Heidi demanded.

Isabel shrugged. "Every other Sunday that I've known about, Roger has a group of people who play guitars and drums and sing really loud songs for a long time before he speaks. They all use microphones so it will be even louder. One Sunday I was sick and it was spring, I had my windows open and I could hear every sound they made. I had to shut my windows. I didn't think it was what I wanted to hear in church."

Heidi looked at Isabel for several minutes, then she said, "He outta have Ms. Sandy play and people sing like yesterday and then he talk, like yesterday. It be what we do at our church. He talk good yesterday."

"Yes, little one, that would be good, but Sandy and Ramon take me to my church in Blairsville, they don't go to that church either."

Heidi turned and looked Isabel directly in the eyes, then she said, fiercely, "Mommy gots her own car. Mommy and me go to Mr. Roger's church on Sunday. We gots to show him we's 'trested in his talk about God."

Isabel smiled. "Little one, if your mommy wants to go to Roger's church, that's okay. When I get home from my church, we'll spend the rest of the day together. I don't mind at all."

Nodding fiercely as if to make it so, Heidi said, "Asides, he be my daddy soon and we gots to stick by him."

Isabel put her finger under Heidi's chin and turning the little face up so she could look into her face, Isabel asked, "Why do you think Roger will be your daddy soon?"

"'Cause I writed Santa a letter. I ask God, too. It be time I gots a daddy. We comed here and Mr. Roger be just right. He help me yesterday, just like a daddy." Heidi put her hand on Isabel's leg and said, earnestly, "Member? He puts food on my plate just like a daddy do."

Raylyn had crept into the room and was standing behind Heidi. Tears filled her eyes, but she was blinking furiously to keep them from falling. She wondered when it had become so important to Heidi that she have a daddy. When she could speak around the cotton in her mouth, she said, "Heidi, just because you sent a letter to Santa and asked God for a daddy, doesn't mean Mr. Roger's going to be your daddy. We live miles and miles away from here. I can't leave my job, we need the money to live."

Heidi turned around and took Raylyn's hand that she had extended toward her child. "Mommy," she said, with all the seriousness possible, "God make a way."

Since Heidi wasn't looking at her, Isabel murmured, "Oh, the faith of a child!"

As Raylyn dressed, she realized she'd never seen Roger except in what he'd worn in his pulpit and to dinner. Heidi was already in her chair at the table and so was Isabel when Raylyn slid into her chair. Gratefully, she pulled the mug of coffee toward her and took a long sip.

Still holding the mug in front of her mouth, she asked, "Grandma, what should we wear this afternoon to Roger's farm? I know he doesn't wear a clerical collar, he didn't yesterday in his pulpit, but does he always dress up?"

Isabel waved her hand and said, "Humph! That night of Sandy's concert that she played *in his church*, mind you! I had to send him home to change into something appropriate for a pastor! I mean, he had on a black tight shirt that showed every muscle and those denim pants all young people wear that looked like skin!" She shook her head. "I tell you, he looked just plain awful! And for a minister who was the host of the concert! Why! It was perfectly dreadful!"

Raylyn was glad she had her mug in front of her mouth it was very hard to hide her smile. It wasn't hard to let her imagination wander a little and know how 'awful' Roger looked in tight denims and a black T-shirt. In fact, just the thought made heat creep up her neck. Before she could say anything, she took another sip of her coffee. It was good and hot, but that helped cover her reaction to Isabel's description.

However, before Raylyn could say anything, Heidi said, "Mommy wear jeans and T-shirt in summer, but in winter she wear a sweatshirt. She be cold-blooded, she says. I not, I wear cool stuff in winter."

Isabel smiled. "You do a lot more running around than your mommy, little one. You don't get cold when you run around. In the real winter I wear lots of clothes to keep warm."

"Can'ts you turn up your heat, Gamaw?"

"Well, I could, but you see, I don't have much extra money coming in during the winter. My cabins don't have many people in them when it's cold. I'm really fortunate this winter, I have a single man living in one of them, but he's gone this weekend."

"How come, Gamaw?"

"He went to some relative over the holiday weekend. He works with Ramon on the trails in the summer."

"You like him?"

Isabel shrugged. "Let's say, I like the rent money he pays me every month. It helps with my heating bills."

"What's his name?"

"Heidi! It's none of our business who Grandma Isabel rents her cabins to."

"But I wanna know!"

"It doesn't matter, really. His name is Duncan Roads. He's a single man and doesn't have much family at all. He said he'd rent one of my cabins as long as he held the job with Ramon, which suits me just fine."

"I should think so! That's really good for you, Grandma."

Roger had just tossed the scoop back into the dogfood bag when his phone rang. He scowled, who would call? His stomach turned over, surely it wasn't Raylyn who'd changed her mind and they wouldn't come! He snatched up the phone and tried for a pleasant tone, "Hello?"

"Oh, Roger! Oh, will you come? Ernest collapsed on the floor well, I can't get him up!"

Recognizing one of his regular parishioners, he said, "Ms. Anna, I can come, but if he collapsed, shouldn't you be calling for the ambulance?" he asked her kindly.

"Well, maybe I should." Roger pulled the receiver from his ear only a second later, since the dial tone was buzzing loudly.

Roger hung up and looked at the clock. It was eight o'clock, surely he'd have time to go be with Anna for a few minutes until the ambulance arrived and she'd go with Ernest to the hospital. He wrinkled his nose, he had to take a shower and change into something presentable other than what he wore to milk his cow. He kicked off his barn boots and headed for his shower. Quickly he lathered his hair, then his body, then rinsed. In less than fifteen minutes he was in the Jeep headed into town.

As he turned the corner onto the street where Ernest and Anna lived he heard a far off wail of the emergency vehicle. He sighed he had beat the paramedics, but not by much. He parked in front of the house next door; the ambulance would probably want extra room in front of the victim's home. He jumped out and ran to the door. The wail of the siren was coming closer. He hated the sound of any siren. When he'd been young an ambulance had come to the ranch where they lived and taken his granddad. He'd never returned.

He knocked and Anna came to the door. When she saw who it was, she yanked the door wide. Tears hanging on her lashes, the older lady put her hand out to him and whimpered, "Oh, come in, Roger! Oh, that's the ambulance already! They came fast too. Roger, he's there in the kitchen! I can't lift him!"

"Ms. Anna, we won't try to lift him, we'll let the paramedics do that."

"But what could be wrong?"

"Has he been feeling bad recently?"

"Well, no, not that he'd tell me. We had our children and their families here for Thanksgiving dinner yesterday and he seemed a little tired after they left, but well, so did I, you know? We went to bed pretty soon after they left."

Roger couldn't answer. There were heavy steps on the porch and Anna jerked open the door for the paramedics carrying their gurney. "Somebody sick here?" the first man asked.

"Oh, yes, my husband, Ernest. He's on the floor in the kitchen. I couldn't get him up and, well, he couldn't do it, either."

"What's your last name, Ma'am?"

"Why, it's Nexton, sonny."

"Thank you, Ma'am," the typical southerner said.

Roger tried to stay out of the way, but Anna grabbed his arm and pulled him along to the kitchen. She was only a step behind the man holding the back of the gurney. When the men stopped, she tried to get around them, but Roger held her back so that the men would have some room in the small space between the kitchen table and the refrigerator where Ernest lay. He was perfectly still, but his eyes were open.

The men put the gurney on the floor then the first man squatted down and picked up Ernest's hand. Roger could tell it was limp. "Mr. Nexton, can you hear me? We're from the Blairsville Hospital, your wife called us."

The man nodded, but didn't speak. "Do you hurt somewhere?"

Roger could tell the man tried, but instead noise came from his mouth. He eyes were open, but his mouth drooped when he tried to speak. "What is it?" Anna looked fearfully from her husband to the man beside him. Of course, Roger could tell from the symptoms, but he wasn't about to say what he thought. He was no medical man and he knew the paramedics weren't allowed to give a diagnosis, either.

The man still held Ernest's hand, but he turned slightly to look up at the lady. "I'm not allowed to give a diagnosis, but these are stroke symptoms, Mrs. Nexton. We'll need to transport him to the hospital and have the doctor there see about treating him. You do have a family doctor we can contact on the way, don't you?"

Nodding, she asked, "Can I ride with him?"

"Of course, Ma'am. Do you have family you should call while we get him on this gurney and loaded?"

"Yes, oh, Roger, will you call my son?"

"Sure, Ms. Anna. Is his name in your speed dial on the phone?"

"On my what? It's in the back of the phone book." She waved in the vicinity of the phone hanging on the wall. "It's there somewhere."

Nodding, Roger said, "I'll find it. Don't forget a coat, Ms. Anna, it's cold out," Roger told the distracted woman.

"Oh, oh, yes." As the men headed out the door with Ernest on the gurney, Anna turned to Roger, who was hanging up and said, "You'll come?"

"Ms. Anna, your son said he'll call your daughter and they'll meet you there at the hospital when you arrive. There'll be too many of us if I come too. I'll come visit perhaps tonight when all the emergency work is finished. You'd better hurry, they're ready to slam the doors, so if you're going...."

Anna grabbed up her purse and ran as fast as her buxom body and chubby legs would allow. The men already had one of the doors closed when Anna reached the sidewalk. Roger stood in the doorway of the house and watched her clamber inside the waiting ambulance. He pulled the door closed and headed for the Jeep. The ambulance made a U-turn, turned on its flashing lights and its siren and vanished from the little town. Roger didn't stick around, either; he also made a U-turn and headed back to his house. There were things he needed to do.

On the way, something came to his mind that had never crossed his mind, even though several of his congregation had been hospitalized before and he'd been called just as Anna Nexton had called him. He should have prayed with the couple! But as he thought about it, there really hadn't been time to even mention it. However, he found a great frog in his throat, none of his people even considered asking him to pray.

He pulled into his parking spot and pushed the stick into park. Before he turned the key to shut off the engine and of course, before he opened his door, he bowed his head onto his hands still on the steering wheel. "God in Heaven! How I have failed these people so miserably! Please forgive me. Please be with Ernest and Anna. Touch Ernest with Your hand and quiet Anna's heart, she is so worried and afraid. I pray in Your Son's Name, amen." He swiped at a tear that leaked through his eyelids, then shut off the engine, opened his door and slid out.

He pushed open the back door of his house and an aroma of cooking beef met him. He inhaled deeply, then looked at the clock and hurried to the refrigerator. He'd lost more than an hour of cooking time for his soup. He'd have to hurry to get his vegetables in so they could be done when Raylyn and Heidi came in about two hours. He washed and cut up all the things he normally put into his hearty soup. His crock-pot was nearly full and he had to add more water. He knew if he didn't he couldn't call it soup.

After putting the top on his pot, he looked around the kitchen. He wasn't the prissy housekeeper his mom was or in need of a paid woman who came to clean and do laundry each week that his sister had because her husband was a slob, but he knew he needed to do a little work on his place before a lady and her child came to visit. He cleaned the kitchen, setting placemats in three places at his table. As he placed the bowls, silverware and glasses on the mats he sighed. He could get used to having a lady and even a lady and her child in his house. It wouldn't be so quiet and feel so lonely.

He got out his sweeper and ran it over the carpet in the other rooms then swiped his finger on one of the end tables beside the couch. He sighed, he hadn't done any cleaning in quite a while and living on a dirt driveway sent dust inside even with all the windows and doors closed for winter. Quickly he found his furniture polish and a rag and set to work making the wood shine. Besides, he wouldn't be watching the clock so much if he kept busy wiping away remnants of his bachelor life.

As they finished breakfast, Heidi said, "Oh, you got amblance here, Gamaw?"

"Well, not here in Vansville, little one."

"But that noise be a amblance. I know, 'cause one comed to my school one time. My friend got hurt and her had to ride in one."

Isabel frowned. "I wonder who it could be for?"

"I guess in a little place like this one can be heard all over town, can't it?"

"Yes, it can. It stopped a street over. Let's see, who lives there?"

Isabel ran down the list of people who lived on the next street over from her. Finally, she said, "I wonder if it's Ernest Nexton? He hasn't been feeling all that peppy since summer. Of course, his wife can't see it, but I've seen him about town a time or two and I can tell. I wonder if he's taking his blood pressure medicine?"

Isabel looked at Raylyn and said, "I guess where you live an ambulance going by is a fairly common thing, isn't it?"

"From our house we can hear when they reach the hospital. Not too far away on the other side of the hospital complex is a very busy intersection. About once a week there's a fender bender and someone gets hurt."

Isabel looked at Raylyn and asked, "Do you like your work?"

"Yes, very much, Grandma Isabel! I get to meet a lot of people and deal with many families who work with me on their finances. I'm so glad I had my degree before Dan and I were married. I took the job before he was deployed and when they came with the news of his death, I had something to take my mind off it at least for eight hours every day. It was hard to go home to the house for a while, but that's eased now."

Isabel smiled. "Is it the kind of job you could do in any hospital?"

Knowing exactly what the older lady was hinting at, Raylyn answered, "I'm sure just about every hospital has someone to do what I do. Perhaps in a smaller one there wouldn't be so many in the department, but there would be at least one spot that would have to be filled with someone like me."

"I wondered." After another minute or two, Isabel sighed and said, "You mentioned Ruth yesterday, how is she these days?"

"Gamaw, we not see Grandma much, she live long ways. I wish Grandma comed to see us sometime."

Raylyn shook her head, looking intently at her sprightly grandma. "Grandma, she's going to take herself to an early grave! She won't get out except to church and the grocery store! She won't meet with people, even those who used to be her close friends. She goes to the store once a week and that's it. She goes to the same store and never shops around. Heidi and I can't go see her too often, but Mom wants me to call at least once a week. I try, but it's hard, between work, Heidi's daycare and things we do there and church, I find myself forgetting to make that call. She'll call and scold me for not calling. Grandma, I wish I could get her interested in something, but it's not just a mile or two to her place."

Isabel nodded. "I had a feeling that's what she's doing. I've written to her and invited her to come for a visit, any time, but she'll write back and say she hates to leave home because you call off and on and she doesn't want to miss your calls."

"Grandma, I think that's only an excuse! She has my number, just like I have hers. Really, it would be so good for her to come visit you! It really would! I'll try to talk it up the next time I call her or see her. Grandma, you're so up beat and you have so many interests, I admire you and what you do. Having these cabins is great! You have some income besides your social security and that's really good. Mom has Daddy's pension, but that's not too much, since he was so young when he was killed. I've looked into it, I know she'd get to keep it even if she remarried, but I can't see that happening. She's worked at a job, but it's not much and she's too young to collect on Dad's social security. I really don't know how she makes it and keeps her house. She never did have a career."

"No, I don't see her getting married again, either, not with how she's handling it now, that's for sure!" She reached across the table and squeezed Raylyn's hand, smiling broadly at her. "I'm so glad you came to see me!"

"Oh, Grandma, so am I! You can't know how glad I am that we came!"

Raylyn didn't want to watch the clock, but Heidi didn't know how to tell time and several times an hour she said, "Mommy, is it time to go yet?"

Finally, she said, "Sweety, I'll tell you when we need to get changed, okay?"

"'K." she sighed. "Mommy, I wants to see Mr. Roger!"

"I know and it will be time soon." She looked up at the kitchen clock once more and said, "I tell you what, you go read Dollie a storybook and I bet it'll be time to get changed when you're finished. Now you show her every picture, she may have forgotten since the last time. You know how much she loves to have you read to her."

"I will, Mommy."

As the child disappeared into the living room, Isabel whispered, "You know, that won't work in another year or two."

Raylyn smiled. "I know, Grandma, but I'm sure glad it still works now."

She reached for her grandma's hand and said, "I'm sorry Heidi bothered you so early this morning and for the way she acted."

Isabel placed her other hand over Raylyn's and patted it. "Honey, don't feel badly. She's obviously quite taken with Roger."

Raylyn sighed, "It seems so. Just the other day she told me one of her friends at the daycare is getting a new daddy for Christmas and a new sister. That's when she 'wrote' her letter to Santa and that night in her bedtime prayers she prayed for a daddy, too. I've tried to play it down, but she took one look at Roger and her mind's made up. Grandma, how could it happen? It's impossible! My job is in Grand Rapids, a thousand miles from here! I'm pretty sure a pastor can't pick up and leave his church at the drop of a dime. And another thing, didn't he say he owned the property where he lives?"

Isabel smiled at her grand-daughter, patted her hand and said, "God works in mysterious ways His wonders to perform. Never say anything is impossible. Remember, God is the God of the impossible. If He wants you here, He'll do it and if He wants Roger there, He'll do that. If He doesn't want you together at all, He'll keep anything from happening. I'll guarantee it."

"Yes, I know that's true, Grandma. I've seen Him work some really neat things, things lots of people thought could never happen. I'll keep that in mind."

Isabel smiled. "Good, I'm glad, Deary."

"Just yesterday I realized that Dan's death was for the glory of God, since he was a believer. It doesn't seem quite so senseless when I think about it that way."

"I'm glad, Honey; that is the way God wants us to see things. If only your mom could see her husband's death in that light."

"Yes, I know."

"Mommy, I read Dollie a whole book. We get changed now?"

Isabel smiled at her grand-daughter, her eyes twinkling. "Better hop to it, girl! That's what you promised, you know."

Raylyn giggled. "Yeah, I know. Must have been a really short book."

Isabel nodded. "Or Dollie remembered all the pictures."

"Yes, that's a thought."

At ten minutes to twelve Raylyn took Heidi's hand and they walked to the car next to Isabel's in the parking lot. Raylyn opened the back door and Heidi scrambled in, excited to be going to Roger's farm. Between the two of them, they fastened Heidi's seatbelt, then Raylyn closed Heidi's door and opened her own. She slid behind the wheel and turned the key, but she realized her hand shook just a little. The car rumbled into life, this kind of cold weather was nothing to this dependable car.

Isabel had given Raylyn directions, so at the street she turned to go through town. She was almost to Ramon's house when she saw a roadblock across the entire two lanes just outside of town. Several cars in front of her turned around, but she knew the only way to Roger's house was on the highway for a little ways and then turn off on a country road. She wasn't like these natives who knew every country road around town.

She inched her way up to the barricade and rolled down her window a little, a bit intimidated by the barricade across the road and the quite large man coming toward her in full police gear, including a revolver on his belt. He was scowling at her and for some reason his hand rested on his revolver.

"Mommy, what's going on?" came a timid voice from the back.

"I don't know, Sweety, we'll see real soon."

A Georgia state police car was parked at the side of the road and a very imposing man in uniform strode to her car. Raylyn opened her mouth, but before she could speak, the man said, in a gruff voice, "Step from your car, Ma'am!"

Raylyn scowled and asked, "Why? What for?"

Without answering her, he said, "It'd be easier for all of us if you do as I ask, Ma'am."

"All of you?" She looked around, but didn't see another officer or another police car. Scowling, she said, "I'm interested to know who 'all of you' are. Officer, I'm here visiting my grandmother with my daughter. I was on my way to visit someone who lives up that next road and I just left her house. What is going on?"

The man took the handle of her door and Raylyn instantly regretted not locking her door when the man walked up. He pulled up the handle and opened the door. His voice, even more ominous, said, "Get out! Your child, too!"

Free Saturdays

Heidi was whimpering in the back seat. Raylyn leaned over to her glove box and was very glad when her registration was on top of the many things inside. She pulled it out and grabbed her purse, then put her feet on the ground, but didn't make a move to stand up. When he realized she still wasn't out of the car, the man turned to grab her wrist, but she leaned back at that moment to grab her keys.

"Leave the keys in the car and get out! Get your child!"

Raylyn shook her head. "Officer, until you give me a good reason to abandon my car, I will not leave it! Believe me, my keys stay with me until you give me reason to leave them while I abandon my car."

The man turned his head and touched a small microphone on his shoulder. "Suspect refuses to leave the car!"

"Drag 'em out!" came the reply. The reply was even more harsh than the words the man in front of her had said.

The officer turned back to Raylyn and said, angrily, "You heard the man! You get out or I drag you out!"

"Why do you think you have that right?" She was becoming quite agitated. She swallowed and tried to calm down. Nothing would be gained if she lost her temper.

"You're a suspect! Get out of the car and leave the keys in it!"

Very obviously disobeying Raylyn, dropped her keys into her purse and zipped it shut. She looked at the officer and said, "It won't happen, mister! I have a right to know what I'm a suspect of. You have been most obnoxious and you are harassing an innocent citizen. Now give me one good reason why you think I'm suspected of doing something worthy of a search."

"You're driving a car with an out-of-state license plate."

"Yes, I happen to live in Michigan. I drove from my home on Wednesday to spend this weekend with my grandmother. I was never informed that that was a crime."

Swallowing, the man said, "Show me your license and registration!"

Making sure her keys stayed in the bottom of her purse and staying firmly in her seat, she pulled her license from her wallet and gave it with the registration to the man. "I hope this clears up whatever misconception you have about who I am. You have no right to treat me as you have. I demand a written apology from you and also your superior! How dare you stop me and treat me as a common criminal!"

The man looked at both items he held in his hand, both things matched and neither was expired. Without answering her, he turned on his heel and went directly to his car, opened the door and slumped onto the seat. Raylyn could see that he was using his in-car phone to make a call. That reminded her that she had her cellphone so she activated it and called Isabel.

She was glad when the older lady answered immediately. "Grandma, there was a roadblock at the edge of town. The officer stopped me as if I was a criminal. Would you call Roger and tell him I'll be a bit late? Oh, here he comes back now. Bye!"

The man scowled even harder at her when he saw she'd used her cell phone. She'd barely dropped the phone back in her purse and zipped it shut when the man reached her car. "My supervisor is on his way. Do you have another picture ID?"

"No. Why should I need another when my picture's on my license?"

"We can't be sure."

"Of what?" Raylyn asked, exasperated. "This is my car I'm the only one who drives it. I renewed my license last year and they took my picture, then handed me the card. What is there not to be sure of?" She glanced at her unhappy child and said, "And meanwhile, you're holding me against my will for no reason while someone who is really a criminal is probably getting away as we speak."

The man shrugged and said, "You could make it much easier on yourself if you'd get out of the car."

Raylyn shook her head. "Nope, not gonna happen! I have done nothing wrong, not at home in Michigan or here in Georgia. You refuse to give me an explanation as to why you're detaining me. So, my keys stay with me, I stay with my car and I demand a written apology."

Roger stirred his soup and looked at the clock. They should be here any minute. They'd decided on noon, because it was during the warmest part of the day to see his farm. He turned the dial on the pot to its lowest setting, knowing the soup was finished, but wanting to keep it warm until they arrived. At ten after twelve he scowled and went to the living room to look out his drive, surely she should be coming up the hill right now. However, the driveway was empty.

Just as the thought entered his mind, his phone rang. He ran back to the kitchen and grabbed the receiver, his heart dropping to his shoes surely it wasn't Raylyn saying she'd changed her mind. "Hello?"

"Roger," an agitated Isabel said, "I don't know what's going on, but Raylyn called and said she was stopped on the edge of town by a roadblock. She said she'd be detained for a bit."

"A roadblock? What for! I'm on my way!"

He slammed the phone back onto the hook on the wall, grabbed his coat and was out the door in only seconds. The Jeep was moving before he even had the door closed. He backed around and headed down his long driveway toward the country road. Skidding around the corner at the bottom, he headed toward the highway only two miles away. He nearly bounced the last few yards to the highway and only about a thousand feet in front of him was the roadblock Isabel had mentioned.

Roger saw Raylyn's car sitting in the middle of the lane heading toward his road. On the side of the road facing the other way was the state police car. Raylyn's door stood open and the imposing police officer stood holding it open with his body. He was looking down and Roger realized Raylyn sat on the driver's seat. He wondered why she still sat in the car the man's height put her at a huge disadvantage.

Almost at the exact minute that Roger screeched to a stop on one side of the barricade, Isabel pulled to the side of the road beside Raylyn. However, she didn't so much as acknowledge the activity. She continued to glare at the officer even though two car doors slammed close by.

Roger's long strides brought him to Raylyn's car before Isabel arrived and he said, "What's going on, Officer?"

"This woman is a suspect. I have demanded that she leave her car with its keys in it, she refuses. When my supervisor arrives, we will proceed to remove her and impound her car."

"She is a suspect for what, Officer?"

"I cannot divulge that information."

Isabel had reached Roger's side by now and heard what the officer said. She recognized him as a neighbor's child when she had lived in Blairsville many years before. "I do believe you are Johnny Markham, aren't you?"

Taking his eyes from Raylyn for a minute, he looked at Isabel. It was a few minutes, but he finally said, "Are you Ms. Isabel?"

"Yes, sonny, I am. This is my grand-daughter. She came to see me for Thanksgiving. Why do you think she's a suspect?"

"I... I'm just following orders, Ms. Isabel."

"And what would those be?"

"We're to stop an out-of-state car...."

"And none other has come this way?"

"Umm, well, no."

Just then another state police car drove up. An older man stepped out and marched purposefully up to the group. "Who are these people?" he demanded.

Before anyone else could speak, Isabel said, "I'm Isabel Isaacson and this is my grand-daughter whom, Johnny, your underling is detaining without cause."

"She has Michigan plates."

"And that would be a problem?" Roger asked.

"We were given a lead to stop an out-of-state car."

"That's it? No description of the driver? No description of the car? Oh, and by the way, there are forty-nine other states, all of which would show out-of-state plates."

Roger barely had the words out when the young officer looked over the shoulder of the older man. There was a car coming through town bearing down on them with such speed that there was no way he could stop in time to keep from hitting Raylyn's car. The big man whirled around and dashed to his car that was still running. He yanked the stick into drive and flashed across the road into the path of the on-coming car. Only seconds later there was a crash and glass tinkled to the pavement. The officer could step from his car, but the other driver definitely could not, his car looked like an accordion and the driver was slumped over the wheel.

Looking at the wreckage from where he stood beside Raylyn's car, Roger said to the older officer, "Could it be that your suspect is sitting behind the wheel of *that* car?"

Chagrined, the man said, "I would say that's a good possibility. Ma'am, I'm terribly sorry for the harassment and any delay we've caused you."

Showing lots more courage than she normally felt, Raylyn looked the man in the eye and said, "Officer, I will not go anywhere until I have my license and registration in my hand. You will take my name and address, both you and your underling will write me a letter of apology. Is that clear?"

"Yes, Ma'am, that will be taken care of today," the officer said, contritely.

The younger officer stepped from his damaged patrol car, but when he tried to put weight on his right foot he grabbed hold of the door. He lifted his right foot from the ground and balanced on his left foot and both hands grabbed the door. He threw his head back and those who watched thought he would scream, but he didn't. Instead he stood there holding onto the door, gritting his teeth. His supervisor turned immediately from Raylyn, noticed his obvious pain and rushed back to him.

"You're injured!"

Through gritted teeth, he groaned, "Yes, I still had my foot on the brake when he slammed into me. I didn't hear anything with the crash of his car, but I felt something in my leg snap. It hurts pretty… bad."

Nodding at the driver of the second car still slumped over the wheel, the older man said, "I'll call for an ambulance now and a towtruck, we'll need one for that critter. Markham, sit back down and take a load off. Oh, where's the woman's license and registration? She said you didn't give it back to her."

"It's…" looking at the mangled mess the passenger side of his car was, officer Markham said, "I'll have to look for a minute. I had it right here on the seat."

The older man stepped away from the wrecked police car and pulled a cellphone from his belt. After speaking into it for a minute, he closed it and said, "An ambulance is on its way and also a wrecker.

You look for those documents and I'll see what I can figure out with this yahoo in this other car."

"Yeah, it can't be far away, it was right here on top of the seat, I called in to headquarters to verify the information. Umm, it all proved ligit," he murmured.

Raylyn still sat in her car. Now that the emergency was past, she couldn't have stood up if she'd wanted to, her knees felt like pudding and her hands were shaking noticeably. Heidi sensed her mommy's discomfort, so she unfastened her seatbelt and climbed over the seat into the front and tried to climb into Raylyn's lap. She put her arms around her mommy and Raylyn welcomed the child's warmth. She was happy enough to hug her daughter tightly in her arms. She put her head down on Heidi's and inhaled the clean scent of baby shampoo.

When Raylyn opened her eyes, Roger was sitting on his heels looking up at her. His voice tender, he asked, "Are you all right, Raylyn?"

She swallowed and murmured, "I think so. It shook me up a good bit."

"Maybe so and I'm sure this whole thing got your adrenalin kicking in, but you sure were strong when you needed to be!"

She gave him a ghost of a smile and said, "Thanks."

The older officer walked up to the little group and said, "Here's your license and registration, Ma'am. My officer's been injured or he'd have returned it. We are terribly sorry for the harassment and for detaining you without cause. We'll get that note written for you as soon as possible. You have a good day."

"Thank you."

Roger stood and looked the older man in the eyes, then turned back to Raylyn and Heidi. There were a lot of things he'd like to say to the officer, but nothing would be gained by saying them, so he kept his mouth shut. He held out his hands and Heidi eagerly put hers out to him. With the attention span of a three and a half year old, she said, "Mr. Roger will you open my door so I can get back in my seat and we can go to your house?"

"Sure, Heidi! That's what I figured you'd want to do. After all, I couldn't put my cow and chickens in my Jeep for you to see."

Roger slid Heidi from Raylyn's lap, but Heidi put her hand over her mouth and giggled. "Oh, Mr. Roger, you're so funny! Cows be in a barn and chickens, too."

Roger opened the back door and placed Heidi on the seat and said, "Not always. Cow is outside most of the time and in the winter the chickens stay in their coop. It's a bit warmer in there for them."

When her seatbelt was fastened, Heidi clapped her hands. "I can't wait to see them, come on, Mommy, let's hurry!"

"Roger still has to get to his car, you know and besides, the policeman must move the barricade before we can go anywhere."

Heidi sighed, "Yes, I know, Mommy."

Isabel came to the door of Raylyn's car and scowling, she said, "Are you all right, my dear? I know he upset you."

"Yes, Grandma, I'm getting there. Thanks for coming. I think you made the man stop to think for a minute. He wasn't about to take anything I said, but when you called him by name, he looked a bit sheepish." She chuckled and said, "When you called him Johnny, I don't think he's been called that in a good long time. Thanks, Grandma, we'll see you later."

She winked at Raylyn. "That's fine. You young folks have a good time." Isabel peered into the back seat and said, "Little one, don't scare that cow now."

"Gamaw, I can't scare Cow!"

"Oh, I don't know! Maybe you will!"

Roger straightened from fastening Heidi's seatbelt and said, "We'll have a great time, Isabel. Have a quiet afternoon."

Isabel turned on her heel and looked at him, her finger gave one wag. "Young man, you behave yourself!"

Holding up his hand, he said, "I will, Isabel, don't worry, I wouldn't think of doing anything else."

"Good."

By now, the officer had removed the barricade. Raylyn turned in the seat and pulled her legs inside the car. Roger closed her door, while she looked in her purse for her keys, which, of course, had slithered to the bottom. Isabel looked over the top of the cars at the wreckage behind Raylyn's car and shook her head, then went to her own car and sank into the seat. This was probably the most excitement the little town of Vansville had seen in over a year and to think her family had caused it! Isabel had to smile. Roger walked to his car and started up. He had to back up and make a U-turn before he could leave the scene.

While Roger turned around the ambulance came, so the officer moved quickly away from the cars that were leaving. Raylyn took a deep breath and started her car. She waved to Isabel then followed Roger down the road. Isabel waved back, turned around and moved slowly by the wreckage toward her home. Before she turned into her drive a large truck that could haul two cars went by her toward the accident scene. Soon there would be no evidence of an accident.

She smiled. "So Johnny Markham became a policeman. How about that!"

They hadn't even reached Roger's turnoff before Heidi asked, "Mommy, why'd that awful man stop us? Him was awful mean! How come he not like Mr. Roger? Mr. Roger be real nice, but that big man was mean!"

Knowing she'd often told Heidi that policemen were our friends she didn't want the child to get a bad impression, even though the man really had been gruff and nasty. "Sweety," she said, as she looked into the mirror, "he was doing his job, at least what he thought was his job. He was told to stop a car with license plates that weren't from here. You know ours aren't from here, they're from where we live in Grand Rapids so he stopped us. He was a bit nasty in the way he treated me, that's for sure, but I don't think he would have hurt me once he found out I wasn't who he wanted."

"How come he wreck his car?"

SIX

Raylyn involuntarily shuddered, remembering how fast the car was coming and knowing what could have happened. "Sweety, if he hadn't pulled his car behind us, the other car that was coming so fast would have ploughed into us and wrecked our car really bad. I think he knew you'd have been hurt badly if the man had hit our car because he was going so fast. I'm glad he had time to get his car between that one and ours. I'm glad we're both safe and okay, so let's go to Roger's and have a good time."

"'K, Mommy. Hurry, Mommy, you gots to catch up so we don't get lost."

"Sweety, we can't get lost, Roger lives up this road a little."

"'K."

Finally, Raylyn followed Roger's Jeep up his long gravel driveway. There was a turn after they left the road and until they went around that turn, she couldn't see the house, but she saw the trees he'd talked about. They were close to the left side of the drive and began on the other side of the small open field on the right side of the drive. Raylyn wondered what kind of house a bachelor preacher lived in. Was it a cabin, barely big enough for a bachelor, a second story on top of his barn so he didn't have to go far to tend his livestock or get out in the weather? She wrinkled her nose at that his place would always smell like a barn! Or a mobile home possibly or was it a house? *Raylyn, aren't you getting the cart before the horse?*

She made the turn and Heidi said, "Look, Mommy, there be his house."

She did look. It was a rustic log house with forest green shutters and blended with the trees that were close to one side. What she could see wasn't very wide, but as she looked more closely, she saw a porch on the right side of the house and a walkway on the other. There was no door that faced her. She decided she was looking at the end of the house. Possibly the walkway led to the front door, because the porch looked out on the large shed.

"Mommy, look!" Heidi nearly screamed. "Mommy, a cow!"

"Yes, Sweety, I see it."

Heidi's face was glued to the window. "And look, Mommy! Mr. Roger gots a dog!" The little girl was bouncing in her seat. Before Raylyn had the stick in park she heard Heidi's seatbelt snap and her feet hit the floor. "Come on, Mommy, turn off the car! I gots to get out and pet doggie right now! Come on!"

Raylyn's hands were shaking a bit from the experience down on the highway, but Heidi had no such problem. The whole episode was completely behind her and she was anxious to get out of the car. She stayed in the car, with her bottom on the seat, until the car engine shut off, but then she pulled the door handle and followed the door as it opened. She started clapping her hands, she was very excited. Of course, Raylyn had to pull the keys from the ignition, but only minutes after Heidi, she was ready to leave the car.

Roger had stepped from his Jeep when Heidi's feet hit the ground. Excitedly, she exclaimed, "Mr. Roger! You gots a doggie!"

Roger came back to Raylyn's car and opened the door for her, but he said to Heidi, "Yeah, his name's Curly."

Heidi came up beside him, still looking at the dog and shook her head. She looked up and slowly, she said, "Mr. Roger, your doggie don't have no curl on him, his hair too short."

"You don't think that's a good name for him?" he asked with a straight face.

Heidi shook her head solemnly. "He don't got no curl, Mr. Roger! Curly not a good name for your doggie."

"But he comes when I call him."

"Well, I guess. Maybe he don't know what Curly mean."

Roger nodded. "Maybe that's it."

Just then the huge yellow and white tomcat bounded through the kitty door in the barn door, heading for the porch on the run, his ringed tail, a flag over his back. He hit one step then bounded onto the porch. Heidi, of course, saw him and clapped her hands. "You gots a kitty! Oh, wow! You gots a huge farm, Mr. Roger!"

"That's Linus."

"Mr. Roger, Charlie Brown's friend be Linus, not a kitty!"

Roger shrugged. "Maybe that's why he doesn't pay any attention when I call him. He'll walk on by with his nose in the air."

"Well, see, it's 'cause he not a boy, but a kitty."

With that kind of logic what was there to argue about? With a twinkle in his eyes, Roger said, "Think we could get your mommy out of the car and inside so we can eat my soup, Heidi? You know it's a bit cold out here."

Nodding, Heidi held out her hand and said, "Come on, Mommy! We 'posed to eat now. Mr. Roger gots our lunch. We can see chickens after."

"I'm coming, Sweety, I'm hungry, aren't you?"

"Mommy, we eat Gamaw's buns long time."

Roger turned from the little girl with a grin on his face, but took Raylyn's arm and with a twinkle in his eyes, he whispered, "Gamaw's buns?"

Raylyn giggled. "Grandma bakes the best cinnamon buns you ever tasted. She warmed up what we didn't eat for Thanksgiving breakfast."

Chuckling, he said, "Ah, I see. Come into my humble abode and sample my home made vegetable soup. I turned down the heat, so it should be fine."

"Oh, boy! Mommy don't make soup much. She make stuff in the cockpot only on Thursday, but not soup."

Nothing like a child to spill your life story to a perfect stranger, Raylyn sighed to herself.

The three went in the door that Raylyn had correctly decided was the back door into the kitchen. Of course, they went through the small mud room first. She breathed deeply of the fragrant air and said, "What a wonderful smell! It's been a very long time since I've had home made vegetable soup."

Roger motioned toward the table, but headed for the counter. "You and Heidi have a seat and I'll have this soup on the table in a jiffy." Looking at Heidi he asked, "Do you like crackers in your soup, Heidi?"

Nodding vigorously, she said, "Yum, yum! Teacher let us squash 'em in soup at school. I like lotsa cackus."

"You were such a good help yesterday, would you like to help me now?"

"Sure!"

Pointing to an easy-access cupboard, Roger said, "There are crackers in that cupboard would you get them out, please?"

"'Course, Mr. Roger, I be big girl and help."

Roger had made it quite obvious where they were to sit. He'd placed two cushions on one of the chairs and Raylyn was sure Roger normally sat in the chair closest to the stove, which was the head of the table. However, it meant that Heidi sat on his one side and she on the other. Raylyn stifled a sigh and pulled out the chair, normally, she sat next to Heidi to help her, but it wouldn't happen again today.

Roger turned off his crockpot and lifted the ceramic pot out of the cooker and brought it to the table. He set it in front of his place then turned to get a ladle while Heidi opened the cupboard door to get the crackers. She rushed to the table, saw the chair with the cushions and pushed the box onto the table. She made a beeline for her chair and climbed up to her perch on top of the cushions.

Grinning, she said, "Mr. Roger, this be great!"

"I'm glad, Heidi and thanks for getting the crackers. Do you like milk or would you like some chocolate mix in it?"

"Oh, choclet, please!"

"Okay. How about you, Raylyn? I have fresh coffee, fresh milk, with or without chocolate and iced tea."

"Coffee's fine. I know your soup'll warm me, but I got really chilled when that guy held my door open for so long."

As Roger poured the coffee into two mugs, he said, "So the man was intent on getting you out of your car?"

Raylyn took the mug Roger offered her and wrapped both hands around it. "Yes, but I was just as intent that it wouldn't happen. I wished there'd been a button to push my seat higher he was so tall I got a crick in my neck looking up at him."

"Yeah, when I first drove up I wondered why you still sat, but then I quickly figured it out. So he never gave you a reason why he'd stopped you?"

"No, he said I had out-of-state plates and I was a suspect."

"Sheesh, how dumb can those guys get!"

Looking around the rustic kitchen, with its huge picture window that looked out on the red barn, as Roger ladled out the thick soup into the bowls, Raylyn decided they'd talked about the incident long enough, so she waved her hand around and said, "I love your place! Did you build it yourself?"

Roger put a ladle full of the wonderful smelling soup in Heidi's bowl and said, "No, I was on sight all the time, watched them dig the well and some other guys put in the septic, but the house is a log cabin package that I bought from a company and their employees did the work. It's a bit big for me, but when I made the purchase I thought there might be a possibility some year of filling it. When I was called here I didn't know how very small the town was."

"What you fill it with, Mr. Roger?" Heidi asked, innocently.

Raylyn's cheeks started to burn, she knew what Roger meant. She swallowed, but didn't know what to say to her child. However, Roger said, "Heidi, I thought perhaps I'd find a lady who would be willing to be my wife. However, this town is so small that the only single ladies who live here are Ms. Isabel and another lady whose husband died three years ago. They're both a bit too old for me."

"Mommie not old, her gots no husband. My daddy died when I be a baby."

"Heidi!" Raylyn's strangled vocal cords hissed out.

"Well, you is, Mommy!" Heidi answered, sincerely.

Roger smiled at the child and said, "But you live miles and miles away."

Heidi dropped her eyes to her soup and said, "I know. Mommy say that, too."

Raylyn couldn't think of anything else to say that wouldn't bring her daughter's one track mind into play, so she concentrated on eating her soup. It was delicious and lived up to the aroma that had hit her when they walked through the door. For several minutes there was no sound in the room other than the tinkling of silverware against the bowls. The seasoning was perfect she decided Roger must be a good cook.

Heidi put down her spoon in her empty bowl and rubbed her tommy. "That be real good, Mr. Roger. You be good cook."

"Thanks, Heidi. I can make a good pot of soup and Curly really likes the bones I cut the meat from. Are you ready to see Cow and my chickens?"

Heidi clapped her hands, "Oh, yes, Mr. Roger! I be ready!"

"Okay, we'll clear away these dishes and go out."

Linus came prancing into the kitchen from wherever his haunts had taken him and Heidi slid from her chair. "Oh, here's kitty! Does he play?"

"I don't know, Heidi. He's usually too stuck up to give me the time of day. He does play with the mice he finds in the barn, once in a while."

Nodding, Heidi said, "I play wif him here."

"That'll be fine we need to finish our soup, Sweety." Raylyn and Roger both took another spoonful of the delicious soup.

Heidi sat on the floor and much to Roger's surprise Linus came and curled up in her lap. He shrugged and said in a low voice, "She's more on his level so he thinks she's his speed."

Raylyn made a face and whispered, "Gives us a chance to finish our lunch."

Roger's eyes twinkled. He was sure he knew what she wasn't saying. "Yes, that's true. Any cure for the miles and miles?"

The pink crept up her neck again, as she shook her head. "I don't see how, Roger. My job is my only source of income. I got a lump sum cash settlement, but that paid for the mortgage and didn't go much farther. It's essential that I work. When Dan was killed, we hadn't been married very long. We had bought that house only a few months before and our baby was about fourteen months old. He was only in the reserves, but they were called, as I'm sure you know.

He didn't make much from them and the little bit of life insurance he had hardly paid for the funeral. I've been able to keep the house because of my job, but there's no splurging. I've saved for quite a while to pay for this trip."

"But you could do that kind of work in any hospital?"

"Oh, yes. Grandma asked me that, too. Every hospital needs at least one financial counselor, but most hospitals have one in place when they open and require someone leaving the position to give plenty of notice when they leave so they can fill the spot immediately. I'm afraid it is a very important position."

Raylyn slid her spoon into her soup dish and picked up her coffee mug. She turned a little so she could look at Roger, who had put another ladleful of soup in his bowl. "So tell me, why did Grandma tell me that your sermons were only readings from a book when yesterday you didn't even use notes."

Roger put the last mouthful of soup in his mouth. It was a large mouthful and he used the time it took to empty his mouth to think about what he wanted to say. Ever since Sandy had played *The Old Rugged Cross* he'd been ashamed of his 'preacher' behavior. Finally, he swallowed and said, "It's a long story. Perhaps after we see the animals and do the outside things I want to show you, there'll be some time to talk."

He'd barely said the words when Linus became bored with Heidi's lap and her hand stroking his back and jumped from her lap. Since he left, Heidi jumped up and came back to the adults at the table. "Mr. Roger," she looked from his empty bowl to her mommy's and said, "is we gonna go see Cow now?"

"So Linus ran off, did he?"

Nodding, she said, "Yes, he had enough pet time, he over there, eating now, and you said we see Cow and Chickens."

"Let's get these dishes done first, Heidi," Raylyn said.

"We'll rinse them and leave them in the sink. We should get outside during the warmest time of the day," Roger insisted.

Jumping up and down and clapping, Heidi exclaimed, "Yea, yea! Mommy, come on! We go see chickens now!"

Raylyn grabbed Heidi's coat, which she was about to forget in her hurry to get outside. She zipped her up and pulled up her hood and tied it, then helped her into her mittens. Roger shrugged quickly into his old coat then held Raylyn's for her as soon as she stood up from helping Heidi. Only minutes later they went out the back door, only to see Cow almost to the trees on the far side of the field.

Unhappily, Heidi asked, "How come she be way over there, Mr. Roger? When we comed she be right here."

"It's like this, Heidi, she didn't know she was going to be on display. I milked her this morning, so she was feeling good except she was hungry and there's still some grass over there that she wants to eat."

"Well, I wanna see her!" she pouted. She left the adults, crossed in front of Roger's Jeep to the fence. From there she called, "Here, Cow, here, Cow! I wanna see you, come here!"

However, the cow didn't even raise her head, instead, she kept munching the grass.

Roger had to cover his mouth and cough to keep Heidi from hearing his laughter. Raylyn also was smiling broadly behind the little girl's back. Finally, when he could speak, Roger murmured, "She is something else!" More loudly, he said, "Heidi, we can go into my barn and see the chickens, if you want. Maybe Cow will come back before we come out."

Heidi spun around and ran back to Roger's side. "Oh, can we, Mr. Roger?"

He held out his hand to the little girl and said, "Sure! Come on! We know we can see the chickens they're all in their coop. I let them outside in the warm weather, but during the winter they stay in the pen." He walked them into his small barn and from a nail took down a pail. "Want to feed them some scratch grain, Heidi?"

"Oh, can I? Oh, what fun!"

With a pail a third full of grain in one hand and Heidi's hand in his other, he took them to the back of his barn. Raylyn followed behind them a few steps down the walkway, seeing Roger's tool room where he kept his tools and also his grain and feed in barrels for his livestock. Next to it was the stall where he milked his cow. At the far end was a door that was closed and that was where he was headed.

She lagged behind, watching this very virile, handsome man holding hands with her little daughter. She was sure that his shoulders went on forever they were strong and moved smoothly to his muscular arms. His one hand gripped the handle of the pail that swung gently next to his leg, but his other hand gently held the tiny hand of the child next to him. He looked totally at ease with doing both. He was blond there was no other way to describe his hair. Raylyn was sure he had at least some Scandinavian blood in him, although he hadn't said so. He looked down at Heidi and said something she couldn't hear, but it made Heidi very happy, she turned and grabbed his hand with her other one and jumped up and down. Of course, her hood bounced off her head.

She moved closer and heard him say, "Go on, you can reach that block. It should move easily, it's a block of wood held there by a nail."

"'K, Mr. Roger, I big, I open it."

"All right, that's the chicken coop."

Heidi rushed forward and jumped up on the wooden step, then reached as high as she could and pushed the block of wood next to the door up. The door came open about three inches and all of them heard the squawking that started immediately. Heidi jumped back from the door and looked up at Roger.

"Is...is that...um...chickens?" Heidi asked, her eyes huge. Shaking her head, she said, "I... I not go in by myself."

"Sure is. Here, I'll go in first and scatter some grain. They'll see that and it'll get them quiet." Roger pulled the door open, and said, "Come on in so I can shut the door. We don't want these critters to get out."

Heidi didn't move from where she stood at the bottom of the step into the chicken coop, so Raylyn stepped up onto the step and went in behind Roger. When Heidi saw her mommy go in, she took that last step and climbed in but stood behind her mommy. Roger reached around them and pulled the door closed. He let his hand linger on Raylyn's shoulder before he turned and dipped his hand into the pail. To Raylyn it felt like lightning had touched her. She barely controlled a shiver.

"Heidi, don't you want to scatter the grain?" he asked, knowing full well what he'd done to Raylyn, because he'd felt it too.

"I watch you first."

"Okay, but it's not hard."

Several of the chickens were sitting on their nests, but most of them were either on the floor raising a ruckus or standing on the ledge in front of the nests. Roger reached into the pail, filled his hand with grain and scattered it in front of them on the floor. Immediately, those on the floor ran to peck on the grain and those standing on the ledge fluttered down to the floor. One of those on a nest jumped up and squawking, jumped down to the floor. Immediately, all the noise stopped and Heidi's eyes opened even wider.

"See, I told you they'd be quiet as soon as they got some grain."

"Do they gotta have more?"

Roger held out the pail to Heidi and said, "Sure, that's why we brought all of this, they'll eat it all. Here, put your hand in the pail and bring out a big handful. You can scatter it around for them."

When the pail was empty, Heidi looked up and saw three hens sitting on nests. When she looked back at Roger she asked, "What about those guys?"

"Those hens are sitting on their eggs. We can shoo them out and you can pick up the eggs that are there and put them in the pail."

Her eyes shining, Heidi exclaimed, "I can?"

Roger nodded, but picked up the little girl with one arm, then went to the first nest where a hen sat. Holding the little girl tightly, he put his other hand behind the hen and gently pushed her. Clucking, she jumped from the nest onto the ledge, then jumped down to the floor and began to scratch with the others. Contentedly, Heidi stayed in Roger's arm, but her head followed every move the hen made.

Heidi craned her neck and whispered, "Mr. Roger, there be a egg there!"

"Yes, there is. If your mommy will bring the feed pail, you can pick it up and put it very carefully in the pail so we can take it inside."

Without looking at her mommy, Heidi said, "Mommy, hurry bring the pail I put this egg in it." Heidi held the egg in both hands until Raylyn had the pail under her hands. Carefully, not taking either hand away, Heidi lowered it to the bottom.

Finally, all the hens were rousted from the nests and there were five eggs in the pail. Raylyn set the pail on the ledge and Roger set Heidi on the floor. However, Heidi wasn't finished with Roger. She turned around and held her arms up to him. He leaned over and saw her sparkling eyes. He nearly lost his composure, but he scooped her up into his arms and her arms went tightly around his neck.

Before he could think, she gave him a big, slobbery kiss on the cheek. "Mr. Roger, I loves you! You be the best man in all the world!"

Roger's throat closed, he swallowed and whispered, "You're a great kid, Heidi."

They were about to leave the chicken coop when they heard a loud "Mooooo" outside the barn. Heidi wiggled in Roger's arms, so he set her on her feet. "Oh, maybe Cow comed back! Can we go see?"

"Sure!"

Heidi was clearly anxious, she danced near the door, but waited until Roger flipped the latch and pushed the door open then she was off down the long aisle. Behind her, Roger picked up the pail with the eggs, then stepped around Raylyn and stepped down onto the barn floor. He turned and raised his free hand to help her down the step. She smiled at him and took his hand, knowing that when she had taken it yesterday it felt like an electric current had buzzed between them. It was no different today, but she let him help her down and he kept her hand in his.

"You don't mind, do you?" he asked, quietly. That smile had turned his stomach into mush. He had to pull his thoughts back, all he could think about was throwing the pail wherever and taking her in his arms to kiss her.

"No, it's fine. I don't want Heidi to get any ideas."

Heidi disappeared outside the barn door, but Raylyn knew she couldn't be hurt, there was a fence between her and the cow. The adults moved more slowly down the aisle and Roger said, "Would Isabel be okay with Heidi? Could you feel free to go to Blairsville with me for dinner at a restaurant this evening?" He hadn't thought about inviting Raylyn for the evening, but he didn't really want their time together to end.

"Probably if we called her."

"We'll have to wait till we're inside, I don't have a cellphone because there's no reception up here the towers are too far away."

"You have one in the kitchen, while you entertain Heidi with the cow, I could go in and call her. The longer she has warning, the better, I'm sure."

He squeezed her hand. "Great!" He winked at her and said, "Why don't you take the eggs in with you, Heidi won't suspect then."

Heidi was at the fence, her little hand through as far as she could make it go, trying to reach Cow, but Cow would have none of it, she stood facing the fence, but back several feet, watching the child dance around. At the barn door, Roger let Raylyn's hand slip through his and she stepped toward the house. Instead of watching the child, however, he watched the lovely lady as she walked gracefully toward his house. It wasn't hard to let his imagination slip several months into the future. Was there a chance that the lady he was watching could be doing that little chore every day? Would God answer his prayer and make this lady his wife? He sighed, he could only hope.

The door closed behind Raylyn and Roger pulled in a long breath. He turned his head to see Heidi and knew that Cow would never let her close enough she was too full of energy and moving too much. He moved behind her and Heidi grumbled, "Mr. Roger, Cow won't come!"

"I see that. I tell you what, why don't I hold you so you'll be above the fence. Cow knows me, so she might come a bit closer. But she's really big, so don't scare her or she might kick up her hooves. If she gets close enough those things can hurt."

"I be real careful, Mr. Roger."

Heidi turned to Roger and held up her arms. When he picked her up, instead of turning immediately toward the cow, she threw her arms around his neck and gave him another slobbery kiss on his cheek and squeezed his neck. She drew back and grinned at him, then rubbed his cheek where there was moisture. Roger nearly turned into a puddle right there beside the fence, but he gave the child a squeeze.

As soon as she'd rubbed his cheek, she said, "'K, Mr. Roger, I ready to see Cow. Hold me real tight so I don't fall."

After he swallowed, he said, "I'll do that, Heidi."

"Good, Cow be too far away for me."
"We'll remedy that right away."

Inside, Raylyn set the eggs on the counter and quickly washed up the dishes they'd used for lunch. Roger was doing so much for them she wouldn't let him do the dishes as well. She pulled the receiver from the wall and punched in her Grandma's phone number, then put the receiver under her chin and picked up the soup container and slid it in the refrigerator.

After the third ring, Isabel answered, "Hello?" she said, breathlessly.

"Grandma, were you napping?"

Isabel chuckled a little and said, "Well, not officially. I was reading, at least I thought I was, but the phone woke me. Is everything all right?"

"Oh, yes! Everything's great. We've seen the chickens and Cow finally obliged us and came to the fence, so Heidi and Roger are there watching her. Roger asked if he could take me to Blairsville for dinner if you could watch Heidi."

"My dear, it will be a joy to watch that sweet child! We'll have beans and weenies and watch some TV together. If it's past her bedtime, I'll get her down."

"Grandma Isabel, that's great! Thank you so much! You know, I haven't been on a date since Dan died. I'm a bit nervous about it, but Roger's a great guy."

"He does seem to be a nice young man. I'll hold judgment on everything for a while. But there's no reason why you two can't enjoy an evening out."

"Thanks, Grandma. We'll see you after a while."

"Yes, dear, have fun now."

"Yes, Grandma, we will."

Raylyn opened the back door, went out onto the back porch and stood to watch. Immediately, a smile came to her lips. Silently, she closed the door and stood there without moving. The big man was totally absorbed with the little girl, holding her protectively while she leaned as far as she could toward the cow. The animal was stretching her neck and holding up her nose so that Heidi could only touch it with her fingers. The cold wetness was making Heidi giggle, but she was having the time of her life. While Raylyn stood outside the door, Curly sauntered up the steps and wandered over to her side. Absently, still keeping her eyes on the pair at the fence, she reached down and scratched the head that rubbed against her leg. Much to her surprise, while her hand was down, Curly's tongue swiped across her hand, making Raylyn jump and leaving several fingers slobbery wet.

She did look down at the dog then, but instead of wiping her messy fingers on her pants, she stroked his head down onto his back until her hand was dry. Of course, she'd have to wash her hand when they went back inside. Curly sat down on his haunches, but kept his head very close to where Raylyn's hand was so she would continue to pet him.

She looked down at the shivering dog and said, "You are a silly dog. I know you get lots of attention, but a little more never hurts, does it?" she said, continuing to pat his head, while his tail thumped the floor. She chuckled. "Wonder why he called you curly? You don't have long enough hair to curl."

When she looked up both Heidi and Roger had turned enough that Heidi said, "Mommy, come pet Cow! She gots a real soft nose."

Smiling at her child, Raylyn said, "Sweety, I just got my hand washed by Curly, I think I'll pass getting my hand wet again by Cow." The dog still sat still beside Raylyn. When Roger looked, Curly seemed to be smiling.

She walked down the back steps and over to the pair at the fence and stood beside Roger, but made no move to stretch her hand across the fence. His eyes twinkling, Roger said, "What, you don't want to have Cow lick your hand, too?"

Dryly, she said, "I think I'll pass. Curly just did it for her."

Roger chuckled. "How sweet of him."

Heidi went back to touching Cow's nose, so Roger asked, "So, what is it?"

"Sure, it's fine."

Roger smiled at her. "Great!"

A breeze picked up in the trees across the field, they could see the tops of the trees move, but as it came across the field it swooped down and came at them full force. Heidi's hood was still off and it ruffled her curls. As it hit Raylyn, she was sure Heidi's hands were getting cold and she could see her nose was cherry red.

Before Raylyn could say anything, Roger said, "That sure is a cold wind, I think it's time to go inside and get some hot chocolate. What do you say, Miss Heidi?"

"Hot choclit? You got 'mallows, too?"

"Hmm, I'll have to make a search."

"Well, you search real good, 'cause I love mallows wiff hot choclit."

"Okay, we'll make a real search and see what we find. I have lots of things stuck in my pantry. Maybe we'll find some marshmallows."

Holding the child in one arm, he turned and picked up Raylyn's hand and took the two ladies across the yard and up the steps to the porch. Since she didn't really want him to let her hand go, Raylyn reached for the doorknob and pushed the door open. With the wind still blowing behind them, the warmth from inside welcomed them.

When the door was closed and Heidi was on the floor, Roger helped Raylyn with her coat and said, "It feels good in here. Of course, I'm from Montana and you're from Michigan, so cold here is nothing new to us, but I've been gone from there for over ten years and the warmth of the woodstove feels pretty good."

"When we saw the snow yesterday I was a bit surprised, but I guess this is in the mountains, isn't it?"

"Yes, it is. We're a few thousand feet above sea level."

Heidi had shed her coat and dropped it close to the door, so Raylyn said, "Heidi, bring me your coat. You need to hang it over the chair and not leave it on the floor."

"'K, Mommy."

After the coat was on the chair, Roger said, "Heidi, wanna help me look for some marshmallows while our milk gets warm?"

"Oh, yes! I help good."

Roger took the child to his pantry and took her close to where he thought he remembered putting some marshmallows several months ago. Heidi saw them immediately and grabbed them off the shelf. "Here they are, Mr. Roger!"

"Why, you found them fast! You're a good helper. I think our milk's ready, so lets get those marshmallows in our mugs right away."

Clapping and dancing, Heidi exclaimed, "Yes! Yes!"

As they sat around the table again with mugs of warm chocolate milk in front of them, Heidi said, "Mr. Roger, yesterday you say we have hot choclit and then go home. Mommy and me be goin' home now?"

Before Raylyn could open her mouth, Roger said, "Heidi, your mommy and I'd like to get to know each other a little. Would you like to stay with Grandma Isabel for the evening?"

Heidi looked at Raylyn and opened her mouth, but by the look in her eyes, Raylyn knew she had to say something immediately. "Sweety, Grandma said she'd fix beans and weenies for both of you and then you'd watch TV together."

Clapping her hands, Heidi said, "Mommy, that be great! I love beans and weenies. Can she read to me and Dollie?"

"I'm sure she can! You'll have to ask her. She might even tell you a story that's not in one of your books."

Nodding, she said, "I ask her. I think Gamaw can tell a good story, lots better than TV. Teacher say it not good lots of time."

"Your teacher's pretty smart," Roger said.

They lingered over the mugs of hot chocolate, but after the mugs were empty and washed up, Roger said to Raylyn, while Heidi was in the bathroom, "I need to milk Cow, could I pick you up say around six?"

"That's great. I'll meet you at the door, so Grandma and Heidi won't be interrupted in whatever they're doing."

"Super!"

Heidi came back and Raylyn was holding her coat. "Come on, Sweety, it's time to go. Tell Mr. Roger what a great time we've had."

Heidi ignored her coat, went to Roger and held up her arms. The man was a sucker for punishment, but he picked her up. She threw her arms around his neck and he knew the slobbery kiss was next, but he didn't mind. She leaned back after the kiss and said, "Mr. Roger, I be so happy! I love Cow and um, chickens, too." She scowled. "Tomorrow be Sunday?"

"Nope, it's Saturday."

Heidi sighed and held up three fingers. "Mr. Roger there be free Saturdays tis week, yesterday, today and 'morra."

"To a little girl it does seem that way, doesn't it, but yesterday was Thursday, today is Friday, but tomorrow's Saturday."

Heidi sighed, "I know, Mommy say that, too."

Roger held Raylyn's coat, then walked them out to their car. The wind ruffled his hair, as he stood beside Raylyn's door. As he opened Heidi's door, Raylyn said, "Roger we've had a wonderful day! Your soup was terrific and Heidi's had the time of her life."

Roger closed Heidi's door, then smiled as Raylyn sat down behind the wheel. "Believe me, it's been great having you come. I'll see you after a bit." At that moment, Roger had the greatest desire to bend down and kiss the lady who sat behind the wheel. Instead, he winked at her and closed the door. Her heart thumping, because she had no trouble reading Roger's thoughts, she left for Isabel's house.

Being out in the cold for so long had made Heidi sleepy. In the few minutes it took to reach Isabel's place, Heidi fell asleep. As excited as she had been about staying with Isabel for the evening, Raylyn was surprised. However, when Raylyn turned off the engine, Heidi opened her eyes and was undoing her seatbelt before Raylyn had her door open. Quickly, Heidi slammed her door the wind that had hit them at Roger's house had decided to blow harder in town. It felt very much like winter was just around the corner.

Heidi immediately started running up the walk, so Raylyn grabbed her purse and hurried behind her. At the door, Heidi reached over her head and turned the knob, just as Raylyn stepped onto the porch. Pushing the door, Heidi called, "Gamaw, we be here now! Can you tell me and Dollie a story afer we eats beans and weenies? Mommy said you said we could watch TV, but I don't like it much."

From her seat in the living room, Isabel nodded. "You're a smart child!"

Isabel sat in her chair close to the window that looked out over the parking lot. She had her sweater over her shoulders and had heavy socks and tennis shoes keeping her feet warm. Her half glasses perched on her nose and a book rested in her lap. She reached out and smiled at the little girl and said, "I think I can come up with a grand story for you and your dollie, little one. It can't be time to eat yet, it's not even dark. When does your mommy have to be ready to go?"

Heidi shrugged. "Dunno, Gamaw. Mommy not teach me clocks yet. She be gonna real soon, 'cause I smart. Asides, Mr. Roger tell Mommy when I be in the bafroom at his house."

"It'll be time soon enough, little one. Don't rush into things, take your time growing up, believe me, it's a lot more fun being a little girl." Isabel pushed herself from the chair and said, "You know what? I didn't check my cupboards, but I think we may have to make a quick trip to Alex's store for those beans and weenies I promised you. Come help me check my pantry. If I don't have any, it's not far, want to walk with me?"

Eagerly taking the older lady's hand, Heidi said, "Oh, yes, Gamaw! We gots to get beans and weenies. I not take my coat off yet, we go now?"

"Sure! Come help me look in the kitchen."

"'K, Gamaw, you think you not got some?"

After a quick search, Isabel said, "Will you bring my purse to the door while I get my coat on? I left it in my bedroom last night."

"Uh huh, I be right there, Gamaw!" The little girl ran to the open door of Isabel's room to where she'd seen the purse. She picked it up and holding the handle with both hands, came back to the hall. The little girl grunted as she lifted it to the hall table and said, "Gamaw, what you keep in here? It be awful heavy!"

While Isabel walked to the closet by the front door, Raylyn, answered her question, "Roger said he needs to milk, so he'll be by about six, Grandma."

Isabel looked at her watch, then slid her arms into her coat sleeves and said, "He ought to make reservations, it is Friday night, after all and lots of those nice places get a line on Fridays. Of course, he has time, he could call now."

Raylyn shrugged. "He didn't say where we'll go, Grandma. Would you mind if I take a bath now?"

"No, that's quite all right. Did you get chilled? I noticed that the wind's picked up since you left this afternoon."

Putting her coat in the closet, she said, "No, not really. It's not near as cold here as it is at home, but I think I need to relax some." Raylyn shrugged. "Maybe that state policeman shook me up more than I thought."

Sliding a button in place on her coat, Isabel said, "That's fine, Deary, you go right ahead. Heidi and I won't be long it's just down the street to the grocery."

Raylyn grinned. "Okay, I'll see you later."

Heidi came up puffing. "Gamaw, your purse be heavy!"

Isabel smiled. "Little one, when you get to be my age you keep everything that's important right where you know where it is. For me, that's in my purse."

"Oh, 'K. Bye, Mommy!"

"Bye, Sweety, I'll see you later."

Heidi took Isabel's hand, reached for the doorknob and said, "Come on, Gamaw, we needs beans and weenies for supper! Dollie want a story, too. She be sleepy afer a while, so we need to get there right now."

"Okay, little one. We'll just hop to it!"

The door closed behind Isabel and Heidi and Raylyn didn't hear Isabel's response, but she was chuckling. She knew her daughter could be persistent when she wanted something, but she was sure Isabel could handle her nicely. She had already several times since they'd come to visit and she was glad for any help she could get. She smiled, anticipating her bath and hurried down the hall.

Isabel kept some bubble bath on one of the shelves inside the tub enclosure, so Raylyn started the water and tested it as it warmed up, then dumped in some of the lavender smelling liquid. While the water ran, she went to the room she was sharing with Heidi and found the prettiest outfit she'd brought with her and laid it on the bed, then grabbed her robe and went back to the bathroom. The steam was already rising from the tub, as she shut the door. She quickly shed her clothes and climbed into the water, then closed the shower curtain to keep the heat in. Only seconds later she was sliding down under the bubbles. Soon, the water reached her chin, so she turned the faucet off.

She'd learned since Dan died that she did some good thinking while she lay in a tub of hot water. She smiled maybe the hot water cleared her sinuses, that might be it, whatever it was she was glad for it. For some reason, Heidi never bothered her while she took a bath and she hoped that would hold true this time. She lifted her hair and leaned back against the sloping back of the tub, then dropped her hair on the ledge. She drew in a deep breath, savoring the lovely fragrance surrounding her. She didn't indulge like this often, but she was on vacation!

Roger hadn't come right out and asked her to move, hadn't even hinted he wanted to spend his life with her and Heidi, but he'd asked if there was any cure for the miles and miles. Was there? Well, at this time in her life there wasn't, but she knew that God was in control of her life and He could do things way beyond her feeble imagination. As she thought about it, she realized He'd been the one who had gotten her the job in Grand Rapids He could surely take it away or give her one here.

SEVEN

Both Isabel and Roger had asked her if she could be a financial counselor in any hospital. Of course she could be, or even in a large doctor's office. However, as she'd told Roger, it was tough to find an opening. Most hospitals worked really hard to keep that position filled, usually promoting from within. She'd gotten excellent references and had made application at just the right time to get the job she had at the hospital where she worked now, otherwise she wouldn't have gotten the job. If she put in her resignation she knew exactly who would get the job and rightfully so.

However, she didn't know anything about the hospital in Blairsville, was it smaller? larger? Did the department have several in it or was there only one counselor? A doctor's office? She knew even less about any such thing in Blairsville. The whole situation seemed moot, she didn't feel there was a clear message, no sign in the sky, telling her to quit in Grand Rapids and move a thousand miles away. Of course, that could change within the hour.

Goodness, she thought, *I only met the man yesterday!*

She sighed and laid the warm washcloth on her face, she loved the scent of lavender. She had no clock behind the curtain, so she didn't know how long she'd been soaking and perhaps she dozed awhile, but after a while, she heard the front door open and knew Isabel and Heidi were back with their beans and weenies. Maybe she should let out the cooling water and start to get ready for her date.

DATE! She hadn't been on a date since Dan had taken her to that perfectly awesome restaurant where he'd placed the lovely diamond necklace around her neck for their second anniversary. It seemed so long ago. They'd both known he was being called up, but of course, they hadn't known how soon or how drastically everything would change. She'd still been nursing Heidi, so they hadn't stayed long after finishing their dinner, really just long enough for Dan to place the necklace around her neck. It had been less than a year later when the chaplain and Dan's commander had come to the door of the little house with the awful news.

She sighed. Sometimes it was hard to grasp the concept that Dan's death was for the glory of God. It was foreign in the secular world. Dan would always hold a warm and special place in her heart, but she knew, especially since her talk with Isabel, that there was plenty of room in her heart and life for whatever God, her heavenly Father, would bring into her life. If that was another handsome man to love, then so be it.

She stood up and grabbed the towel she'd slung over the bar. She shook herself, not only to get the extra water off, but to dispel any morbid thoughts that had bombarded her. She pushed the lever to let out the water then dried herself as much as possible to keep from getting cold when she stepped out onto the floor.

Making a point of it, she turned her thoughts to the man who had asked her to go to dinner with him. She was glad he looked nothing like Dan, he'd been handsome, but dark complected. Roger was tall, blond and handsome. She didn't know, but she wondered if he was of Scandinavian decent. His skin seemed tanned, but not as dark as some blonds she knew. He had told her he was from Montana and she knew many Scandinavian immigrants had settled in that area over several generations.

She drew her robe around her and just before the last of the water gurgled out she swished it around the tub to clean it out. She put the bath towel over a rack and placed the bathmat over the side of the tub, as she had found it, then picked up the clothes she'd worn to the farm and opened the door to go back to the bedroom.

Heidi stood in the hall in front of her and said, "Mommy, we gots beans and weenies for our supper. When you go? Gamaw say we can't eat 'em till afer you get gone. Mommy, you not even dressed yet!"

Raylyn chuckled at her vivacious daughter. She hadn't looked at the clock in the bathroom, but the sun was still shining, so she said, "Sweety, I haven't seen the clock, but since the sun's still shining, I don't think it's quite yet. Remember, Mr. Roger said he had to milk Cow first. I know that takes him a little while."

Heidi sighed, "'K, Mommy, I guess Gamaw and me doesn't eat now. We went to Mr. Alex's store for our beans and weenies."

Nodding, she said, "That's really good. After that big lunch at Mr. Roger's house, you surely can't be hungry yet! Heidi, you need to go play with Dollie or read a book, because I need to dress to go to dinner with Mr. Roger." She smiled at the child. "Believe me I don't need any help from the peanut gallery." Raylyn knew already what response she'd get from that remark. She'd said those words before.

"Mommy, I are no peanut! I not got a shell on me, you know. I just Heidi." she said, indignantly, but turned on her heel and ran back to the living room where her dollie patiently waited for her. Raylyn watched Heidi skip down the hall, then closed the bedroom door and chuckled at her daughter.

Heidi jumped backward onto the couch and said, "Gamaw, I seen Mr. Roger's cow and chickens tis day!" She shook her head and continued, "Cow not like me much, she only let me pet her nose. It was all wet, Gamaw!"

Isabel chuckled and pulled her sweater closer around her shoulders. "Well, little one, she didn't know you. Did you find any eggs?"

Grinning broadly, she clapped her hands and exclaimed, "Oh, yes! I gived Chickens stuff from the pail and they scratch around on the floor. Me and Mr. Roger pushed some lazy ones out and finded five! Mommy taked 'em in the house when she call you."

"Five! I bet that was exciting."

"Oh, yes! I be real careful wif 'em. Mr. Roger say they break easy and I din't wanna break 'em, we not have the right box, so I picked 'em up wif bof hands and puts 'em in the feed pail. But Gamaw, them eggs was brown. Are them good eggs?"

"They're the best, Heidi. I haven't had fresh, brown eggs in years. I know you only get white ones in the store, but brown are better."

Dubiously, Heidi said, "Maybe."

Isabel chuckled at the city child. "Yes, definitely."

Roger watched the red lights of Raylyn's car receding down his driveway. He took a deep breath, then let it out and went back inside his big, empty, quiet house and looked at the clock. It took about twenty minutes to milk, then he'd need to shower and dress, but all of that would take about thirty-five or forty minutes. The trip into town would only take ten. It was now four o'clock. Which gave him over an hour to kill. He shrugged he guessed if he put his mind to it he could find plenty to do. Yes, now that he wasn't doing readings from his book, he needed to come up with something to give to his people on Sunday.

He walked to the mud room, Cow didn't care when she was milked he could do that any time soon. He hadn't taken milk to Sandy, so he could get cleaned up and take it on the way. Another thing, he could use some quiet time at his office to think of what to say on Sunday that would be more than reading something out of a book. God had really convicted him that there was more to say from His Word than what some men put together in a book. He slid off his good pants and pulled on his barn pants and his old boots. His work coat would cover him on top. He pulled on a bill cap, grabbed the milk pail and went out into the breezy afternoon.

Cow still stood by the fence, the breeze making her tail sway gently. When the back door closed, she looked at him and raised her head. "Moooooooo!" Roger sighed, "I can't say I'm happy to see you!" Cow's only response was another impatient "Moooooo!" "But since you asked, I guess we'll get this over with."

Roger opened the door into the barn, filled the feed pail and went to the side door where he let Cow in. He opened the door and she met him. When Cow was in her stall chomping contentedly on her feed and Roger was directing the milk into the pail, he turned his thoughts to the lady he planned to have a rewarding time with over a nice dinner in a couple of hours. He knew the place he wanted to take her and they wouldn't need reservations, he knew the owner personally and the man would always have a table for two open, he'd told him as much many months ago – not that he'd ever taken the man up on his suggestion. The food was exceptional and the atmosphere perfect.

Raylyn was a lovely lady. She was very pleasing to look at, with beautiful auburn waves that played loosely around her face. He wondered if she always wore it down. Both times he'd seen her that was how she wore it. Her blue eyes sparkled most of the time, because she smiled most of the time, too. He had to admit, there was nothing about her he didn't like. She was conscientious, beautiful and a loving mother to her child. Not that he'd been displaying much of his Christian up-bringing up till now, but Raylyn was also a Christian lady. She was obvious about it and she was raising her daughter in the ways of the Lord. As he saw it, the only problem was that she lived in Michigan and he in Georgia, a thousand miles apart.

Actually, there was another problem. He didn't have to think too long to know that his income wouldn't give her the lifestyle she and Heidi were used to, he hardly made it himself. If it weren't for his little farm, the milk and eggs he always had, he'd be sunk. The pastor of a village community church didn't make enough on his own to support a wife and family. She wouldn't have to make house payments, or utility payments, which she was obviously doing now, but was that enough of a reason for her to leave her good paying job? Another question to tack onto that one; could she find a suitable job in the area if it came to that? How would you ever find that out?

The last squirt went in the pail and since he knew how Cow acted, he took the pail in one hand and the stool in the other. As he pulled the stool forward, he stood up and took a step back. Almost immediately, Cow's right back foot moved forward, just as he'd expected. When he'd first gotten her, he'd lost several pails of milk and gotten a few bruises on his left shin before he realized what her habit was.

Setting the stool down several feet away, but keeping the milk pail in his hand, he smacked her on the rump and encouraged her to back out of the stall. She looked at him with her big brown eyes. "Mooooooo!" Shaking his head, Roger said, "I don't understand cow talk, but your supper's over and it's time for you to head on out. I have a date! A date, you hear! with a lovely lady and you're not going to interfere, so get on out in the field." Just to be ornery, she landed a wet, smelly plop at his feet.

"Thanks a lot!" he grumbled. "I do believe you are the most ornery critter this side of Blairsville! And don't you include me in that evaluation either!"

Roger opened the barn door and hit her rump again, shoveled out the mess and took the milk to the house, then ran it through the strainer into a container. He set it by the back door he would take this gallon to Sandy. It couldn't get any fresher than this. He quickly shed his barn clothes and hung them in his mud room, then headed for the shower in the master suite. He didn't like the odor that lingered on him. That plop hadn't helped the situation any. As far as he knew, there was no men's cologne named barnyard fresh. Just before he stepped into the shower, he looked at the clock; he had over an hour before he was to pick up his date. His date! WOW! How long had it been?

He'd never been one to sing in the shower, but the words, "Showers, showers of blessing, showers of blessing we need…" rolled off his tongue as the water poured over his body. He chuckled, showers of blessing - was that the cow plop or the date he was anticipating? He didn't know at this point.

He'd been alone so long he hoped and prayed that those days would soon be over. He knew he could love and cherish Raylyn and Heidi as his own. His heart skidded a bit it seemed Raylyn wasn't immune to him, either. He lathered his hair, then rinsed it and scrubbed his body. He didn't want any of the barn smell to remain on his body when he went to pick up his date. He didn't usually shave at night, usually it was peach fuzz when he did, but as soon as he left the shower he pulled out his razor and shaved.

He dressed carefully, he hadn't washed his white shirt, but he had a good looking polo shirt that was clean that he hadn't worn much since last Christmas when his sister had given it to him. He pulled it on and pulled his dark slacks from the hangar. He pulled on dark socks and stuffed his feet in his dark shoes, then splashed some aftershave on his face. For the restaurant he had in mind he was dressed quite properly. If only Isabel didn't see him, she'd probably think he should appear in a dress shirt, tie and suit jacket. He sighed, his suede jacket would have to do he didn't even own a suit.

He still had about an hour, so he shrugged into his suede jacket, stuffed his wallet into his back pocket and picked up the gallon of milk. When he stepped outside he looked around and saw that Cow had left the lot and was across the field again. Her tail swished in the breeze, but she was obviously munching grass. He'd thought all the good grass was gone by now, but she must have found something that interested her over there. He shrugged, he didn't care he didn't have to deal with the animal until tomorrow morning. He started up and only a few minutes later he pulled onto Ramon's parking lot and walked toward the front door.

As soon as he knocked on the door a cheery voice inside said, "Come in!"

Roger opened the door and heard Sandy's chair motor humming as she came from the kitchen. Seeing the gallon jug, she exclaimed, "Great! You brought my milk! Will you bring it to the kitchen for me please, Roger? I guess I could take it on my lap."

Walking up beside her, he said, "Of course, Sandy! Sorry I didn't get it here this morning like I promised, but one of my parishioners called, her husband collapsed on the kitchen floor and she called me, wanting me to get him up. I stayed with them until the ambulance came and took them to the hospital."

"That's okay. Ramon never had fresh milk to drink, so he used up the last of what we had on hand on his cereal this morning." She grinned and pulled the refrigerator door open for him. There was a large open place on the top shelf, so Roger slid the gallon in. Mischieviously, Sandy said, "He'll get used to it now. I'm looking forward to having some again."

"I never thought to ask before, but if you lived in Philadelphia, how are you familiar with fresh milk?"

"Mom has three sisters, all older than her. Two of them married brothers and they run a dairy farm in the country close by the city and they belong to a dairy association that supplies milk for Philadelphia. Each day, before the tankers come, they skim off a gallon or two and when any of the family run low, they make a trip out to the farm and get a gallon or two. Mom always has cream available for coffee, Mom made cheese and butter and we had plenty to drink and use in cooking. I've missed it, but never thought to ask you about it until yesterday. I knew you'd be coming, so I put your two dollars in my little purse here on my chair."

Sandy looked at the handsome young man and asked, "So what brings you to town this time of day, Roger?"

"Um, well, I'm going to my office at the church to do some thinking for Sunday's service then Raylyn and I are going to Blairsville for dinner."

Her eyes sparkling, Sandy asked, "Have you convinced her to move here yet?"

Roger sighed, "No, her job in Grand Rapids is very important to the hospital where she works and it's essential for hers and Heidi's livelihood."

Just as seriously as she'd been when she played 'The Old Rugged Cross' she said, "You'd be more than happy for her to move here, though?"

As Roger took Sandy's money, he said, seriously, "Sandy, I know she and Heidi could fill the huge empty place in my heart and add joy and laughter to my big, silent, empty house. If there was any possible way, I'd be a happy man."

Roger stuffed the bills into his pocket and Sandy held out her hand. "Roger, let's pray about it right now."

"Thanks, Sandy," he murmured.

He took her hand and bowed his head as she did the same. "Father in heaven," she prayed, "You know Roger's heart, You know he's lonely and a good Christian lady is sometimes very hard to find, especially for a pastor. Raylyn has come for a visit to Vansville. She seems to fit Roger's needs exactly, but she lives far away and has a job she can't leave. However, 'we know that in all things God works for the good of those who love him…' (Rom 8:28) If it is Your will for Roger and Raylyn to be married, we know You can make it happen. Thank You! We praise You and pray in Your Son's matchless Name, amen."

"Amen," Roger murmured. He raised his head, squeezed Sandy's hand and in a voice too choked to do anything but whisper, he said, "Thanks." As he turned toward the front door, he swallowed and asked, "How often would you like a gallon? Believe me, I have plenty so any time you need one it'll be no problem."

"I'm not sure. Why don't I call you when I run low and we can work out a schedule?"

Roger nodded. "That works for me! Thanks."

"Of course! Thank you!"

Roger slid behind the wheel and started up. His lighted dash clock showed that he still had about forty-five minutes before he should pick up Raylyn. He roared out of Ramon's parking lot and more sedately hurried through town to the church. He parked in his usual place, then let himself into the dark foyer, locked the door behind him and hurried to his office behind the piano, without turning on any lights. He flipped on the light in his office and sank into his desk chair behind the huge desk that the original Bradford Thomas had.

The verse in Romans that Sandy had quoted in her prayer burned in his mind. It was a verse and reference he'd learned as a child and it seemed most relevant today. He opened his Bible to the chapter and read it all the way through twice. The book of Romans was such an awesome book and how much he'd been missing of God's Word! There was so much meat there, he knew he'd have to come back tomorrow and work through it again. He sighed he'd been ignoring so much of what God had for him.

He bowed his head. "God in heaven, I've really let You down these years. I'm sorry. I lost so much when I went to that school and under those professors. Please use me now, I pray. It took Sandy, being her dynamic self and bringing me up short every time she saw me to bring me back to You, but now I want to let You have Your way in my life. If You'll give me Raylyn as my helpmate, I would be so happy! But God in heaven, You are now in control of my life and I'll accept Your plan, whatever it is. In Your Son's name, amen."

He didn't raise his head much, just opened his eyes and started reading and writing. He became so engrossed he wasn't aware of the time until his watch beeped. When the sound registered, he jumped from the chair, shooting it back until it slammed into the wall. He grabbed his jacket from the other chair and ran through the sanctuary. He nearly took off several fingers when he grabbed the door, because he forgot that he'd locked it. He pressed the lock behind him and bolted down the steps to his Jeep. He did a U-turn and sent the vehicle down the street. Fortunately no traffic had been on the street.

Only seconds later he skidded to a stop in front of Isabel's house. He only had time to push the stick into park when the door opened and a lovely lady walked out. The porch light was on and Roger groaned her hair looked like rich mahogany. She'd tamed it a little with a sparkling comb on one side. Her coat made her look elegant. Maybe a suit should be his next purchase. Another thought hit him, *Well, duh, didn't a groom wear a suit to his wedding?*

The young man bounded from his seat and hurried up the walk to meet her. "Wow! This is what I get to escort in town? You are an awesome lady!"

Embarrassed, Raylyn giggled. "Please, I didn't expect to go on a date when we came to visit Grandma Isabel. I thought I'd wear this to church on Sunday." She made a face. "I'll still have to wear this to church on Sunday."

"You will look lovely, believe me."

She smiled. "Thanks."

Roger took her elbow as soon as she reached the walk. In the sun, the snow from yesterday had all melted and the walks were dry, but Roger wanted very much to touch Raylyn and this was the best way to do it legitimately, so he escorted her all the way to the passenger side of the Jeep. He helped her in and silently enjoyed the view of the sheer stocking-clad legs as they slipped inside. As soon as he closed the door, he hurried to the driver's side and slid in.

"You know, it's been an age, or it seems like it, since I've been to Blairsville! Daddy was still alive, so that had to be at least four years ago."

"So Isabel had never seen Heidi before?"

"Yes, being Mom's mom, she came north when Heidi was born and stayed for a week. Dan and I lived outside Detroit then, close to our parents. We moved to Grand Rapids nine months later because he got a promotion. When he was called up, I had just gotten my job."

As the car shifted into cruising speed, Roger said, "Blairsville downtown hasn't changed too much, but they've added a mall on both the east and west sides. The restaurant I have in mind is close but not inside the mall. I know the owner personally. He's a nice guy and always has a table. At least he told me he always would."

"Do you eat out much?"

"Goodness no! We don't have any restaurants or fast food places in Vansville to go to and to take myself out to eat in Blairsville is a waste of gas money. Alex, the grocery store owner and I are on first name basis. He keeps his freezer stocked with simple meals for one and I keep the stock rotated for him."

She chuckled. "You fixed a really hardy, nutritious vegetable soup today."

"Mmm, I do well with breakfast, since I get eggs every day and about once a week I fix vegetable soup and give Curly the bone. Mac and cheese is my other specialty, but that's about the extent of my culinary skills." He glanced over and grinned at her. "Of course, I shouldn't be telling you this, it blows my image. Besides, it's a bore to cook for just me, I always fix way too much and then I'm stuck with leftovers. Pardon the pun, but they can get old."

"I like to cook, but I had that problem right after Dan shipped out. He was a hardy eater, so it was hard at first to scale down for Heidi and me. Actually, it was just me for a while Heidi still was eating food out of a jar."

There was a question he wanted to ask, but how? He shrugged, might as well be out with it. "You're not bitter about your husband?"

Raylyn sat and watched the night deepen for several minutes while she thought of Roger's question. Finally, she said, "You know, I think I was. I didn't let it consume me like my mom has done, I'm not sure she's passed the mourning stage yet, but when I went to church it was to go and be seen by the people I know. Of course, I had Heidi to consider. I felt pretty far from God and didn't particularly feel anxious to get back."

She sighed and shook her head. "You know, I felt like shaking my fist at God for what happened. Grandma Isabel and I had a long talk Thanksgiving morning and it finally dawned on me that God was glorified in Dan's death. He was a great Christian and in several of his letters he told me of men he'd led to the Lord and others he'd helped, so when God took him home, his work here was finished. I hadn't thought of his death in that way until she and I talked."

Roger reached across the console and squeezed her hand. "That's a wonderful attitude, Raylyn! Not too many widows feel that way."

Raylyn made a face before she said, "No, and I didn't until just yesterday. When I go home, I'm making it a point to see my mom as soon as possible. I don't know if I can help her much, but with God's help I intend to try. Mom used to be so vibrant and joyful, she and Dad sang in the choir and she hosted the ladies meetings often. Now she's only a shell that gets up in the morning and goes to bed at night. She rarely goes out and never even tries to see her old friends. She's too young to do that."

"I agree with that."

He entered a parking lot over half full and said, "Here we are, I hope you're hungry!"

Raylyn chuckled. "I'll do my best. After all, you fed us that delicious soup for lunch. I don't usually eat so much I'll have to run it off tomorrow. It's a good thing I brought my running shoes. With all the food I ate yesterday and then today… If I don't get a little exercise, I'll look like the side of a house."

Roger shook his head. "I don't see why," he murmured.

Just as Roger believed, his friend who owned the restaurant had a table for two that looked out on the lighted garden behind the restaurant. Raylyn was enchanted with the ground lights that lined several paths. Of course, in the summertime there would be flowerbeds spilling over onto those paths and probably millers and butterflies flitting around those flowers, but now it was the paths winding between gently rolling grass cover. As they sat looking over the menu, they became aware that there was soft music playing in the background. As she listened, Raylyn was astonished that she knew the tunes; hymns were playing throughout the restaurant.

Raylyn looked up from the menu and said, "There are hymns playing!"

"Yes, this man makes no excuses for his Christian faith. I've envied him for years he's much more bold than I am."

"Why is that, Roger?" she asked, seriously.

Before Roger could answer, the waiter came and took their meal orders. After he was gone, Roger shook his head and said, "I know it really doesn't make sense. I've been a Christian all my life, I was raised in a wonderful Christian home and even as a kid I felt God wanted me to be a pastor. I went to college with that in mind, then went to seminary." He put his elbows on the edge of the table, looked intently at Raylyn and said, "It was in seminary where my faith got clouded. I'm sorry to say that several of the professors weren't what you'd call dynamic Christian scholars. Oh, they were dynamic scholars, but not with Christianity. It's easy to become skeptical when your teachers are that way."

Raylyn shook her head. "That is so sad! In a place where young men and women are supposed to be learning how to lead a fellowship of believers and assist them in knowing how to lead people to Christ, they are led astray. It's unconscionable!"

"I agree."

"But you had a wonderful message yesterday! Grandma Isabel reluctantly admitted as much and Sandy congratulated you at dinner. I thought you were as good as my pastor at home and that's saying something!"

"Sandy will get her reward for that! From the very first time I met her, she has been bombarding me with Scripture and my need to preach from it. A few days before Thanksgiving, they invited me to their home. Well, Ramon called and asked me to come help him paint some on their new addition, but then I stayed for supper.

"After we ate, she gave us a concert. I don't know how she did it, but very effectively she moved into playing 'The Old Rugged Cross' and as she finished the chorus she let it die away and while it did, she asked me how many people I'd led to that cross." In a choked voice, he murmured, "I ran out the door! I fled to my Jeep and roared away. I felt like the demons of hell were after me!"

"You were under conviction."

"Was I ever!"

The waiter brought their dinner and as he set down the plates, he said, "Enjoy your meal, folks. I'll be back with refills."

"Thanks, we plan to," Roger replied.

After they had eaten in silence for several minutes, Raylyn asked, "So that was it? You prepared your message?"

Roger shook his head. "I was still intent on using my same old books and give a reading on Thanksgiving, but God had other plans. I went to my office there at the church, but when I opened my book and looked up the Thanksgiving section, I realized I'd used them all before. There was a footnote calling attention to several praise and thanksgiving Psalms."

He shook his head. "Would you believe I didn't have a Bible there at the church except the big one that always sat on the table below the lectern? I went out to the auditorium and picked it up, but it was covered with dust! I took that big Book back to my office and God hit me between the eyes with that Psalm I used. He put the words in my mouth yesterday, I never even used the notes I'd prepared that day. I have determined from now on that God is in control and can use me any way He wants."

Raylyn reached across the small table and grabbed Roger's hand. She looked into his eyes and said, "Praise God! I'm so glad!"

He turned his hand over and squeezed hers. Content to hold her hand he nodded and agreed, "Yes, praise God. I know He put those words in my mouth." He sighed, "I may lose the pastorate over it, but it's in God's hands."

As they finished dessert and were sipping their last cup of coffee, Roger exclaimed, "Oh, wow!" He struck himself on the forehead and said, "I totally forgot a promise I made to a lady from my church this morning! How horrid of me!"

"What's that?"

Shaking his head, he said, "She called me early this morning and asked me to come to her house because her husband had collapsed and was on the floor. I think she wanted me to get him up for her, I told her I'd come, but she needed to call the ambulance and not try to move him. She must have called right away, because they were only a few minutes behind me. When the ambulance took them away I promised her I'd come see them tonight at the hospital. It totally slipped my mind until this minute."

Raylyn placed her cup down on the saucer next to her empty plate where her cheesecake had been and slid her hand across the table again. "Roger, I don't mind waiting in the visitor's lounge at the hospital if you want to go from here."

"Are you sure?" he asked, turning his hand over and grasping her fingers again.

"No, not at all. I'm very familiar with hospitals they don't hold any dread for me at all. Shall we go now?"

"If you don't mind. I'm sure that all I can do is pray with them." Roger's eyes turned bright with unshed tears. "You know, I never prayed with them before they left for the hospital, in fact, it never even crossed my mind until I was back home. That..." he vowed, "...will never happen again as long as I'm a pastor."

Earnestly, Raylyn said, "I'm glad to hear that."

Roger kept her hand and helped her to her feet, then lifted her coat from the back of her chair and helped her into it. He quickly shrugged into his own jacket and placed his hand on Raylyn's back to escort her from the restaurant. Of course, they stopped at the register and Roger forked out some of his precious dollars to pay for the meal. Again he took her to the passenger side of his Jeep and helped her in.

In the darkness, while Roger went to the driver's side, Raylyn realized she was curious and glad that Roger needed to visit the hospital. In the back of her mind she had a feeling she would get to know this place somehow. She didn't know yet how it would happen, but it seemed God was working in her world. Since her talk with Isabel, she knew she was willing for whatever God had in mind for her.

Only moments later, Roger pulled into a spot in the three story parking garage that was very close to the entrance. Raylyn grinned. "Well, isn't that convenient! They have a parking spot marked for clergy and it's empty, just for you."

Roger chuckled. "There are some perks in this business." When he reached her door, he took her hand and asked, "You're sure you don't mind waiting for me in the visitor's lounge?"

"Of course, not, Roger! Of course, it's infinitely better that Heidi isn't here, but I don't mind at all. In fact, I may look around the first floor while you're gone."

He grinned. "That's fine with me." *Will she be looking around because she's thinking of moving here?* He could only hope!

He led her to the walkway from the garage to the waiting area and took her into the well lighted lounge. Much to his surprise, Roger spotted Ernest's daughter-in-law sitting on a two seater couch. Playing quietly close by were her two children. Roger kept his hand on Raylyn's back and went to the little group. "Hi, Polly, I guess I didn't expect to see you here, but with your children, I should have known. How is Ernest doing?" He looked at Raylyn and then at the other lady and said, "Polly, this is a friend of mine, Raylyn Keys. Raylyn, meet Ernest Nexton's daughter-in-law, Polly Nexton."

The young woman smiled up at Raylyn and said, "It's nice to meet you. Dad's doing as well as can be expected, the doctor says. He's convinced that there's no more damage than there is because he arrived so soon after it happened. Mom's convinced that's because you talked her into calling for the ambulance. Thanks for doing that, Roger. Will you go see them now?"

"Yes, is that okay?"

"Oh, sure, I know they'll be glad to see you. Dad's awake now, but I'm sure he'll be settling in for the night soon."

Roger nodded. "I'll hurry right up there now." He looked at Raylyn, "You're sure you'll be okay for a bit?"

"Of course, get on with you!" She turned to the other woman and said, "If you want to go up with Roger I'll watch your kids for you."

"You'd do that?"

"Sure! I have a little girl myself."

Polly smiled and said, "Thanks, that's great."

Raylyn sat down as Polly stood up. Polly got the attention of her children and said, "Hey, guys, this lady's going to watch you while I go see Grampa, you behave!"

"Yes, Mommy," they said, solemnly.

Raylyn watched as Polly and Roger left, but he never once touched her. Before they disappeared into the elevator, Roger looked back at her and grinned. Just the way he looked at her sent her heart into a flutter. She smiled back at him, but to her astonishment, Roger winked at her before he turned back. Silently, without moving her mouth, she said, *Be still my heart!*

The older child, who was about eight, came over to Raylyn and asked, "Who are you? How come you came with him?"

Raylyn smiled at the little boy. "Do you live here in Blairsville?" When the boy nodded, she asked, "Do you know your grandparents' neighbor, Isabel Isaacson?"

"Yeah, that old lady who's got those cabins?"

"Yes, that's right. I was sure you'd know her. She's my grandma and we came to see her for Thanksgiving. My little girl and I live in Michigan, but we came for this long weekend. What's your name? Are you in school?"

"Yeah, I'm in accelerated second grade. It's 'cause I'm smart!"

"That's great! What's your name?"

"I'm Jeffery Allen Nexton and that's my little brother, Jerrod Alfred Nexton. What's your name? How come you don't have your kid here?"

"I'm happy to meet you Jeffery and Jerrod. I'm Raylyn Keys and my daughter's back in Vansville with my Grandma Isabel."

"Oh." The little boy looked up briefly at Raylyn and momentarily, his brother went back to play with blocks with him. Neither one of them looked back at Raylyn. They played very quietly and Raylyn knew Heidi would never have been so quiet.

It was about fifteen minutes later that Roger and Polly and her husband Ernest Jr. returned. After introducing Raylyn to the other man, Roger shook his hand and said, "Ernnie, I guess we'll be leaving. Like I promised, I'll be back tomorrow sometime to see your folks. I'm glad your dad's doing so well."

Gripping his hand and shaking it heartily, Ernnie said, "Hey, Roger, you're the reason he's doing as well as he is, believe me! Thanks. I'm sure Mom would have hemmed and hawed around and Dad would have gotten much worse if you'd not intervened. I'll go try to talk Mom into going home with us for the night, but it's probably a lost cause. I don't think they've ever been apart overnight. We'll see you again, Roger. It was nice to meet you, ma'am."

Raylyn nodded. "Same here. I hope your dad improves quickly."

Ernnie smiled. "Yes, I sure do too. Mom would have a very hard time adjusting to being a widow, believe me."

When they were walking to the parking garage, Roger sighed, "I guess you didn't get to walk around much, did you?"

Raylyn chuckled. "I sure didn't. Their eight year old gave me the third degree while you were gone. I never got to leave that seat."

Roger chuckled. "Did he tell you he's smart?"

"Oh, yes! Before he would tell me their names."

Before they reached his Jeep, Roger took Raylyn's hand and said, "I'm not surprised. I hear about him from his grandparents every Sunday."

"I suspect he's their first grandchild?"

"I believe so, their daughter isn't married." After he had the Jeep running and was leaving the hospital garage, he asked, "Are you free tomorrow at all?"

"I don't know, Roger. My intent was to see Grandma Isabel and except for Thanksgiving Day, I haven't spent too much time with her. She hasn't said anything about tomorrow."

"I need to spend some time on my sermon for Sunday, but could I call you, say around lunch time and see what's on for your afternoon?"

Enthusiastically, she said, "Sure, that'd be great! I'm sure that'll give us enough time to decide on what we'll do for the day."

Back in Vansville, Roger turned onto Isabel's gravel parking lot and stopped right beside Raylyn's car. He hopped out and came to her side to open her door. When he had her hand, she stepped out and he closed the door, putting his hand immediately onto her back. As they walked up the walk to Isabel's front porch, he said, "Raylyn, I've had the best evening I've had in many, many days, believe me. Thanks for going with me tonight and coming out to the farm with Heidi this afternoon. Both events have made my day special."

"Roger, the pleasure's been mine! I know Heidi had the time of her life and I haven't been on a farm in years. In fact, I can't remember when I was last on a farm. Believe me this evening's been special for me, too." She looked at him, her eyes twinkling, "I must admit, I haven't been on a date in a *very* long time."

He chuckled. "Even the stop at the hospital?"

"Yes, even that."

He turned the knob on Isabel's front door and pushed it open. As she crossed in front of him, he squeezed her waist and said, "I'll call you tomorrow."

"Great! I'll be waiting."

Roger closed the door and Raylyn hurried to the nearest window to watch him drive away, until she couldn't see his tail lights. It was only then she realized she stood by Isabel's chair. Isabel could see the going's on from that chair. She tiptoed farther into the silent house. There was one little light on over the kitchen sink, so she hurried to it and turned it off still it wasn't totally dark in the house. By the light from the streetlight in the center of Isabel's parking lot she made her way to her room and as silently as possible, she undressed and pulled down her covers. Just before she crawled into bed, she gazed down at her child sleeping contentedly in the next bed. She was turned on her side clutching her dollie in her arms. A child so young looked totally innocent in sleep.

Overcome with love for her child, Raylyn leaned over and kissed her cheek. As she straightened up, she murmured, "I love you, Sweety. Goodnight." Heidi never woke up, but she did move in her sleep and let out a long sigh.

. Raylyn stretched out on her bed and pulled the covers up to her chin, luxuriating in the comfortable warmth. It wasn't cold in the house, but it was comfortably cool for sleeping. She closed her eyes, but that only brought the man from her thoughts more clearly into her mind's eyes. She'd had a wonderful time with him this evening. He'd been gracious and kind, making sure everything was perfect for her. They'd enjoyed their dinner and the conversation and he'd been so apologetic about going to the hospital. She sighed, she knew her body had tingled each time he'd put his hand on her. She had to admit, it had felt very good and she knew she'd missed male company in the last couple of years.

It took her several minutes to settle down enough to go to sleep. She knew anything could happen life could change, or stay the same. The most important thing; what was God's plan? Very often our plans didn't mesh with His and even more often we humans were in much more of a hurry to see results than our Heavenly Father. She was determined to watch and wait for God to act.

Roger reluctantly slid back into the Jeep and left Isabel's parking lot. He'd had a great time with Raylyn and wished it was only the first of many. He had already decided he missed female company, but Raylyn didn't seem to be just female company, she was a very special lady. Was there any way he could convince her that he was the man for her and that they should spend the rest of their lives together? He guessed that wasn't the problem. That still lay with the thousand miles between their homes and their work.

He drove back onto the road through town and drove home and parked in his usual spot. The house was dark, he hadn't thought to leave a light on when he'd left, of course it had been daytime. Without thinking, he pulled his keys from the ignition and stuffed them in his pocket, then went to the back door. Curly's doghouse was on the back porch, but he didn't even hear the mutt's tail thumping on the wooden floor. He didn't give it a second thought, but opened his back door and stepped inside.

He hadn't even crossed his mud room when he smelled a foreign odor. He stepped back and threw open his back door, then flipped the switch for the light in his mudroom. There was no mistaking the odor of propane. It had to come from either his cook stove, the furnace or the water heater. However, he was sure it was the stove, since the smell was so powerful in the kitchen. What surprised him was that the woodstove was only one room away and no spark had ignited the fumes.

His heart thumping, and taking a deep breath at the back door, he hurried into the kitchen. He didn't turn that light on, but with the light from the mudroom shining on his stove, he saw that the knobs had all been turned on, even the oven, but none of the burners were lit. Quickly, he turned them all off and threw open the window over the sink. With the cross draft from the back door, he hoped to air out the kitchen quickly and keep any fumes from spreading into the living room, which was only a few steps through the open archway.

EIGHT

Taking another deep breath at the sink, he hurried into the living room, but the odor was not near as strong, for which he was instantly relieved. It became less and less noticeable as he made his way down the hall. The bedrooms were fine. The two guest rooms he kept the doors closed and his was the farthest away from the kitchen. He still wondered about the water heater and his backup furnace, but they were in the basement, so after he checked each room, he went back to the mudroom and opened the cellar door. No fumes greeted him, but he cautiously flipped the switch for the ceiling light downstairs and went down anyway. Both the water heater and furnace were fine and his gas dryer didn't have a pilot, so that wasn't a concern.

When he came back upstairs, he couldn't smell anything and the cold air was blowing his barn coat. He closed the back door, sure that he'd taken care of the problem. It was only then that he realized that he hadn't heard Curly make a sound in his house and with the back door open for so long, surely the dog would have been at the back door wanting to come in or at least want some attention. Linus hadn't appeared either, but he could be sleeping in the barn. He hurried into the kitchen and pushed the window down to within an inch of the sill. There might be some stray fumes that he couldn't smell and he wouldn't take any chances.

Roger still had his jacket on, so he turned on the porch light and went to the dog house. Curly was there, but stretched out with his head toward the back. "Curly," Roger said, but the dog didn't move. His heart in his throat, Roger bent down and put his hand on the dog's side. To his relief, the dog's sides were moving, he was asleep, but there had to be something wrong, the dog never slept this soundly. Roger knelt down and put one hand around a leg and the other across the dog's backbone, he pulled him from his house. The dog never roused.

Roger stood up and as he looked at the dog in the porch light, he noticed a piece of paper curled around his collar. Pulling his gloves from his pockets, he pulled them on then reached for the paper. It was curled tightly and the porch light was too dim to read the message. Roger stepped into his mudroom and unfolded the paper. His heart began thumping, Vansville was a tiny town in Georgia he was a Yankee to these people. What did they think he'd done wrong? He had no idea! Until now he felt he had no enemy among the towns people. Who did this?

He smoothed out the folds and looked closely at the writing. There was no greeting and the message wasn't signed. There was one line of messy hand writing that said, "No more preaching or you're out! Got that?"

Roger leaned against the back door and dropped the hand holding the note to his side. Any fatigue he felt coming back from town had fled the moment he'd smelled the propane. He had only preached from that lectern one time in five years and that had been yesterday. He tried to think of who had been in the audience yesterday for the Thanksgiving service, but the building had been packed, which meant there had been over a hundred and fifty people there for the service. Even so, he pictured the audience in his mind and tried to imagine who might have been angry enough to do this.

He read the note again, shook his head and muttered, "All the regulars were there, even husbands that don't usually come. There were quite a few from town who don't come, but wanted to be in a Thanksgiving service. It makes no sense! Who could have done this?"

From the porch he heard a loud doggy snort and let out a long breath. He was sure that meant that Curly was starting to come around. He pushed away from the door, feeling sure that the dog would soon wake up, but he knew he must report what had happened. If he hadn't come home when he had, it was no telling when his house would have gone up in flames. The gas fumes only had to reach his woodstove. It was anyone's guess how soon that would have been.

"*Thank You, God!*" he murmured.

The fumes were gone from the kitchen, so he closed the window, shed his jacket and picked up his phone. To his astonishment, there was no dial tone. He even pulled the receiver away from his ear and stared at it for a minute. Somebody was serious and meant for him to get the message! He looked at his watch, it was eleven thirty and in Vansville, that meant everyone was in bed. Perhaps Ramon and Sandy would still be up, but he didn't want to disturb them. However, he felt this was important.

Keeping the note in his hand, he went to the front door and locked it, something he hadn't done since he'd moved in, then went back through the kitchen and out the back door, locking it as he went. He kept a house key on his ring with his Jeep keys, but he'd never used it before. On the porch, the dog's tail thumped, but he didn't get up. Roger bent over and patted the dog's head. Curly tried to raise his head, but it only came up a fraction off the floor. Giving the dog another pat, Roger went down the steps to his Jeep.

When he came into town, Ramon's house was the first place and he noticed lights were still on in the house, so he whipped onto his parking lot. He dashed to their front door and banged on it. After several minutes, a scowling young man dressed only in his jeans, opened the door. "What are you doing here at this hour, man?"

Ramon opened the door wider and Roger walked in, as he said, "I got home about half an hour ago from Blairsville and smelled gas in my house. When I investigated, all the burners on my stove were on, but none were lit. My dog was drugged and my phone line cut." He held up the note. "This note was around Curly's collar when I pulled him from his house."

Ramon's eyes were like saucers as he quickly led Roger to his office. He shook his head. "In the country, in Vansville? That's unbelievable! There's the office phone, call the sheriff."

"Thanks."

Roger didn't even sit down, but picked up the phone. Ramon followed him in and sank into a chair by the desk. Vansville had no police department the county sheriff was the only law enforcement for the tiny town, so Roger dialed the emergency number listed for Vansville.

When the voice answered, Roger identified himself and told his story. When he hung up, he said to Ramon, "Thanks for your phone, I'd better get home, the man said he'd be out in twenty minutes."

"Sure! No problem, man! I cannot believe this!"

Sandy appeared at the doorway. She had on a lovely robe, but she'd obviously heard most of Roger's talk with the sheriff, because she said, "Roger, you've got a minute, let's pray."

"Yeah, thanks, that would be great."

She brought herself into the room, held out her hands so both her husband and Roger took one, then the men completed the circle. They dropped their heads and she said, "Heavenly Father, we don't know what's going on, but You do. We pray that as Roger goes home that You will keep him safe and that You will bring this trouble-maker to justice. We know that You are in control and that You work for our good. Thank You, in Your son's matchless Name, amen."

Letting out his breath, Roger said, "Thanks, Sandy. Thanks for your phone, too."

"That's the least we could do!"

"Still, I needed a listening ear."

Feeling some better for talking with his friends, Roger drove home. The porch light was on, just as he'd left it. He turned off the engine and cut the lights, then pocketed his keys, but decided he'd wait for the sheriff before he left his Jeep. He cracked the door just a little, planning to listen for any sound, but hoping not to hear anything he didn't recognize. He couldn't remember ever feeling so paranoid in his life before. Just as the darkness and silence surrounded him, he saw movement beyond the fence and heard a welcome, "Mooooooo!"

He sighed, "Well, at least she's okay."

He never heard any other sounds before lights appeared coming up the driveway, then the sheriff's car pulled up behind him. The man left his lights on and stepped from his car, so Roger also stepped out of his. Immediately, the man asked, "Roger Clemens?"

"Yes, I'm Roger."

"Okay, so let's get this figured out." Reaching back into his car, the sheriff brought out a large flashlight and flipped it on. "You say your phone line was cut."

"Yes, the lead in is on this wall of the house."

The man flashed his powerful light starting at the front then moved slowly toward the back on the side that faced them. The phone box was a different color and was easy to spot. When his light illuminated the box, they both saw the wire hanging down below it to the first clip. "Well, I guess we know where that break is."

"I'd say so," Roger agreed.

The man started walking toward the house and Roger fell in beside him. The man was big, he was no taller than Roger, but he probably outweighed him by fifty pounds of all solid muscle. Plus, around his waist was a belt full of paraphernalia, including a revolver. Roger thought perhaps he felt a little more protected with the man beside him.

He took a deep breath and said, as they reached the steps to the back porch, "I guess it's similar to closing the barn door after the fox got the chickens, but I locked my door when I went to call you."

"Hey, it's not surprising, nobody locks doors here in this little town and you're out here in the boonies, why would you?" As they climbed the steps to the porch, a welcome sound reached them, Curly's tail started thumping.

"Oh, yes, you said something about your dog."

Looking down at the moving tail, Roger said, "Yes, I'm sure he was drugged. Obviously it wasn't too big a dose, since he's coming around. Actually, he started coming around before I left to call you, but when I first came home he didn't move or respond, which he usually does when he hears me outside. After I opened up and checked all my gas pilots, I pulled him from his house out here onto the porch so I could see him in the light and that's when I found the note around his collar."

The sheriff held out his hand. "Do you still have it?"

"Yes, here." He held up the small piece of paper. "I've held it ever since I found it. I never touched it with my fingers. I haven't contaminated it."

From his back pocket the sheriff produced a plastic Ziploc bag. He opened it in front of Roger who dropped the note into it. "That was very smart." The man immediately zipped the bag shut. Through the plastic, the man saw the writing, but it was too messy and the porch light didn't give enough light, so until he shined his flashlight on it he couldn't read it. Frowning, the sheriff said, "Haven't you been the preacher here for a while? Why are you just now getting a note about preaching? Maybe I'm a bit dense, but isn't that what a preacher does in church?"

"I'm sorry to say I've only preached one message at that church. I had a Thanksgiving service at the church and I gave a message. Every other time I've had a service at that church I've given a reading, but never preached."

"So this had to come from someone who was in that service on Thanksgiving Day. Is that what you're saying?"

Nodding, Roger said, "I would assume so."

"Hmmm, let's go inside."

Roger opened the back door and the sheriff took a deep breath, as he stepped through. "Yes, I can still smell the propane faintly. You were very smart to open the door and windows right away. So you're sure it was just your kitchen stove? Furnace, water heater, any other appliance on gas?"

Glad to be in out of the cold and also happy there was no longer the gas smell, Roger said, "Yes, everything else that's gas is in the basement. I went down there and checked it all out. The pilots on both the furnace and water heater were both lit and my dryer is electronic ignition, but all the burners on the stove were turned on but nothing was lit. My first thought was the fumes reaching the wood stove."

"Absolutely! So it had to be someone in that Thanksgiving service. Can you think who was there who could have done this?" The sheriff gave him a slight smile. "Got any enemies that you know about, Preacher?"

Slowly shaking his head, Roger shrugged and said, "I have tried to think, but the room was packed, every seat was full. That means more than a hundred and fifty people. Most of those who were there were my regulars, some husbands who don't usually come were there, but there were quite a few who don't attend here in Vansville. I can only narrow it down to my regulars, the others don't come, so they wouldn't know if I preached or did a reading. Believe me, I am totally baffled."

"Okay, I'll take this back to the station and send it for analysis. Of course, you know it may not turn anything up, the person who wrote it might have worn gloves, too. Did you lock your Jeep before you left it?"

"No, it's not a habit, so I never thought about it." Roger chuckled and held up his keys. "I even brought my keys in usually I leave them in the ignition."

The sheriff chuckled, too. "Yeah, that's good, although the Jeep wasn't here. I'll lock it when I go out. Why don't you bring your dog inside. Give him plenty of water, that'll help wash out what he's had. Just because he's waking up, doesn't mean whatever he had won't hurt him internally. I'm sorry about that. Keep me posted about anything else and if you come up with a name let me know."

"Thanks, Sheriff, I'll do my best. Sorry to have to bring you out so late on a Friday night, but I felt it was important."

"Of course! No apology needed, Roger! It's important in a situation like this to take care of it right away."

They shook hands and the sheriff walked out the back door. Roger followed him and locked it behind him. Back in the kitchen he looked at the clock, it was one o'clock. He felt like having a hot drink and almost turned the burner on under his teakettle, then remembered he needed to light the pilots before he'd get any flame. He found his matches, lifted the four black heat spreaders off to one side then lifted the top up. Not only had whoever blown out the pilots, they hadn't meant for them to be lit right away, someone had stuffed a plastic shopping bag under each cover across the pilots. If he'd tried to light the burners with a match, he'd had a fire on his hands! Who could it be that had such a vendetta against him?

He pulled out the plastic from both sides of the stove, then lit a match and lit both pilots. He sighed, he was too tired to worry about the oven he could do that some other time. When he had his stove top back together, he filled his teakettle, turned on a burner and set the kettle over the fire. A few minutes later his teakettle whistled, so he poured the water over the coffee crystals. He dumped the cream into the cup and sat down at the table. While the coffee cooled, he pulled his Bible to him, something he wouldn't have done even two months ago, but now, he knew he needed God's encouragement.

A verse of Scripture came to his mind. He opened to his concordance and found the reference. Psalm forty-six was where he needed to read:

"God is our refuge and strength, an ever present help in trouble
Therefore we will not fear, though the earth give way
and the mountains fall into the heart of the sea,
Though its waters roar and foam and the mountains quake
with their surging…
The LORD Almighty is with us, the God of Jacob is our fortress."
(vs1-3,11)

Roger sat with his Bible open and sipped his coffee. He reread the verses, he had nothing to fear, God was his refuge and strength, any trouble that came his way, God knew about it already and was with him. He would be with him no matter what came about. Just as he'd said when Sandy prayed, "*Thanks,*" he murmured. "God in neaven, I needed that verse and thanks for Ramon and Sandy, they are truly friends."

Swilling down the last of his coffee, he took the cup to the sink and rinsed it, then set it on the drain board to use for breakfast. He shut off the light and went to the wood stove in the living room. He put a large piece of wood from his woodbox in for the night then realized he wouldn't have needed such a large piece, it would soon be morning. He closed the door and went down the hall to his bedroom. He left the door open, as he usually did so the heat would circulate in. He flipped on the light and went straight to the bathroom. He reached around the corner and flipped on the light, then stood in the doorway and gapped at what he saw, his heart began immediately to thump wildly. He hadn't reported everything to the sheriff!

Whoever had been in his house had come to the farthest, most private room. This was unbelievable! Whoever wanted him out, *really* wanted him out! The drain in his tub in the master bathroom had been closed and the overflow had been taped over with several strips of heavy-duty duct tape. The faucet was running a stream and the tub was only a scant millimeter from spilling over. He sighed and turned the water off, pulled off his shirt and plunged his hand in to get at the plug. He shivered, the water was ice cold. Reporting this could wait until morning after he'd reattached his phone line. As soon as he heard the water gurgling away, he ran into the hall bathroom, but nothing was wrong in there.

He climbed into bed and let the first line of the psalm run through his mind again: "God is our refuge and strength, an ever present help in trouble." He closed his eyes and murmured, "*Thank You, God.*" Lying in bed, the covers up to his chin, he realized he felt as calm as he'd ever felt in his life. God truly was his refuge.

Cow woke him at her usual time. Roger pulled the pillow over his head and went back to sleep for a few minutes until she bellowed several times in a row. He pushed the pillow away and sat up, shivered, because it was rather chilly in the room. He went to the bedroom door and pulled it open all the way, then went to the bathroom for his morning shower. He needed the shower to wake up this morning.

He quickly dressed in old clothes then from the nail in the mudroom, he pulled off his barn coat and bill hat. Stuffing his feet into his old boots, he went out the back door with the milk pail. Cow met him just across the fence and bellowed at him again. "I hear you! I'll be right with you, you old cantankerous female!"

However, when he went into his feed room, his heart sank. The barrels holding his cow feed and chicken scratch grain had been turned over and someone had walked through the piles mixing them together. He set down the milk pail and righted the barrels. Cow was already at the side door bawling to get in. He found his scoop against the wall and when he picked it up he found it was cracked, but still usable. However, the handle fell off in his hand, so he gripped the scoop itself, but his heart was going double time.

Scraping across the floor several times, he was able to get enough feed from the mess on the floor to fill his pail, so he took it to the trough, emptied the pail into it and opened the door for her. "Come on, you ornery thing. I sure wish you could tell me who has it in for me!"

Of course, Cow's only response was "Mooooo!"

Shaking his head, he muttered, "Didn't bring anyone to mind."

As he sat and milked, his thoughts went to the service he'd held on Thanksgiving. There were only a very few who had been there that knew he was gone last night. In fact, only Sandy, Isabel, Raylyn and Heidi knew for sure he wasn't going to be at home. He eliminated all four of them instantly he knew none of them had anything against him. Besides, Sandy's chair couldn't have gotten to all the places where the culprit had been. Whoever came only took the chance he would be gone.

He tried to think of the people who greeted him after the Thanksgiving service. Had any of them voiced any displeasure with what he'd said? Had anyone walked out without saying anything to him? That particular action was rather hard to accomplish, since he stood in the doorway of the double doors. His hands slowed on the cow's teats as he thought. However, nothing came to mind, no one's face stood out. He sighed and finished the chore.

He moved away from Cow and set the milk pail by the door to the hall, well out of the way of errant hooves. Cow had finished her breakfast, so she went willingly outside. After that door was closed, he went back to the feed room and looked around more closely. The barrels were solid they'd only been turned over. Whoever had done the job was fairly strong, both barrels had been more than half full and they were heavy, even when they were empty.

He looked around for the lids, at first he'd thought they might be under the piles of feed and grain, but as he looked, he saw one lying under the shattered window. The logical deduction, the other lid was outside that window. He'd have to fix the window, at least board it up to keep the inside dry.

With the feed scoop, he tried to salvage as much of the feed and grain as possible. He was glad, both the cow and his chickens would eat each other's feed, but he tried to sort it out as much as possible, because the cow feed was prepared especially for cows, not chickens. When he had the floor as clean as he could get it with the scoop, he retrieved the lid he could see and covered the feed barrel. He must remember to get the lid that had to be outside, but he could do that when he found something to cover the window with.

Finally, he filled his feed pail with scratch grain and went down the hall to the chicken coop. He opened the door and his heart sank again. A quick count told him all the chickens and the rooster were there, but the hay in the nests was either scattered on the floor or it was ruined from the eggs that the intruder had smashed everywhere. Roger scooped up what hay he could from the floor, then scattered the scratch grain and went for a shovel and more hay. The chickens didn't let the mess bother them they started right in on the grain.

Roger came back with several sections of hay under one arm and a black plastic garbage bag in his other hand. As he started to clean out the nests he found two eggs that had obviously been laid this morning. Carefully, he put them in his feed pail, then dug out the sticky hay from the nests and stuffed it in his black bag. That's when he remembered he and Heidi had gathered eggs yesterday afternoon. Think of the mess if those five had still been there!

When the coop was cleaned and new hay put in the nests, he pulled the strings on the bag, picked up his pail and left the coop. He sighed, put the pail beside the milk and went outside to retrieve the other barrel top. He found a piece of plywood, some nails and a hammer in the room and covered the window. For now, that was the best he could do.

On his way back inside he looked at his watch. A job that normally took less than half an hour had taken well over an hour and a half. He shed his barn coat, hat and boots in the mud room then carried the two pails on into the kitchen. As he strained the milk, his stomach reminded him he hadn't eaten since last night and it was well after nine now. He quickly heated his frying pan and broke the eggs into it, popped some bread in the toaster and turned the fire on under his teakettle. That reminded him that his oven still wasn't lit, so before the eggs were done, he lit it, glad it didn't explode in his face.

After eating, he fixed the phone line, called the sheriff and reported what more he'd found. When he finished speaking the sheriff asked, "You didn't by chance take any pictures of all this, did you?"

Roger sighed, "Sheriff, I don't own a camera. No, I didn't think about doing that, sorry."

"So all your livestock is okay?"

"Yes, my cow greeted me last night and woke me this morning. I counted the chickens and they were all there and in good shape. I haven't seen my cat, but he's an independent sort, so that doesn't surprise me."

"You still haven't come up with a name?"

Shaking his head, knowing he'd tried every avenue to come up with something. "No, I've run it through my brain several times, but nothing seems to come together. I'm on my way to the church now, maybe that'll bring up some images."

"We can only hope. Keep me posted. I've recorded our conversation I'll add it to my report. I sent that note in for analysis, so we'll see what that leads us to. Of course, you know, being Thanksgiving weekend, it'll be a while before they get to it. Sorry for this, Preacher."

"Thanks, Sheriff."

As he hung up, Roger looked at the clock. It was ten o'clock and he'd promised to call Raylyn at lunch time. He'd planned to spend about three hours at the church this morning would she still think he'd call if he waited until one o'clock? He pulled on his jacket, picked up his Bible, grabbed his keys from the little hook behind the mudroom door and headed out. Vansville was supposed to be a nice, quiet, pretty little town.

Curly went out with him, wagging his tail and flopped down on the porch. Across the backyard streaked a yellow and white blur. Roger let out a sigh all his animals were alive and accounted for. Curly had suffered the most, but he seemed to be in fine shape this morning. He'd eaten his normal breakfast and enjoyed a doggie snack, as well as emptied his water bowl. Linus made a figure eight around Roger's legs then went off to rub against the dog. Roger made sure the door was locked then headed for the Jeep.

He drove into town and passed Ramon's house. He and Sandy were two of his best friends, but he didn't want to trouble them with the rest of his problem, so he drove on. Isabel's place was beyond the church on the other end of town, but he could see the parking lot from where he parked in front of the church, both Isabel's and Raylyn's cars were still parked side by side, as they'd been last night. He smiled a little, so the trooper had stopped her because she drove an out-of-state car. He could sincerely hope that could be changed soon.

Roger took a deep breath as he shut off the Jeep. He picked up his Bible, locked the Jeep and headed for the steps up to the front door. Inside, he made a beeline for his office and flipped on the light. He rounded the desk, but he saw another half sheet of paper sitting on his blotter.

Be warned, no more preaching from this lectern or you'll find a hot seat.

Before he even sat down, Roger lifted the receiver. He was surprised to find there was a dial tone. Quickly he punched in the sheriff's number. When he answered, Roger said, "Sheriff, it's me again. I just arrived at the church and this narrows it down a bunch. The church is always locked, even when I'm here alone, but there was a note on my desk when I arrived."

"Will you be coming into Blairsville at all today?"

"I wasn't sure what my afternoon would present, but I definitely can."

"It won't call so much attention if you put that note into a plastic bag and bring it in to my office rather than me come there to the church."

"I'll do that right away. I'll see you later."

Roger found a plastic bag in a file drawer and without touching the paper, worked it into the bag and closed it up. He pushed the bag to the side of his desk and brought his Bible in front of him. He opened it to Psalm forty-six and began to read. His eyes still intent on the verses, his hand fumbled on his desk until he found a pad of paper and his pen. Only moments later he was madly writing notes, his pen trying to keep up with the words flashing through his mind. He had to smile, if nothing else, God was using this mishap in his life and for His glory. He sighed, how much of God's blessings he'd missed since seminary.

Across the street, a man looked out the front window of the gas station/hardware store in time to see Roger's Jeep pull up in front of the church. He smiled, only a raising of one side of his mouth, and wondered what he'd done about the mess he'd found at his place. Oblivious to the scrutiny, Roger locked his Jeep and made his way up the steps. As he watched the young man's progress, he decided the fellow must have come home before his house burned down, because no fire trucks had come through Vansville last night, but all he'd done there on that little farm could have produced a lot of damage and sent a clear message.

The door closed behind Roger and the man in the store moved from the window. Hmm, he'd locked the Jeep, not his usual trusting soul. That half smirk appeared again, there was still one more thing, he hoped the young pup got the message and went back to his readings and quit meddling. He had the clout; he could get him set out on his ear. He'd do it, if he had to.

At breakfast Saturday morning, Raylyn sat across the table from Isabel and cut the sausage on Heidi's plate. After she'd pushed the plate back in front of the child, she used the knife and cut up her own sausage. After putting a bite in her mouth and savoring it a moment, she asked, "Grandma, what's on for today?"

Isabel reached across the small space and patted Raylyn's hand and said, "My dear, I'm content that you two've come to see me. I haven't seen my daughter in several years and that hurts me, but I'm blessed that you decided to come for this long weekend. I'm so happy to see this sweet child and to have you both here is the best present I could ask for. Why, do you have something in mind?"

"Roger said last night that he would be busy all morning, but he wondered what we were doing this afternoon. I told him I'd ask you if you had anything on."

Before Isabel could answer, Heidi exclaimed, "Oh, will Mr. Roger come here?"

"I don't know, Sweety, we'll have to see when he calls."

"My dear, if you and Roger want to do something together, that's fine. I planned to do a little Christmas shopping one day soon, but it doesn't have to be today and it doesn't need you two along. I still drive myself anywhere I wish to go. Somehow, this time of year, my days aren't very full. I only have one cabin occupied and the man told me he didn't want me cleaning his place, that he'd do it himself. Once a week I dust the cabins, but I did it before you came and I won't do it until after you leave. So feel free."

"Mommy," Heidi said excitedly, "will Mr. Roger want us to go back to his house?"

"Sweety, I have no idea what he wants to do. He only asked if he could call."

"I hope we does stuff wif him. Mommy, is it Saturday?"

"Yes, Sweety, it's Saturday. Tomorrow's Sunday and then we leave Monday for home."

"But Mommy, what 'bout Mr. Roger?" Heidi's eyes were big and soulful.

Scowling, Raylyn asked, "What about him?"

"I wants him for my daddy!" She added, "For Christmas."

"Little one," Isabel spoke immediately, even before Raylyn could get her thoughts and her tongue to get together for a response. "God is in control of that, maybe God has other plans for you for a daddy. Maybe he wants you to be patient, Christmas isn't far off, perhaps it's not God's plan for you to have a daddy for Christmas. I know you asked Him for a daddy and I'm sure He heard your prayer, but sometimes He doesn't answer right away, sometimes He has us wait for His answer."

"But Gamaw, Mr. Roger be a nice man. He does stuff wif me, and...and he hold me like a daddy last day," she said earnestly.

Raylyn's eyes were shining with unshed tears. She swallowed before she could get any words out, but she said, "Sweety, I know he did, but you must remember that we must go back home on Monday. Mommy has to go to work and you must go to daycare. We can't stay here, we have things we must do back home."

"Can't Mr. Roger come wif us?"

"No, Sweety, his job is here. He is the pastor of this church and you remember it's the only church in town. If he leaves, where will those people go to church?"

Pushing out her bottom lip, Heidi grumbled, "Where Gamaw goes!"

Raylyn shook her head. "Sweety, it doesn't happen that way. Roger's church people expect him to be here to be the pastor of that church. He can't run off and come with us to Grand Rapids. This is his job, like Mommy's job is at the hospital in Grand Rapids. Besides, Curly and Linus and Cow and Chickens wouldn't have anybody to feed them if he ran off."

Still pouting, Heidi said, "He could bring 'em."

Isabel chuckled, but Raylyn laughed. "Pumpkin, he has a Jeep. He might be able to fit Curly and Linus in that, but he couldn't fit Cow and the chickens in. Besides, where would we put all his animals?"

Slamming her fists on her hips, Heidi said, determinedly, "In our back yard. Anyway, I want him for my daddy!"

Pushing back her chair, Raylyn said, "Come here, Sweety." Heidi slid from her chair and came to Raylyn. Picking Heidi up, she said, "You told me you asked God for a daddy. We've met Roger since you prayed and he's a very, very nice man, we both like him. Honey, you need to learn something and I don't think you're too young. God is in control of our lives. He loves us so much and He wants what's best for us. It's important that we listen to what God says. We must be sure we don't hurry ahead of God or jump into something He doesn't want for us."

Isabel stood and moved to Heidi's chair. She sat down and held out her hands. "I have an idea. Why don't we hold hands and ask God right now to help us find His will for us?"

Nodding, Heidi took Isabel's hand and said, "'K, Gamaw, I ready."

Keeping one arm around Heidi, Raylyn reached for Isabel's other hand. The three bowed their heads and Isabel said, "Dear Father in heaven, we want to ask You to help my dear granddaughter find the perfect man to be a daddy for my sweet great-granddaughter. We know that You love them in a very special way and we know that You have that very special man to be Raylyn's husband and Heidi's daddy. We pray that You will bring that man into their lives and help all three to know beyond a shadow of doubt that they are to be together. We love You, Lord Jesus and we pray in Your name. Thank You for answering our prayer, amen."

The two older ladies had barely raised their heads when Heidi said, "Gamaw, you din't say nothin' 'bout Mr. Roger."

Pulling her hand from Raylyn's she patted Heidi's hand and said, "Little one, perhaps he's not the one God wants to be your daddy. I was asking God to send the right man into your lives, there's a good chance that Roger's not that man and I don't want to limit God or tell Him what He should do."

Letting out a loud sigh, Heidi muttered, "I s'pose that's okay, Gamaw."

"Yes, that's the way Jesus wants us to pray."

Dishes were washed, Isabel and Raylyn sat in the living room talking and Heidi was playing with her dollie when the phone rang. Raylyn jumped from the couch and rushed to pick up the receiver. "Hello?"

Without identifying himself, Roger blurted out, "How about us three heading into Blairsville for a coney dog at the mall and an afternoon together?"

"That'd be great! We're all ready."

"Great! How about we go in your car, mine's not got a back seat for a little one and it's not nearly as well heated."

"Sure, but I'll let you drive."

"Okay, I can be there in five minutes."

"We'll be ready!"

Heidi was beside her mommy immediately, her eyes shining. Dancing from one foot to the other, she asked, "Mommy was that Mr. Roger?"

Chuckling at the child's reaction, Raylyn answered, "Yes, Sweety, it was. Let's get our coats he'll be here in a jiffy. He must be in town, because he said he'd be here in five minutes."

Instantly, Heidi grabbed Raylyn's hand and pulled. "Yea, yea! We gets to go someplace wif Mr. Roger!" When Raylyn didn't come quickly enough, Heidi dropped her hand and raced back to the living room where Isabel sat in her chair and exclaimed, "Gamaw! We gets to go wif Mr. Roger someplace!"

"I heard you say that. You're a bit excited."

"Oh, yes!" She raced away to the coat closet and flung open the door. She was pulling on the edge of her coat as Raylyn hurried to join her. "Come on, Mommy, he be here now! We go wif Mr. Roger!"

The Jeep pulled up beside Raylyn's car and stopped. Isabel watched as the handsome young man stepped from his car and pocketed his keys. Raylyn heard the car on the gravel, but she still stopped long enough to zip Heidi's coat, then swung her purse strap onto her shoulder and grabbed her keys where she'd dropped them on the hall table.

Raylyn opened the door and Heidi called, "Bye, Gamaw, we be gone now!"

Before closing the door, Raylyn looked back at the lady and said, "I don't know our plans, Grandma, we'll see you."

Before the door closed fully, Isabel called, "Tell that young pup to come for supper!"

Raylyn laughed and pushed the door open again. "Okay, Grandma, I'll ask him. Are you sure you have enough to fill that man up?"

Isabel laughed. "I'll fill him up, don't worry. Besides, Alex's store is a block away."

Isabel watched through the lace curtain as Roger met the two on the walk. He had a broad smile for Raylyn and as she watched, Roger scooped Heidi up and hugged her. Her heart twisted as Heidi took his face in her hands and plastered a big, wet kiss on his cheek. The child really longed for a daddy. Would the Lord work in both their lives to bring those two together? In her heart of hearts she prayed that would happen. If what he had confessed at the Thanksgiving table was true, he was a worthy candidate now. Roger opened the back door on Raylyn's car and placed Heidi on the seat, then fastened her seatbelt. After closing that door, he put his hand on Raylyn's back and walked her around to the passenger door and helped her in.

"Well," Isabel murmured, "he knows his manners, anyway."

Unaware that Isabel watched, Roger closed Raylyn's door and walked around to the driver's door. Soon he backed around the car still sitting in the lot and pulled onto the street. "I know the best place for coney dogs." He looked in the rearview mirror at the little girl behind him and said, "You don't like coney dogs, do you, Heidi?"

With a scowl, Heidi said, "Mr. Roger, I *loves* coney dogs! Acourse I think they best!"

"You do! Why would you like coney dogs?"

"'Cause they be *really* good, Mr. Roger. Don't be silly!" The child's grin was broad and she clapped several times.

Roger placed his hand on Raylyn's leg and said quietly, "I found a problem after I got home last night and more this morning that I wasn't aware of. When I reached the church there was a note on my desk that I must take to the sheriff in Blairsville. We'll do that after lunch."

Her eyes wide, Raylyn said, "A problem at your house? While we were out together somebody came to your place?"

"Yeah, everything's fixed now." He chuckled. "I locked my doors this time."

"But a note on your desk at church? Why? What did it say?"

"I'd find myself in a hot seat."

"Whatever for? A hot seat? That's crazy!"

Nodding, Roger continued quietly so Heidi wouldn't hear, he whispered, "I'm not to preach any more."

"Roger! A note on your desk! That's awful!" she exclaimed. "You keep that door locked, don't you? Somebody broke in?"

"Yes, I keep the door locked and nobody broke in. There was no forced entry. Only a few people have a key, but I'm not sure who does have one and I'm not sure how to find out." He grinned at her and squeezed her leg. "Hey, lovely lady, let's have a coney and a good time."

"I'll try, but you're taking that note to the sheriff, right?"

"Oh, yes! I told him I'd be by this afternoon with it."

"Good! That's awful!"

A man followed a customer from the cash register to the front as Roger locked the door of the church and hurried down the steps to his Jeep. The man who paid for the gas got into his car and left, but the other man stayed by the front window to watch where Roger went. Noting that he went on from the church and didn't turn around to go back to his home, he wondered where he planned to go. Why didn't he go home to guard his house? The man shrugged, it was daytime he couldn't do anything in broad daylight. Besides, he had work to keep him busy.

After their coney dog, Raylyn insisted that they go by the sheriff's office. Obliging her, Roger did as she asked, even though he didn't want to take the time he had with her and Heidi to do it, but it did have to be done. He drove up to the building that housed the city offices and easily found a place to park. Every office but the sheriff's office and the county jail were closed for the long weekend.

He looked at Raylyn, but before he could say anything, she said, "Heidi and I'll wait here you get that note to the sheriff."

With a grin on his face, he saluted her. "Yes, Ma'am!"

Raylyn let out a sigh and grinned back, but she said, "You know I'm not trying to boss you, but I am really concerned."

"I know you are, it's okay."

Roger knew that the only unlocked door into the Justice Building would be into the jail but the sheriff's office was in the same area. Thankfully it was around the corner, out of sight of where he parked. He hurried around the corner and soon stood in front of the jailer. Roger scowled and said, "The sheriff said he'd be here today, I need to see him. Is he available?"

The man looked up from his newspaper and said, "Actually, he's down the hall with a prisoner right now." Nodding toward an open door on the opposite side of the room, the jailer said, "If you'd like to talk with him, step into his office over there. He'll be back in a few minutes, I'm sure."

Roger headed for the open door and said, "Thanks."

Only a few minutes later the big man walked into his office and rounded his desk. "Mr. Clemens, you have that second note?"

"Yes, Sheriff, I do." He pulled the folded plastic bag with the paper in it from his jacket pocket and laid it on the desk. "I never put a finger on it. When I found the bag I used another piece of paper to push the note into it."

"Good. I haven't gotten any word back on that other one, but since it's Thanksgiving weekend, I didn't really think we'd hear anything until Monday perhaps."

Roger nodded. "Not surprising."

The sheriff picked up the clear plastic bag and read the message. Still looking at the writing, he asked, "Could you change the locks on the church doors without anyone seeing you?"

Roger made a face. "Not until after dark. Right across the street is the hardware store/gas station. It's open from eight to eight every day and from the display windows at the front of the store is a clear view of the front of the church."

The sheriff made a face. "Here's another thought. Are there two doors on the church, one that's not visible from that store?"

"Yes, it goes into my office, but I'm not sure I even have a key for it."

After a minute's thought the sheriff said, "Okay, here's what you need to do. Today, here in Blairsville, you buy a whole new lock set and a deadbolt. Tonight after dark, park somewhere away from the building and preferably out of sight and get inside. On the front door install the deadbolt, then go through to your office and put the new lock set on your door. That way, you'll secure the building and no one will see you doing it. It won't matter how many keys are out, you'll have the only key to get into the building. After we solve this business is soon enough to change that front lock and produce more keys, if necessary."

Extending his hand and with a grin on his face, Roger said, "Will do, Sheriff. That seems like a good plan."

NINE

The sheriff took his hand and shook it warmly. "Still no idea who could do this?"

Roger shook his head. "Like I told my friend, there are several keys around town. I have no idea who all has them. A longtime town resident gave me mine when I came and I've made a few copies myself to give to people who need to get in early. Except to raise suspicion, I have no idea how to find out. If there aren't any fingerprints on those notes I can't imagine how to find out unless someone comes forward."

The sheriff nodded and said, "For now, keep it under your hat. Don't let on anything just install the new lock and the deadbolt. Keep in mind who complains about not getting inside that may give us a clue."

"I'll do that, Sheriff. Thanks for your help. I really hope I don't have to call you again with anything else happening."

Grinning at the younger man, the sheriff winked, as he asked, "Planning on preaching tomorrow, Preacher?"

Roger turned to go, but grinned back at the sheriff. "Yup! That's my intention."

"Keep me posted!"

Raylyn and Heidi kept up a conversation while Roger was gone, but after a few minutes, Heidi became restless. Since it was her own car, Raylyn felt under the passenger seat and discovered one of Heidi's books that they had both thought was lost. She pulled it out and said, "Heidi, look! I found that book we thought we'd lost."

Heidi's seatbelt clicked and as she scrambled over the top of the front seat, she exclaimed, "Mommy! Oh, read it to me! I almost forgot what it say!"

Raylyn chuckled. "I don't believe that for a minute, Pumpkin!"

With Heidi cuddled close inside Raylyn's arm. Heidi listened raptly as Raylyn read the story. She had only read three pages when a siren began its shrill wail and only seconds later a big ambulance appeared at the corner of the building. Both Raylyn and Heidi jumped when the noise started. Of course, Raylyn stopped reading and they both watched as the truck raced away.

"Mommy, that be scary!"

"I know, Sweety, it scared me, too."

Heidi's eyes glistened. "I hope it wasn't Mr. Roger!"

Minutes later, Roger came jogging around the building toward them and the sheriff's car with its lights and siren going wheeled around the same corner, but turned the opposite way and followed the ambulance down the street. Before the sheriff's car disappeared completely, Roger opened the driver's door and fell in. After he shut the door, Roger said, "That's a first! I've never heard an accident reported first hand. I was leaving when the word came." Roger chuckled a bit and said, "I've never seen a man his size move so fast."

"An accident?"

"Yeah, on the highway between here and the interstate."

Roger felt the little body squirm between himself and Raylyn, so he looked down and said, "Hmm, who's here?"

Heidi looked at Roger and smiled. She was a beautiful child, the image of her mommy. Raylyn was probably watching herself grow up. "Mr. Roger, Mommy finded my book we lost long time. We be reading when that amblance scared us."

Roger opened his door again and stepped out, then turned around and held out his hands. "I guess you need to get back in your seatbelt before we can go, don't you?"

Heidi came to him quickly. As Roger picked her up, she put her hands on his cheeks and said, "Mr. Roger, you catch bad man?"

Realizing how he had compromised his problem, he shook his head and said, "No, the sheriff didn't either." Very seriously, he continued, "Heidi, can you keep a secret for me?"

Nodding, she said, "Uh huh."

"The man who left in that car told me not to tell anybody. You and Mommy already know, but the three of us can't tell anyone else, okay?"

Nodding vigorously, Heidi said, "I not say nothing, Mr. Roger!"

"Okay. We're in this together. Not a word." Roger set the child down on the seat, then pulled the belt across and snapped it.

For emphasis, Raylyn said, "Remember, Sweety, not a word!"

Roger drove to the mall then went straight to a hardware store. Heidi found something interesting in one aisle and Roger took Raylyn to the aisle with locksets and deadbolts. He picked up one of each and whispered, "After dark I'm to put the deadbolt on the front door of the church and change the lock on my office door. We'll see who complains the loudest."

Raylyn shook her head. "I hope she doesn't tell. I'm not sure she's ever had to keep a big secret like that."

Roger shrugged. "It's water under the bridge. I'll have you back to Isabel's before I go to install these."

Nodding, Raylyn grinned and said, "Oh, Grandma said I should invite you for supper."

Roger chuckled. "The lady has mellowed. Back in September she came off Sandy's lift madder than a Banty rooster. Before I could say a word to her, she lit into me and sent me home to change my clothes. She said I wasn't dressed properly for the host for such a grand concert. Now she's inviting me for supper? And she doesn't know what I'm wearing while I escort her grand-daughter?" He shook his head.

Raylyn giggled. "Roger, I'm pretty sure she knows what you're wearing. Her chair sits in such a way that she can see out both sides. One window looks out on those beautiful mountains, but through the other she has a clear view of the parking lot. As Heidi and I headed for the door she was very intent on the view of the parking lot."

Roger chuckled as they rounded up Heidi and headed for the cash register. "She's worse than a dad on a girl's first date, isn't she?"

"Almost."

Instead of going to Raylyn and taking her hand, Heidi reached for Roger's and said, "Mr. Roger, you comin' to supper at Gamaw's house?"

"Why, Heidi, I wouldn't dare not do what your gamaw wants!"

"But when you milk Cow?"

Picking up the bag from the cashier, he rubbed his chin with his other hand. "Hmm, I guess I have two choices. You and Mommy could go out to the farm and wait while I milk Cow or I could wait until after I get home tonight after our supper."

"Oh, Mr. Roger, that be too late. Cow be sleepin' then."

Roger chuckled as he picked Heidi up to put her in the back seat. "No, she wouldn't be asleep, I'm sure of that. She'd be making all kinds of noise by then."

"That not good! She wake up Curly and Linus. We go now?"

Roger looked at his watch. "I don't think we need to go just yet. Remember that picture Miss Sandy gave to you and Mommy the other day?"

"Uh huh."

"Would you like to see the place where she painted that picture?"

"It be a real place?" Heidi exclaimed.

"Sure! Sandy loves to drive and she'll go to different places with her paints or her camera. If she takes a picture, she'll paint her picture from what she took. Since it's a winter scene, I'm pretty sure her painting is from a picture she took, but I know right where it is. Want to go there?"

"Oh, yes!"

"Okay! We're off!"

Roger stayed at Isabel's house until it was time for Heidi to get to bed. She insisted that he read her a story, so after she was in her jammies and had brushed her teeth, she took his hand and led him down the short hall to the bedroom she was sharing with her mommy. She pushed him down onto her bed, picked up the book she and Raylyn had been reading in the car, then climbed up onto Roger's lap and opened the book. She looked up at the young man and smiled and Roger was glad he was sitting.

"Start here, Mr. Roger. Mommy only read two pages." The young man started reading and tried to make it interesting.

After he had finished the short story, Heidi said, "Come on, Mr. Roger, we gotta say my prayers. We gots to kneel aside my bed." When they were both on their knees, Heidi said, "Put your hands like this and close your eyes real tight. Now we ready."

Roger was glad he didn't have to pray, he felt so honored that Heidi wanted him, but he couldn't have said a word in his normal voice. Heidi immediately began, "Dear Jesus. You needs to catch the bad guy from the church. Make it quick, 'cause Mr. Roger don't need a hot seat. Bless Mommy and Gamaw and Miss Sandy and Mr. Ramon and…and acourse, Mr. Roger. I love You, Jesus, goodnight now, amen."

Roger opened his eyes, quite concerned about Heidi's prayer, but Heidi's eyes were still closed and she said, "Mr. Roger, you gots to pray. Mommy aways do."

Roger closed his eyes again he felt like sand scratched his throat this child did strange things to him. Finally, he murmured, "God in heaven, thank You for this happy day we've had together. Bless Heidi and her mommy and Isabel. Bless us as we all go to church tomorrow. Thank You for loving us, in Your Son's Name, amen."

Heidi opened her eyes and stood up. She patted Roger's hand and said, "That be good, Mr. Roger. Tell Mommy to come now."

"Okay, Miss Heidi, I'll call her."

A few minutes later Roger left Isabel's house. Raylyn saw him to the door. He didn't let her turn on the porch light, but before he crossed the porch, he took her in his arms and kissed her tenderly. They had discussed what he would do, so as she watched him from the window, he took the bag with the locks from her car and walked away from the parking lot. It was chilly and the breeze blew from the north, but Roger felt warm right down to his toes. He'd kissed the lady he'd love to marry and he'd put the child to bed he knew he could love as his own. The only thing that had marred the day was the threat on his desk this morning.

From the sidewalk, he looked up and down the street. Vansville rolled up its sidewalks as soon as the hardware store closed at eight o'clock, so no one was out and no porch lights were on. Of course, he knew there were still several families and couples who were out of town for the holiday weekend. He turned toward the church and in only a few minutes he walked up the church steps. Looking around again, glad for the little covered stoop where he could stand and not have the street light shine on him, he took one more step to the front door and unlocked it. Quickly, he stepped inside and locked the door behind him.

The small foyer had two narrow stained glass windows on either side of the big double doors and one dim light that hung down from the ceiling, but he had to turn it on to see to install the deadbolt. As quickly as he could, he ripped open the package, pulled out the screwdriver he'd taken from the Jeep and put in his pocket and began to attach the device to the door. When all the screws were secure, he pushed the bolt silently into place and turned out the entry light. Before he started across the dark auditorium he listened for any noise.

Satisfied, he moved quietly across the back and down the side to his office. He opened the door and stood in the opening for several seconds to be sure no one was there then closed the door behind him. He didn't turn on the overhead light in the room, but reached for the small desk lamp on his desk. With the dim illumination, he looked around the room for anything out of place or added, but found nothing.

He opened the back door and was glad there was a stormdoor in place. He flipped the lock on the storm door, then began to remove the lock set on the sturdy wooden door. He'd never assembled a knob on a door before, but he studied the instructions and working them backwards to take out the old set, he replaced it with the new. Before he finished, he tried the key in the new set and was satisfied that he'd be able to get in for church the next morning. He shut off the light, let himself out and hurried to his Jeep

Sunday morning, Isabel's phone rang about seven thirty. Isabel had filled her coffee pot, so she moved down the counter to answer her kitchen phone. Sandy said, "Isabel, are you going to church here or in Blairsville?"

"Why, at my home church, of course!"

"Okay. We wondered if Raylyn had talked you into going here to hear Roger or if you're still going to our church."

"I guess we have divided interests. Heidi has made it quite clear that she and Raylyn will be going here, but I'm still planning to go to my church."

"That's fine, we'll see you at the regular time."

"Yes, Deary, that you will!"

Heidi came in the kitchen in her Sunday best dress. She had to have heard Isabel's side of the phone call. "Gamaw," she said, "you be goin' wif us to Mr. Roger's church today." It was not a question.

Isabel sat down in her chair and pulled Heidi beside her. "Little One, listen to me. I'm going to my church that I have gone to for many years in Blairsville today. I went to the church here in town on Thanksgiving Day because my church wasn't having any service. That's the only reason. It's all right with me if you and your mommy go to this church if you want, but I'm not going there today."

"But it be Mr. Roger's church," Heidi said, tears collecting in her eyes.

"I know that, Little One, but I have my Sunday school class and my friends at my church and I love my pastor. You go to Mr. Roger's church if you want, that's fine."

"'K," Heidi murmured.

Roger milked his cow, then took a shower and started to dress. He wondered if Raylyn would come to his church or if she would feel obligated to go with Isabel to Blairsville. He remembered what she'd said when he'd asked her about spending time with him yesterday. He felt a twinge of conscience he had taken her away from Isabel quite a lot during the weekend. Besides, as things stood now, she would leave in the morning for Grand Rapids and probably never be back. Why shouldn't she go to Blairsville? He didn't have any hold on her. A lump settled in his throat, he wished he did.

He finished shaving and splashing on his aftershave then went to his closet for his white shirt and a pair of dress pants. He looked out the window and saw the tall trees swaying back and forth in the winter wind. He shivered a pair of wool slacks would feel really good today. He hadn't worn any yet this year, so he pushed the more lightweight clothes forward to see what else he had. Much to his surprise, there hung the suit he'd worn when he graduated from seminary. It even had a suit jacket to go with the slacks. It was a bit dated, but so what? That was the beauty of small town living, high fashion wasn't first priority.

He checked his watch he had to remember he must be first into the building. His praise team would be champing at the bit. It was the first time he'd thought of them in several days. He wished there was some way he could dismiss them and have Sandy play for the service without hurting anyone's feelings. He shrugged, first of all, Sandy didn't come to his church she'd only come on Thursday because there was no service at hers.

After breakfast, he grabbed up his Bible, shrugged into his suit jacket, then into his suede jacket and headed out the door. After taking one step, he stepped back and locked his door, then went on to his Jeep. Linus dashed across from the barn and into Curly's house with him and he noticed Cow was across the field again. He left his place, wondering what would become of him once this day unfolded.

In town, his usual place in front of the church was open, but there were other cars parked along the street and one was in the hardware store parking lot. He pulled into his place, shut off the engine and opened the door. As he reached to lock it and step out three of his praise team members left their cars and came toward him.

The bass player reached him first and said, "Hey, how come we can't get in?"

Roger held out his hand to the man and said, "Had some trouble since Thursday, so I had to take some precautions."

"In Vansville?" the man asked, incredulously. "You have got to be kidding! When was the last time the sheriff was here?"

Roger shrugged, but only answered the man's first question, "Seems so. I'll have the door open in a jiffy." He never climbed the steps, but walked down the sidewalk to the corner, then turned onto the other street and disappeared from view.

Across the street, from the window of the hardware store the man watched as the members of the noise-makers group came and tried to get into the church. He scowled, they put their key in the lock and it turned, but the door wouldn't open. He watched as each one came and none of them could open the door. The big man even shook the door, but it didn't budge. Finally, they'd all gone back to their cars to wait for the man who called himself the preacher.

The man was on hand looking out the window when the Jeep appeared. The young man locked his vehicle and all the people swarmed around him, but he didn't even go up the steps! He left them all and went around to his office door. Only a few minutes later the front door swung open, the preacher holding it open for those wanting in. The door closed behind them and the man stepped away from the window. He scowled, that was a new development. He pounded his fist on his counter; that also meant his key wouldn't get him into the church! That was not a good thing, not a good thing at all!

Isabel told Heidi several times before Ramon and Sandy came for her that there was no Sunday school at Roger's church. It made no difference she and her Mommy were going to Mr. Roger's church. The time of the service was posted on the sign out front, so there was no reason to be there early. The light blue van pulled onto the gravel parking lot and Isabel went out, but Raylyn and Heidi stayed behind.

Only moments later, Heidi said, "Mommy, it be time to go to Mr. Roger's church? We not be late, you know."

Raylyn sat down on the couch, knowing it would be a long hour to wait to get to church. "Sweety, remember Grandma and I both told you Grandma's church has Sunday school, but Mr. Roger's church doesn't. It isn't time to go there yet. Besides, it takes a little time to get to Blairsville you remember we went there yesterday."

"'K," the little girl sighed.

Heidi cuddled beside Raylyn, who said, "We can have our own Sunday school! Okay?"

"'K!" Heidi said, enthusiastically. "Tell me about the man up the tree!"

"You mean Zacchaeus?"

"Yes, him!"

"Want to sing the song first?"

Heidi nodded, but started singing and using the hand motions, so Raylyn joined her:

> "Zacchaeus was a wee little man, a wee little man was he.
> He climbed up in a sycamore tree, the Lord he wanted to see.
> But as the Savior passed that way, He looked up in the tree,
> And He said, 'Zacchaeus, you come down, for I'm going
> to your house today,
> For I'm going to your house today.'"

Raylyn told a wonderful story and soon the kitchen clock said it was time to leave for Roger's church. Raylyn zipped up Heidi's coat and as she did, Heidi said, "Mommy, will the bad man be there?"

Knowing this was very important Raylyn crouched down in front of her and looked into the little girl's eyes before she said, "Sweety, I don't know. We don't know who the bad man is, so we mustn't say anything about it, especially not at church. Will you promise me not to say anything to anyone, not even Mr. Roger about it?"

"Yes, Mommy, I not say nothin' tis morning."

"Thank you, Pumpkin. Remember, it's very important."

Roger went to his office and closed the door as the praise team started their warm-ups, their mikes and instruments making lots of noise. He sat behind his desk and opened his Bible, then spread out his notes. He prayed, then read the Scripture and read through his notes. However, it was hard to concentrate the instruments in the auditorium seemed even louder than they had in the weeks before. Roger wondered if they'd always been this loud, perhaps they had been, but now he was trying to concentrate on a still, small voice that was being drowned out and that voice was much more important than the noise of the praise team.

The next time Roger looked at his watch it was quiet in the auditorium and the time was five minutes to the hour. He laid his note papers on top of his open Bible then closed it around them. Quickly he stood up from his desk, but before he opened his door he saw the knob turning and his heart climbed into his throat. He had no idea who would be coming to his office door before the service!

The door was two inches off the latch, but he couldn't see anyone, when a little voice said, "Mr. Roger, you be here?"

Swallowing quickly to get the huge lump from his throat, he laid his Bible back on his desk and crouched beside his desk. "Yes, Heidi, I'm here. Come on in!"

Heidi pushed the door open a little more, then walked in and looked at the man. Even though he was crouched down to her level, she stopped a few steps from him. "Mr. Roger, you gots a suit on! You looks pretty awesome, you know?"

His eyes twinkling, he laughed. "You are precious! Thank you, Heidi! So you came to my church, with Mommy and Isabel?"

"Mommy comed, but not Gamaw. Her went to the other place."

Instead of Heidi kissing Roger, he held her close and kissed her cheek. "I'm glad you came here today, Heidi. You'd better go back to Mommy, okay?"

"'K, you come out now?"

"You go ahead, I'll be right there."

Heidi skipped out the door and disappeared. Roger stood and straightened his tie, even though it didn't need straightening. He swallowed the lump that was back to his throat and pulled out his white handkerchief. He wiped his nose then ran the cloth across his eyes. As he stuffed the cloth back in his pocket, he picked up his Bible and went out to the auditorium. A sea of faces greeted him, but his eyes sought only two. Those he looked for were on the second row, three seats from the middle aisle. Both the big and the little girls were smiling right at him. For the second time that morning, in fact in less than fifteen minutes, his heart turned over.

The praise team had their mikes in position, waiting for the sign from Roger to begin. The clock on the back wall pointed to the hour. However, instead of signaling them to start, he walked onto the platform to their control box and gave the main knob a twist then he walked to the lectern and laid his Bible down on it.

"Let's open with prayer." Most of those present were shocked, but they all lowered their heads, as Roger said, "Dear Father, God, we've just celebrated Thanksgiving, but we have much to be thankful for. If we spoke of only one of Your blessings each day, it would take a lifetime to say them all. Thank You that we have freedom to worship in this building today. May we go away from here knowing that You have been here with us. In Your Son's Name, amen."

Roger turned to the praise team leader and said, "Web, let's hear three songs, but then, since we have a little person here today, I think we need to sing 'Jesus Loves Me,' Maybe you don't have the sound track for that, but with your guitar we could sing it, don't you think?"

With a perplexed look on his face, the man nodded and Roger moved to a chair out of the way of the praise team members. The music began, but he glanced quickly at the little girl nearby and saw her smile. Before he looked away, she blew him a kiss. Where was that handkerchief when he needed it? *God in heaven! Surely You mean for these precious girls to be in my life! You know my heart better than I do.*

The praise team ended their third number. The volume hadn't been near as loud as it had been on other Sundays, thanks to Roger turning the dial down. The man named Web turned to Roger for direction, since what he'd asked was totally foreign to anything they'd ever done before. The people were already standing, so Roger made his way back to the lectern then looked at the man with the guitar, who strummed a chord.

Heidi was never bashful and she knew that Roger was having everybody sing her favorite song just for her, so in her loudest voice, she began, "Jesus loves me..." Roger and Raylyn joined her, then the others on the platform joined and soon everyone in the auditorium added their voices to finish the verse.

After the song, Roger said, "Folks, please sit down. I have an announcement to make before we take our offering." He waited as the people made a bit of noise and chairs squeaked, before he said, "As most of you know, I'll be gone starting the Monday before Christmas until the Saturday before New Year's. There will be no service here on Christmas Day unless someone else wants to hold that service. However, the Sunday before Christmas Sandy DeLord has agreed to perform a matinee of Christmas music here at the church. My thought is that the program will start at two thirty and after she is finished, our ladies could supply dessert and Christmas punch. Would that meet with everyone's approval?"

He looked around to see many nodding heads and smiles from the ladies and grins from the men. "Great! Well, I guess that's settled. Let's take the offering."

As the men took the offering, Roger turned around to the others on the platform and said, "One more song, folks and let's turn down the volume a bit more, okay?"

"As you wish, Roger," Web said.

Roger waited for those of the praise team to take seats in the audience. There was quietness in the room for a change. He opened his Bible, then spread out his notes beside it and looked out at the group gathered before him. "Folks, I will not be reading to you any more from my big book of readings, but I will be giving a message that I feel has been placed on my heart to give you. There is a verse in the book of Psalms that says exactly what I want to say today. It's in Psalm forty and verse three. It says: 'He put a new song in my mouth, a hymn of praise to our God. Many will see and fear and put their trust in the LORD.' I would like to talk a little about those words and how they pertain to me and to you."

When Roger closed his Bible there wasn't any sound in the room. He nodded to Web who reluctantly brought his team back to the platform. Instead of another noisy sound as they usually did on other Sundays after Roger's reading, the man said, "Let's worship while Joe plays for us." Joe played a song that hadn't been played in that church in a very long time, but Roger had heard it only a little over a week before. No one sang the words, but almost everyone knew them from a time in their childhood. Roger couldn't have sung any of the words, his throat felt like a ball of cotton.

> "On a hill far away stood an old rugged cross,
> The emblem of suffering and shame;
> And I love that old cross where the dearest and best,
> For a world of lost sinners was slain.
> So I'll cherish the old rugged cross,
> Till my trophies at last I lay down;
> I will cling to the old rugged cross,
> And exchange it someday for a crown."

As the single guitar continued to play, Roger made his way to the back of the church. When the man stopped playing, Roger said, "Go and God be with you!"

Many in the service congratulated Roger on his new worship service, however some criticized him. With each one he smiled and shook hands. He'd done what he felt God wanted him to do, actually what God had called him a long time ago to do and he hadn't until today. It was the first time in a long time that he felt good after his Sunday morning worship service.

The worship team was still packing up when the last person walked out. Roger turned back into the auditorium and much to his relief Raylyn and Heidi still stood in the aisle. When he looked back, Heidi left Raylyn and ran to his side. She held her arms up and Roger picked her up. She placed a slobbery kiss on his cheek and rubbed it in.

"Mr. Roger, you be really good. Thank you for singin' my favorite."

"Thanks, Heidi..."

Raylyn was beside him and before he could say anything else, she laid one hand on his arm and squeezed. The smile she gave him nearly sent him to his knees, as she said, "Roger, you were terrific! I was proud of you. Every word came right from your heart. It showed on your face and in your voice."

Two tears shimmered in Roger's eyes, but he wouldn't let them fall. He took one arm from around Heidi and pulled Raylyn to his side. In a choked voice he said, "Thanks, Sweetheart. You have no idea what those words mean to me."

Roger still held both Raylyn and Heidi when the four people from the platform came toward them. "So Roger," Web said, "you gonna do things like that again? You know, we could almost do without that sound system if we did."

Nodding, Roger said, "Yes, Web, that's how I plan on the services from now on for as long as I'm allowed. Heidi and her mommy must go back home tomorrow, so probably we won't be singing 'Jesus Loves Me.' but it'll be three songs the people can sing with, a meditation song before my message and one at the end. Joe, thanks for playing 'The Old Rugged Cross,' that hymn means a lot to me."

"Sure! That's a favorite of mine, too. See you next week!"

Web turned and asked, "Will you be here earlier next week or do we get a key to get in?"

"I'll have to see what develops, guys. Thanks." That was all he could say, he had no idea how things would pan out.

The men walked out and closed the door behind them. Roger set Heidi on the floor then followed the men. He turned the lock in the knob and pushed the deadbolt home, then turned back to Raylyn and Heidi. "My coat's in the office. We'll go out the back door."

Roger had just closed the door from the auditorium when the phone rang on the desk. He scowled, but lifted the receiver and said, "Hello?"

"Glad I caught you, man! We're on our way back to Vansville. Would you three join the three of us at our house for dinner?"

"Listen, if it's Sandy's cooking, you don't have to twist my arm! We'll be waiting at your door in a few minutes."

"So you're still alive?"

"Yup, still in one piece, so far."

"Great!"

A man walked away from the counter after paying for his gas and the man followed him to the front window of the store. People were leaving the church, but the noise hadn't made it beyond the closed doors today. One of those who had been in the service drove up to a gas pump and filled his tank, his wife still sat in the car.

When he came inside, he saw his friend and said, "Say, you should have been there! That Roger was in a suit and tie! Can you believe it? He didn't let those fellas blast us out and he gave a message! He didn't read from a book."

"What'd he do, preach?"

"Yeah, I guess that's what you'd have to call it, but he was really good! At the end only one guy played and you know what he played? 'The Old Rugged Cross'! It was a great service today and I enjoyed it a lot."

"Yeah, well, we didn't bring him here to preach!" the man said, scowling.

He friend looked at him. "Ain't that what a preacher's supposed to do?"

"He ain't no preacher!" the man said, pounding his fist on the counter.

"Well, he was today. He sure was today! Yes, sir, it was a great service!"

Raylyn had decided that she needed to leave Vansville by eight Monday morning. She hated the thought of subjecting Heidi to an all day buckled into her seat, but knowing she must work on Tuesday and Heidi go to daycare, she decided that daytime travel was the only option.

Much to Raylyn and Roger's surprise, Isabel invited Roger to come for breakfast. Of course, he didn't refuse he hurried through milking Cow and was showered and dressed when it was still barely light. He was upset with himself, but he had nothing to give Raylyn as a reminder of their days together. He shrugged he knew he'd never forget this Thanksgiving as long as he lived, or the two people who had made it memorable. As he drove to Isabel's house he had to wonder why God had brought these two lovely ladies into his life when having them stay seemed to be out of the question.

It was the delicious smell from the kitchen that woke both Raylyn and Heidi Monday morning. Raylyn lay in bed for a moment savoring the smell of baking cinnamon buns, a recipe passed to her mom, then her from her grandmother. She knew she must get up she not only had to get ready for the day, get Heidi ready, but she also had to pack their things. She so much didn't want to leave that she'd put off packing until this morning.

Before she could bring herself to leave the warm bed, Heidi popped up and scrambled from her bed to climb onto Raylyn's. She snuggled down beside Raylyn and a fat tear slid from the corner of Heidi's eye, as she asked, "Mommy, we gotta leave? We can't stay in this little house wif Gamaw or marry Mr. Roger and he be my daddy?" She hiccoughed and said, "Mommy, I want him for my daddy so bad!"

With a lump in her own throat, she nodded and said, "Yes, Sweety, we must leave right after breakfast for home. You know you told Teacher you'd see her on Tuesday."

"Mommy," the tear dripped on Raylyn's cheek, "we leave Mr. Roger? I love him so much, you know!"

In barely a whisper, she said, "Yes, Sweety, Mr. Roger has to stay and be the pastor of this church. Remember we talked about it before. He's the only pastor this town has, it's important for him to stay and help these people know about Jesus."

Heidi shook her head. "Mommy, that be good for them, bad for us."

Raylyn could hardly speak for the great lump in her throat. "I know, Sweety, but God's in control, He must make the change if there is to be one."

Heidi sighed, "I know, Mommy."

Finally, Raylyn knew she couldn't put it off any longer. She threw back the covers, took Heidi's hand and they went to the bathroom together. She helped Heidi take a quick bath then took a quick shower herself. They brushed their teeth, and Raylyn collected all their things from the bathroom and went back to their bedroom. Heidi dressed in the clothes Raylyn laid out for her then dashed from the room down the hall to join Isabel in the kitchen. The old and the young seemed to get along very well together and Heidi was a big help to Isabel. She'd learned where things were to set the table without asking or being asked to do it. She did the task very carefully, as Isabel watched.

Raylyn quickly dressed, then stripped the beds and put her suitcases on the mattress. She took the clothes from both the dresser and the closet and reluctantly began filling both suitcases. When everything she could find was packed, she closed and zipped both bags. After she set them by the door, she picked up her brush and brushed her hair until it shown. She had pushed the brush into her purse when the doorbell rang and her heart started jerking around in her chest. Of course, anyone in the house could hear Heidi's feet pounding on the hardwood floor of the living room and her shout, "Mr. Roger be here! Mr. Roger comed for buns!"

Before Raylyn could grab the suitcase handles and her purse, Heidi had the door open, exclaiming, "Mr. Roger! Oh, you comed for buns!"

He was chuckling as he scooped her up into his arms. "Yes, little lady, I comed for your gamaw's buns."

Heidi kissed Roger's cheek, but then she squirmed until he set her down. By this time, Raylyn had reached the living room, pulling her two bags. Without saying anything to her mom, Heidi skipped back to the kitchen, which left Raylyn and Roger alone in the living room. With a sad smile, Roger held out his arms and Raylyn quickly stepped into them. After a kiss, she laid her head on his chest and he put his cheek down on it.

In a whisper, he said, "Sweetheart, you have no idea how I'll miss you after you leave. These days have been perfect with you here."

Her words choked because of the lump in her throat, Raylyn said, "I think I will you can't miss me any more than I'll miss you." After a few minutes, she pulled back so she could look at him. Her voice a bit stronger, she said, "You said yesterday that you'll be gone from here from the Monday before Christmas until the Saturday before New Year's. I was thinking about that last night before I fell asleep. Would you make a detour on your way to Billings and stop in Grand Rapids, maybe for overnight?"

His heart in his eyes, as he looked back at the lovely lady, he said, fervently, "I would most happily make a detour to Grand Rapids! Absolutely! Perhaps I could even spend a couple of days there."

"Would you? That would be so awesome and make us both happy." Raylyn stood on tiptoe and drew his face down for her kiss, before she said, "Heidi already asked if we couldn't take you with us."

"I wish, Love, I wish."

A voice from the kitchen said, "Come on, you two. The icing's melting on these cinnamon buns. They need to be eaten now!"

Roger placed a quick kiss on Raylyn's lips, then raised his voice and said, "We're on our way, Isabel; be right there. I've heard about these buns you make, but never had a sample. And the smell…"

"Well, then, get your posterior out here!" she groused.

He and Raylyn reached the kitchen. Heidi was already in her elevated seat and Isabel had her coffee at her place. She was picking up great circles of steaming hot, iced dough from the pan on the counter and putting them on a large platter. "Go on, sit, I'll get these out, we can say grace and I'll pour your coffee."

"Will do, Isabel."

Roger pulled out the chair beside Heidi and held it for Raylyn. Once she was seated, he gently squeezed her shoulders and when she looked up at him with a smile, he winked at her. As Isabel turned toward the table, he went to Isabel's chair and pulled it back from the table and held it for the old lady. He helped her up to the table then went to the only other chair at the table. It was opposite Isabel's and at right angles to Raylyn's. On his way by her, he touched Raylyn's shoulder again.

"Young man, I do believe your mama taught you well. I can't fault you for your manners. Since you're the preacher, you say grace."

Roger nodded and bowed his head. "Father in heaven, thank You for this time we've had together getting to know each other. Thank you for this food that Isabel's prepared. I pray You will take Raylyn and Heidi safely over the many miles they must travel today. Be with us each one. I pray in Your Son's Name, amen."

Isabel had made a huge batch of cinnamon buns. They ate the sticky, delicious delights until they couldn't eat any more. When they had eaten their fill, the adults had each had a coffee refill and Heidi had finished her mug of hot chocolate, Isabel found two large Ziploc bags and divided the buns that were left. As she gave one to Roger and the other to Raylyn, she said, "Okay, there's too many to eat them all at one sitting. If you warm them in the microwave, they taste good for several days."

With a twinkle in his eyes, Roger said, "Isabel, I'll remember that, but you must know that breakfast's my biggest meal."

"Listen," she clucked, shaking her finger at the young man, "you eat all those tomorrow and I guarantee you'll be sick!"

Eying the bag of gooey delights, Roger said, "I'll try to refrain, Isabel. Of course, I wouldn't want to be a glutton, you know."

Isabel only shook her head, her eyes solemn. She turned from Roger and looked at Raylyn and said, "It's a good thing there's someone strong to help you load up. I stuck my head out the back door before you got up and it's a bit cold out today for my old bones and the wind's sharp, so I'll say goodbye here inside."

Raylyn came to her and they put their arms around each other. After she kissed her on the cheek, she said, "That's fine, Grandma, I wouldn't want you to get a chill. I would feel really bad if that happened and you got sick because of us."

Isabel said, "My dear, thank you so much for remembering your old Grandma and coming to see me for this weekend. Some of my friends have grandchildren who live far away and they never see them, not since they've left home. You take right good care of that sweet daughter of yours and be careful on your long drive."

Raylyn kissed Isabel's cheek and said, "Grandma, I'm so glad we came, it's been a super time. Heidi and I've had a great time here and it's been a time to remember. You take care, too. I'll get after Mom and send her down for a visit. I know you'd both have a good time together."

"Yes, that we would, Dear."

Isabel turned from Raylyn and leaned over to look into Heidi's eyes. "Come over to my chair, will you, little one?" Heidi followed the lady to her favorite recliner and as Isabel pulled out a small gift, she said, "Little One, you grow up to be a good girl. Just remember your old 'Gamaw' loves you."

Snuggling close in Isabel's arms, Heidi said, "Gamaw, I miss you and I loves you. 'Cause you and Mr. Roger can't come wif us, you take good care of him."

Chuckling, Isabel said, "I'll think about it, Little One. Open your package, what is it?"

The child tore open the wrapping paper and found a new book. Her eyes sparkling, the little girl kissed the old lady on the cheek. "Gamaw, this be great! I not got this book. Mommy read it soon." Moments later, she went to the couch and picked up Dollie and her other books. Looking at Isabel, she said, "I ready to go. We be gone soon as Mommy say bye to Mr. Roger."

Looking at the couple, Isabel said, "That may be a while, Little One."

TEN

Raylyn had turned directly from Isabel's arms into Roger's. He'd walked her several steps away from the other two, then put both arms around her and pulled her close. His eyes were stinging, but as he held her, he swallowed, willing the tears from his eyes and the clog from his throat. There had never been another lady for whom he felt such love as he did for Raylyn. He'd only had four days with her and now he must give her up, it felt like he was ripping out his own heart. He had promised to come to Grand Rapids in two weeks, would he ever see her again after that? The great odds were that he wouldn't.

He knew the visit he'd make to Grand Rapids would be much different. There would be no Isabel and instead of Raylyn and Heidi being on vacation and he under obligation for only two meetings, Raylyn would be working and probably Heidi would be at her daycare. He'd have to entertain himself for the daytime and only see her for a short time in the evening. He swallowed a sigh; he'd do it just to see her again.

He kissed her. He really didn't care who watched, he was giving up the light of his life and he wanted her and anyone else who cared to know. She held him around the waist and stood on tiptoe to make sure their lips met and sealed. Raylyn was so glad she and her grandma had had their talk. She had no guilt in her heart as she felt Roger's lips seal with hers. If there was any possible way for her and

Roger to become man and wife, she would work every avenue to make it happen.... as soon as possible.

A little voice at their side heaved a big sigh and said, "Mommy, Mr. Roger, it be time to go. We gots to trabel long time and I gots to go to daycare to see Teacher tismarra, you know."

Keeping their arms around each other, Raylyn reluctantly drew her lips from Roger's. Raylyn let out a sigh and said, "I know, Sweety. Mr. Roger's helping us put our luggage in the car and then we'll go. You said goodbye to Grandma?"

"Mommy, 'course I did! You was kissin' Mr. Roger all time. You din't even see the book Gamaw gave me."

Roger smiled down at the little girl and said, "I sure was, Ladybug, it's really cool kissing your mommy."

She dropped her things on the floor beside the couple. Looking up at the young man, Heidi said, "Mr. Roger, I needs a kiss, too."

Still keeping one arm around Raylyn, he held out his other arm and said, "Well, I'll give you one if you come on up."

Before Roger knew what she was doing, Heidi went back to Isabel and ran to Roger. At the last minute, she jumped and if he hadn't been braced with both feet and watching her intently, she would have caused him to stumble. As it was, his arm scooped her up and she put her arms around his neck and hugged him. He kissed her on the cheek, but then she pulled her hands from his neck and put them on his cheeks.

Turning his face toward her and looking him square in the eyes, she said, "Mr. Roger, I kiss you like you kiss Mommy, on the lips." If he wanted to protest, he couldn't, she placed her lips on his and kissed him.

At that moment Roger had never felt more like he was holding his family.

Moments later, Raylyn zipped up Heidi's coat, grabbed her purse and keys and Roger grabbed the handles of the two suitcases. Heidi picked up her Dollie and her books then one last time both Raylyn and Heidi turned and waved to Isabel, who was sitting in her chair watching them. Both Raylyn and Roger now knew she'd be watching them through her window.

Raylyn opened her trunk for Roger then opened the back door for Heidi. Carefully, Heidi climbed onto the back seat, but didn't sit down for Raylyn to buckle her in. Instead, she knelt on the seat and arranged her things. When Raylyn told her to sit down, Heidi shook her head. "Mr. Roger buckle me. I wait for him."

Roger couldn't help but hear the little girl. The lump he thought he'd swallowed reappeared in his throat. He sniffed and slammed the trunk hoping the noise would cover his sniff. He came to the back door, his eyes bright with unshed tears and Heidi said, "Mr. Roger, you buckle me."

Around the lump in his throat, he said, "Okay, Heidi, I'll do that." He buckled the belt and kissed her on the way out, then straightened and closed her door.

Raylyn still stood beside the car and Roger stepped up to her. Immediately his arms slipped around her and he drew her close again. His heart in his eyes, he said, "Sweetheart, please drive safely. Would you call me when you get home?"

Nodding, she whispered, "Yes, I'll call you. It'll probably be late, though."

Shaking his head, he said, "I don't care what time it is! I really want to know you arrived safely. We both know that this time of year is when the snow starts in your neck of the woods."

"Yes, I know. Thank you for the most wonderful weekend I can remember having in the recent past." She put her right index finger on his cheek and said, "Remember, when you're making your flight plans make your trip go through Grand Rapids and two days later go on to Billings. I'll take off and meet you. We'll spend two days together."

"Love, you can do that? You can take off?"

"Sure I can! I have a good boss and vacation time saved up. Besides, she's been trying to get me married off for a very long time." She chuckled.

"Sweetheart, I'll do that! I'll let you know right away. I can't wait!"

Roger watched the taillights grow bright at the end of the parking lot then waved as the car made the turn. A little head barely appeared above the back window and a hand waved vigorously. From the front seat another hand waved. Then the car was gone. With feet that weighed a ton, Roger walked around the Jeep then waved at the window across the porch, because he was sure there was an old lady watching him and slid behind the wheel of his vehicle.

Roger went immediately from Isabel's place to Ramon's. Soon after he walked inside, Sandy grinned at him and said, "Cheer up! You'll see her again."

"Yeah, two days on my way from here to my folks. What'll that do for us?" he growled. "I mean, after all..."

"You never know! That's a couple of weeks away a lot can happen in two weeks. You could get fired, she could get fired, you could get a call to a church in Grand Rapids, she could take a position in Blairsville."

"Let's hope not all those things happen!" Roger said. "We'd be in the same situation we are now." He scowled at Sandy, "Besides, how do you know I could get fired? Do you know something I don't?"

Sandy shook her head. "Not at all, I'm listing the options. Why, did something else happen after you came and used the phone the other night?"

Nodding, Roger said, "The next morning I found more stuff the perp had done outside the house while I was gone that evening and when I went to the church after that, there was another note on my desk."

"Someone had broken in?" she gasped.

"No one broke in. They had a key or had a way to get one."

Sandy gasped, "Roger that ought to narrow it down, right? I mean, surely not everyone in town has a key."

"It would, if I knew who has keys, but I don't. The locks weren't changed when I came, It was Brad Thomas who gave me mine. I've made a few and given them to some folks since I came. Anyway, I came for your program and picture for your concert. I announced it yesterday and everyone's looking forward to it. There'll be desserts and punch for afterwards."

"That's great! Yes, I have the program right here."

Ramon walked into the kitchen and said, "I hear you preached a good sermon yesterday and kept the music toned down so nobody heard it outside."

"Thanks for the compliment and yes, I turned the volume down myself." He took a deep breath and let it out. "While they practiced I had a hard time hearing that still, small voice that I wanted to hear."

Sandy grabbed his hand and when he looked into her face, she said, "Roger, that's an answer to my prayer."

Nodding, he said, "I know it is, Sandy. Thanks for praying for me. Thanks for keeping after me. The Lord honored you, believe me."

Sandy's trademark smile covered her face, as she said, "Praise God!"

As Raylyn crossed the line into Michigan she decided they needed to stop for supper. It was after Heidi's usual suppertime, but she'd been traveling so well that Raylyn didn't want to stop. However, there was a huge sign for a family restaurant at the first exit. Raylyn glanced at her gas gauge and knew she had no choice, she must stop for gas. She pulled to the pump, not sure if she shut off the car without filling up if she'd get it going again. As they stopped, Heidi was wide awake and looking around.

"Mommy, we not be home yet."

"No, Sweety, but we're stopping for supper."

Raylyn stepped from the car and started the gas. As she sat down to drive up to the restaurant door, Heidi said, "Mommy, it be snowing!"

"Yes, I see, Sweety. I don't like to drive in snow, but we must get home. After we eat supper, you play quietly with Dollie until we get home, okay?"

"Yes, Mommy. I wish Mr. Roger comed."

"He is coming in a couple of weeks. We'll see him."

"Oh, yippie, yea!"

The next morning, Raylyn and Heidi were up early. Tuesdays were Raylyn's early day at the hospital. Neither of them was very talkative, the last two hours of the trip last night had been hard. The snow that had started while they ate supper had only gotten more persistent the farther north they went. By the time they reached Grand Rapids, there were three inches on the ground and Raylyn had wished she'd stayed in Vansville where the snow barely covered the ground and only lasted until the next morning when the sun had burned it off and warmed the breeze. However, this was Michigan…

After dropping Heidi off at daycare, Raylyn went on to her office in the hospital. She turned the key in the door and tried to push it open, but it only moved about four inches. Her heart sank, that meant only one thing, the box the mailslot opened into was so full many of the papers had overflowed and were now on the floor, keeping the door from opening. She'd only been gone over a holiday weekend! Carefully, she kept pushing on the door until it was open enough that she could slip in sideways. She sighed as she looked down at the pile, not only in the box on the door, but the much bigger pile on the floor. Her day was off and running today would be catch up day. How could so much come in over a holiday weekend? Of course, that didn't count anything new that would come in in the next eight hours.

News travels fast on the grapevine in a small town and soon Roger's plans to be away for nearly two weeks over Christmas were common knowledge in Vansville. Roger stopped in for gas Monday afternoon and Brad Thomas said, in his usual, very grouchy way, "So, I hear you'll be outta town in a few weeks."

"Yes, just like other years I'm going to Montana to my folks for Christmas." Since the man hadn't come to church on Sunday, he didn't feel it necessary to tell him he planned to stop in Grand Rapids to see a lady.

With a touch of sarcasm threaded through his voice, he asked, "So what'll happen to the church while you're gone?"

Not answering Brad's sarcasm with anything but sincerity, Roger smiled and said, "Nothing, I hope, Brad. Other years it's been closed that Sunday. Like I told the people yesterday, if anybody wants to hold the service, I'd be more than happy to let them, but if no one comes forward, it'll stay closed."

He continued in his brusk manner, "So you're just walkin' out? Nobody comin' in ta take over for ya?"

Roger laid his money for the gas down on the counter. Brad always seemed a bit greedy and grabbed it up, before Roger said,

"Brad, I'm not walking out, I'm taking a vacation of under two weeks long. Most people take their vacation in the summer, but I take mine at Christmas. I know you take a day or two throughout the year off, the store's closed once in a while. I've heard you even close on Christmas."

Brad waved his hand, discrediting Roger's words. "Yeah, well, this here place is open ever day, no matter, but the church house ain't open but one day a week and you'll close it on the most important day for them people who calls 'emselves Christians. Gotta be a law about it!"

Still answering Brad's grouchiness with friendliness, Roger said, "Far as I know there isn't. You want to hold the service? I know you work most Sundays, but that one should be pretty slow. I read in the history book in my office it was your grandad who started that church back in the twenty's or thirty's was it?"

Scowling, Brad said, "Don't you go bringin' my grandad into nothin'! I ain't takin' no service, nor preachin' no words from that lectern!"

Roger shrugged. "No need to get upset, Brad. You seemed concerned, that's why I asked. You have a good day now."

"Humph!" Brad grumbled, as Roger walked out. Brad had no customers at the time, but he didn't follow Roger through the store. Instead, he picked up the phone and started dialing. The door closed behind Roger before anyone picked up. When the person answered, Brad said, "Hey, we need a church business meetin'."

"What for?"

"Alex, you know he's aclosin' up the place over Christmas!"

"Yeah, so he said yesterday. It's his church, he can do that."

"No, it ain't, it belongs to the town."

"Brad, we all voted him in to be pastor. Yesterday he done it right. If he needs a few days off, he deserves 'em. What's your beef?"

"Da know," Brad grumbled and slammed down the receiver. He punched a few keys on the register and muttered, "I'll find sompin!"

As Sandy prepared for the concert she was to play on the Sunday before Christmas, more and more she felt the need that the people who came needed to sing or see the words while she played the music. Many of the composers were staunch Christians, intending that their works and the words glorify God and His Son. She planned to play some selections from The Messiah and other great Christmas works by some of the masters long dead. The words that the music had been written for were powerful and people in Vansville needed to hear or see them. The carols she planned to play weren't ones that people normally sang at Christmas, but had powerful messages and many people didn't know the words. All the oratorios had a great message through out the verses, too.

One evening, after their supper, Sandy sat at the piano and as she played one of those numbers as background, she said to Ramon, "Honey, it's only half a program if it's just the music that's played especially all these Christmas numbers."

"But isn't that what you're supposed to do?"

"But Honey, Christmas is about the Child, the Redeemer, who came as a Baby, but grew up as a sinless Man and became the Savior of the world! The songs, all of them have words that tell about Him."

"Sweetheart, you know you have the best voice in town, do you want to sing each song that you play?"

Sadly shaking her head, Sandy said, "You know I can't do that. Perhaps I could sing maybe every third or fourth one, but I can't play and give the music its rightful rendition and sing and give the words their rightful place." She swallowed, "You know I can't do it all, some of those pieces are classical works which would take all I have just to play."

Ramon thought for several minutes, before he said, "I've heard that they use songs in their meetings that they project the words on the wall so people can sing along. Why don't we see what Roger thinks of something like that, Love?" Ramon put his hands on Sandy's shoulders, leaned over and kissed her.

After a moment's thought, she nodded and said, "Yes, that's best. That would work really well." She turned her face up to him and smiled, expecting another kiss. His eyes twinkling, he willingly gave her another.

Roger made his plans for his trip to Billings. His flight from Atlanta left at some before dawn hour, but that was as he wanted it, it would arrive in Grand Rapids soon after breakfast on Monday before Christmas. He planned to stay Monday and Tuesday then have Raylyn drop him at the airport on her way to work on Wednesday morning. The second leg of his trip would land him in Billings nearly at the same time as he'd left Grand Rapids because of the time zones. He was excited and at the same time a bit depressed, in the two days it had taken him to set up the itinerary he could think of no reason to keep in contact with Raylyn and Heidi. Their worlds were a thousand miles apart and there didn't seem to be any hope of bringing them together.

He sighed. He felt sure God had His reasons for their meeting on Thanksgiving Day. Things had worked out so that they could spend quite a lot of time together and get to know each other quite well, better than he knew most others in town. Heidi had said several times she wished he was her daddy. He could think of no higher calling than be the daddy for a child whose daddy had been killed in the line of duty, protecting his country. Raylyn was a beautiful Christian lady. God surely had a purpose for them.

Shaking his head, he muttered, "I must not get discouraged and I need to take my hands off and watch God do whatever He plans to do in our lives. Actually, we serve an awesome God, He can do awesome things!"

Wednesday morning Roger had just strained his milk when the phone rang. He dropped the pail into the sink and picked up the phone. "Hello?"

"Roger, it's Alex Mallard."

"Hello, Alex! Did you get a new line of microwaveable, succulent dinners in you want me to help you market?"

The older man chuckled. "No, nothing like that, although I've noticed you haven't been in for your weekly purchases yet."

"Alex, between Thanksgiving dinner eaten out and several other meals eaten out over the past weekend and all the food people gave me in pity, because I'm a lonely bachelor, I haven't had to make a trip to the grocery for a bit. I've about run out, though so I'll be in soon. What's your call about, if it's not about food?" Roger asked, truly perplexed. Alex had never called him before, and to call now? not about food? strange.

There was a pause before Alex said, "You haven't called a business meeting in some months, you know? There are a few of us who'd like to get one together, like before you leave for your vacation."

Noting Alex was less than his usual jovial self, Roger asked him, "When did you have in mind, Alex?"

"Uh, tonight."

He sucked in his breath, then let it out so Alex couldn't hear, he said, "Well, since I don't have a heavy date and the TV reception isn't that great up here on my hillside and none of my critters is about to deliver an offspring, I guess I'm free. Since you called, I assume that you want me there?"

"Yes, as a matter of fact, Brad, the old cuss, says you've done something to the locks on the church and none of our keys work, so you'll have to let us in."

"I'll be there. In fact, I'll go in now and turn up the heat. During a business meeting I wouldn't want anyone's fingers or nose to fall off. What time is this meeting scheduled for?"

"Oh, 'bout seven."

"Fine, thanks for calling, Alex."

"Yes, sir, not a problem."

His heart thumping, Roger hung up. Would he find out tonight who the culprit was who had played the malicious games last week? Why did they want to call a meeting on such short notice? What kinds of things did they want to talk about in this business meeting? Why did they want him there at the meeting?

He shrugged. He guessed he'd have to go to find out.

Before seven o'clock he drove back into town. His place in front of the church was full, as were both sides of the street for two blocks and the parking lot in front of the hardware store was full except for the gas pumps. To his surprise, the pumps were dark and so was the store. Brad Thomas must be planning to attend this meeting. That was a shock, the man never darkened the door for services. He looked on passed the church and saw one space in Isabel's parking lot, so he hurried to it. Someone had been busy on the phone!

As soon as people saw his Jeep go by, they began to leave their cars and by the time he walked back, the ramp, the stairs from the street, the walkway and the stoop in front of the door were full of townspeople. Most of the people were surprised when Roger didn't even come to the front door he turned beside the church and went to the door to his office. He unlocked the door, went in and locked it back behind him, then went through the auditorium to the front door, slid the deadbolt free and opened the door. He stepped back out of the way as the people piled in and quickly found seats, pretty much ignoring him. There were several in the crowd who never came to the church for services.

Roger didn't know what to do with himself. Should he head up to the platform and present himself as the moderator or should he sit in the audience and let someone else preside? He didn't know. As he stood in the back watching the seats quickly fill up, he decided since he hadn't called the meeting he'd stay in the background and let someone else take the lead.

The last person came in and closed the door. Brad Thomas looked at his watch and stood up, then walked purposefully to the lectern. "Folks," he said, grabbing the lectern and trying to be friendly in his unfriendly, gruff way, "we have a situation here that needs to be addressed before it gets out of hand."

Much to Roger's surprise, the person who raised his hand was someone who never darkened his church door. Derek Casbah raised his hand, but before Brad would acknowledge him, he said, "And what situation would that be, Brad?"

Brad obviously didn't expect to be interrupted, especially by the richest man in town, so he cleared his throat loudly. "Well, see, it's like this. This here Clemens fellow…" Roger sucked in his breath. At that moment he was sure he knew who had done the deeds at his house and had left his dog for dead with a note and written the note on his desk. "…he's a taken to medlin' and preachin', not sompin we can tolerate around here."

The words were hardly out of his mouth when the door opened once more. Roger turned to look as Sandy and Ramon and Isabel came inside. The purr of Sandy's motor was unmistakable, as she made her way down front where the only free seats were. Isabel scooted in first, then Ramon sat on the end and Sandy stayed in the aisle.

"What was that you said, Bradford?" Isabel asked.

A bit embarrassed now, he said, "I, ah, said, that man of the cloth standin' back there, he's taken to medlin' and we can't tolerate it!"

"How do you know that? Were you here in the last month or so to hear him?"

Shifting from one foot to the other, he cleared his throat and said, "Well, no, you know, Isabel, I got a store to run seven days a week."

"Oh, you do. So you haven't heard his medlin' or preachin' for yourself."

"Well, not exactly. Got reliable reports, though."

"So why did you call this meeting?" Sandy asked.

"We need to vote 'im out!"

"Why should we do that?" Alex asked the question everyone had on the end of his tongue. All over the crowd heads nodded and people murmured in agreement.

"'Cause we can't have none of that!"

Isabel poked Ramon in the arm and said, "Get these people to hush, would you?"

Raising his trail voice, Ramon said, "Quiet, Isabel has something to say."

Isabel stood up and turned to look at those behind her. "You know I don't come here to church, I haven't since Mr. Clemens started here, but I came for the Thanksgiving service he held. Folks, I have never heard a better message, not from my own pastor or any other preacher, than I heard that morning from this young man. He did not meddle, he didn't preach empty words, he read Scripture and spoke from his heart and I believe they were words that God put there. I hear he did the same on Sunday. Friends, isn't that what a man of God is supposed to do? Is he supposed to be run out of town for doing what God has called him to do?"

She turned and looked directly at Brad Thomas and said, "Bradford, as I recall and my memory hasn't started to fail one bit, it was your granddaddy who started this church in his home, then when they had the money, built this church. Did people run him out of town because he preached the gospel?" Isabel had said her peace quite forcefully and sat back down.

By now, the lectern was empty, Brad had slunk to a seat behind the lectern and sat, his head bowed. For several long minutes there was silence in the auditorium. Pastors and pianists are not geared for silence in churches. Roger shuffled his feet, but determined not to move from that spot, or say a word; after all, he was the man in the hot seat, so he stayed where he was.

Alex Mallard was usually a soft-spoken man. He'd come to church occasionally with his wife, but rarely stood up to say anything. Finally, as the silence stretched, he stood up in his place three rows from the back. He cleared his throat and heads turned. He swallowed and said, "Unlike Isabel, my wife and I go here to this church. Last Thursday, Thanksgiving Day, was the best service I have ever attended in this church. My heart was truly blessed. Ms Sandy played the piano and I do believe she was truly touched from God. Pastor Roger read from the Psalms and then gave us a message truly from his heart. On Sunday, we didn't have Ms. Sandy's superb playing, but the music was tasteful and again Pastor Roger read Scripture and preached from his heart." He looked around at all those gathered. "Folks, I really like this new Roger. In fact I'd like to keep him for as long as I have strength enough to come hear him. And folks, I think the man deserves a raise, not to be run out of town."

As Alex sat down people started clapping only a few at first, but then more and more joined in until everyone but Brad and Roger were clapping. Derek Casbah stood up and turned toward the rest of the crowd and motioned for silence. When the clapping stopped, he said, "I don't go here to church, in fact, I haven't been in a church since my daughter-in-law played in September. However, from what I hear from Ms Isabel and Alex, I think it's about time I did. Starting this next Sunday, I will be here in church and with my contribution I do believe there will be sufficient funds to give this young man a good raise. What do you folks say?" People started clapping again and Derek said loudly over the noise, "Shall we give the man a standing vote of approval?" Still clapping, people jumped to their feet. Many of them turned around and smiled at the young man still standing at the back. In his loud voice, Derek said, "Come up front, Pastor. You've got a word for us, I'm sure."

Roger swallowed, dampness rimming his eyes, truly overwhelmed, he made his way down the aisle and stood in front of the large table. Derek wasn't satisfied. "No, not there, up there where you belong, young man."

Roger mounted the steps reluctantly and moved to the lectern. Unbelievably, he was the only one on the platform. Somehow Brad Thomas had disappeared. Roger stood silently, looking out at the full auditorium until people stopped clapping. In the silence he looked down at Sandy and said, "Ms Sandy, could you go to the piano, please?" As she made her way across the front, he looked out at the sea of smiling faces and said, "Friends, you have no idea what this meeting has meant to me. I thank you from the bottom of my heart. Recently, I had an experience where the Lord spoke to me through some verses of Scripture. These are what I spoke from on Sunday, let me say them again:

'He lifted me out of the slimy pit, out of the mud and mire;
He set my feet on a rock and gave me a firm place to stand.
He put a new song in my mouth, a hymn of praise to our God.
Many will see and fear and put their trust in the Lord.' (Ps. 40: 2,3)

Before he could say another word he whipped that white handkerchief from his back pocket and wiped his eyes and nose. "I want to thank you all for your vote of support this evening. Believe me, I have never felt so loved. In closing, I would like very much for Sandy to play two songs that have become my favorites. Let's start off with one verse of The Old Rugged Cross and close with Jesus Loves Me, This I Know."

Sandy's face was radiant as she gave each song a beautiful introduction, then people joined in from their hearts. When the people had finished singing, Roger said, "Shall we close with prayer. Our Father, thank You for this meeting tonight. Bind our hearts together. Our town only has this one church building, but in the time of the apostles there was only one church and they were all united in the goal of reaching the lost for You. May that be our goal starting this evening. Dismiss us with Your blessing. In Your Son's Name, amen."

While Roger prayed and the people had their eyes closed, Brad quietly slunk down the side aisle and beat a hasty retreat to the back of the church. The door hinge squeaked as he opened it to escape and he froze, but when Roger finished praying, Brad was no where to be found. People didn't seem to remember that he was the one who had called the meeting or had tried to spread his malicious venom. They crowded around Roger the minute he left the platform. Several of the ladies hugged him and most of the men shook his hand. When the auditorium was half empty he finally made it to the door. However, Ramon, Sandy and Isabel let everyone else in front of them.

When there were only the four people left, Roger turned to his friends and said, "Isabel, you can't know how much I appreciate what you said. I am truly honored by your vote of confidence. Sandy, thank you again for providing the mood we needed for those hymns." Ramon had his hand out and Roger took it and said, "Friend, what can I say? My life is rich because of friends like you."

Ramon gripped his hand and shook it warmly. "We're behind you one hundred percent, Man! Keep up the good work!"

Wishing there was a lovely lady in his arm, he whispered, "I think I could do it a hundred percent better with a lovely lady by my side."

"Yes," Isabel agreed, "I'm praying for that, too." She grinned at the young man. "Any man is twice the man with a good woman by his side." Silently, Roger agreed. He thanked God that he had this wonderful Christian lady on his side.

Raylyn made it an early night for both her and Heidi on Tuesday. She'd worked hard to do catch-up at work and she was extremely pleased that she'd been able to see the entire pile of mail she'd picked up on her way in taken care of before she went home. However, by the time she and Heidi arrived at home, supper and dishes were all she could handle. Supper had been large, healthful sandwiches that didn't generate too many dishes and those could all be washed in the dishwasher. She and Heidi both took a warm bath, then Raylyn read Heidi's new book for her bedtime story, then they both fell asleep as soon as their heads hit the pillow. Neither of them was upset that they were back in their own beds.

However, during the night, Raylyn had a dream that featured a very handsome, tall, blond man with blue eyes and a beguiling smile. He held out his arms to her as he had at Isabel's and she ran to him. They held each other and savored a long kiss, but when she awoke, her arms were empty and half her bed cold. She couldn't keep a tear from sliding down her cheek. She buried her head in her pillow and let some tears flow.

After supper Wednesday evening, Raylyn was about to pick up the phone when it rang. It startled her, but she picked it up quickly and answered. The caller immediately said, "Where have you been? I tried to call you over Thanksgiving."

Raylyn's heart sank surely her mom wasn't becoming senile, was she? "Mom, remember I told you I planned to take Heidi to visit Grandma Isabel for the long weekend. We left Wednesday afternoon and got back Monday evening."

Ruth sighed, "Yes, I guess you did tell me that. I must have buried the thought, since I wanted you to spend the day with me. Did you have a good time? eat lots of turkey? I know Mom can fix the best food."

Enthusiastically, Raylyn launched into her answer. "We had a fantastic time! The whole time we were there was super, Mom! We had Thanksgiving Dinner with a couple and the pastor of the Vansville church…"

"The what? Mom has told me that man is not worth hearing! She's told me she wouldn't go across the street to hear him. How can he be worth spending a meal with?"

"Mom, that doesn't mean he can't spend time eating with people who invited him. Besides, we went to hear his Thanksgiving Day message and it was great! There's a new lady in town, she came from Philadelphia and lives there now because she married a local man. She plays the piano like a pro and paints professionally. She supplies a gallery back in Philadelphia with her paintings. Anyway, she and her husband invited the three of us and the pastor for Thanksgiving dinner. We spent some time on the pastor's little farm, too."

"You mean Mom went to a farm while you were there? Surely that has to be a first."

"No, I didn't say that. Heidi and I visited the pastor on his farm on Friday."

"That was nice. Heidi got to have a new experience."

"Yes, she had lots of fun and had several new experiences, but then he and I went out to dinner Friday evening."

Ruth gasped, as the words her daughter said registered. After a moment, she said, "You... you went out alone with a man? Why would you do that?"

Even though she hadn't said why she asked, Raylyn knew, so she said, "Because he asked me, I wanted to go, so I said yes. We had a lovely dinner."

"But...but, Dear, Dan's only been gone two years!"

This was the response she'd expected, so she said, "I know that, Mom and he'll always have a special place in my heart, but he is gone, he won't come back to be my husband and Heidi's daddy. Mom, because of his death, God was glorified. We may never know how while we're here on earth, but *He was glorified*. We are here on this earth to bring glory to God and when He sees fit, He'll take us home to be with Him. Dan's in heaven rejoicing with the other redeemed, just like Dad is, Mom."

Raylyn heard Ruth suck in a long breath between her teeth. "Raylyn, don't speak of your father like that!"

"Why? It's the highest praise I can say! Don't you think Dad's in heaven rejoicing with other redeemed people who have gone on before?"

There was a very long silence, but Raylyn knew her mom had not hung up, so she waited. After several minutes thought, she hesitantly said, "Well... of course! But it just sounds so... I don't know... irreverent to speak of the dead that way!" She pulled in a breath and added passionately, "It was so senseless that he died!"

"Yes, I agree, Mom and I thought that about Dan's death for a long time, but Grandma Isabel and I had a long talk before the Thanksgiving service. She helped me see that because both of them were born again believers that they are at home with the Lord and that their deaths were not senseless in His sight."

"You believe that?" Ruth asked, in a whisper.

"Yes, I do, Mom. I didn't always, for two years I only thought of how senseless Dan's death was, but I do believe now that his death was to glorify God. There is a time for grieving for someone whom we've loved, we miss them, there's a hole left in our lives, but if they are believers when they die, we'll see them again and we shouldn't spend our lives mourning for them, because they wouldn't want us to stay in our grief. They are happy in God's presence and they would surely want us to move on and to live life, 'Life more abundantly' as the Bible says."

"You… you really think that's true?"

"Yes, Mom. Grandma Isabel helped me see that."

"She's a wise lady."

"Yes, she is, Mom. She misses you, you should go see her."

"I should, shouldn't I? I'm not really very busy maybe I'll give her a call and go down for a week or so."

"That'd be great, Mom! In fact, you could go for Christmas! Get there so you're there for the Sunday before Christmas and you can hear our new friend, Sandy, play. She's giving a concert in the Vansville church that day."

"I should go then? What about you and Heidi? You'd be here alone."

For some reason, Raylyn didn't want to tell her mom her true feelings for Roger yet. She wasn't sure why, but she didn't, so she said, "Mom, you were here alone over Thanksgiving, it won't hurt us and believe me, it's warmer there than it is here. The snow they had was gone with the sun, but we still have the snow that fell the day we came home."

Ruth chuckled. "I'm convinced, I can do without this snow we're having so early. Yes, you've convinced me. I'll call her and take a trip down."

"Great! I'm glad you'll go. She'll be so glad to see you. She said a couple of times that she's missed you a lot."

"Tell me, how old was this pastor you went out with?"

"I'm not real sure," she hedged. "He's been the pastor there in Vansville for five years now. He went to college and seminary before that."

"Mmm hmm, you, my dear, have been out of college for more than five years. Could it be you're about the same age?"

Chuckling softly, Raylyn said, "Yes, Mom, he's handsome, too and very well built and very considerate and many other terrific things."

"So, why did you come home?"

Stunned by her mom's question, she had to think a minute before she said, "Mom, I have a job here, I don't there. I have a house that I can't just vacate, I'm making mortgage payments and my job is very important to the hospital. My little girl depends on me to be responsible and keep her in clothes and food and give her a place to live. Besides, he didn't ask me to stay, he didn't propose marriage. You know I wouldn't stay with him without marriage. Besides, you always taught me to be responsible and think things through before I leap in the dark."

"How did Heidi take to your grandma?"

"She loved Grandma Isabel, believe it or not, she was perfect with her. She helped all she could without being asked and before you ask, since I know you're going to, she loved Roger and wanted to bring him home with us."

"Roger, that's the pastor's name?"

"Yes."

"Well, I'm definitely going down there soon."

Laughing now, Raylyn said, "Mom, it better be soon, because he's leaving for Montana the Monday before Christmas and won't be back until the Saturday before New Year's Day."

Ruth chuckled. "You've done your mom good tonight, Dear. I'm sure Heidi's in bed already, so give her a kiss from her grandma and I'll see you sometime."

"I will, Mom, thanks for calling."

"Oh, Raylyn, you have helped me much more!"

"I'm glad, Mom."

Thursday morning, before Raylyn went to work at ten, the phone rang again and when she answered, a mellow, masculine voice said, "Hi, Sweetheart. I have my itinerary worked out, so I thought I'd call and tell you."

"Oh, Roger," she sighed, "I'm so glad you called. I've missed you so much and Heidi's impossible these days since we came back. Yes, when will you be here?"

"I'll fly in about eight o'clock Monday morning then leave Wednesday about the same time. Will that work for you?"

"It sure will! What's the flight number so I'll know where to go at the airport?"

When he had given her that information, he said, "I found out last night who played the pranks at my place that night and left the note at church."

"You did? How?"

"Brad Thomas, the hardware store owner, called a meeting for the whole town last night, but Alex, the grocery store owner called me so I would have the church open for them. I guess word has spread that I've got the only key to get in the building. Brad got up there with all kinds of venomous words and wanted to run me out of town, but Isabel and Alex immediately put him down and Alex wanted to encourage me by giving me a raise. Ramon's step-dad was there and said he'd be coming and his contribution would give me a substantial raise. Old Brad vanished while I gave the closing prayer."

Totally indignant, Raylyn exclaimed, "Why, that old coot! He did all that because you preached? For goodness sake! He wasn't even there, was he? How would he know how your message went? Will you press charges?"

"No, I don't think so. Nothing was hurt, the only damage was the window in the barn that I'll get him to pay for and we'll call it square. I called the sheriff and told him to call off his investigation. He was reluctant, but he said he would."

"You're forgiving, Honey. Much more than I'd be, I think."

Stunned into silence for a second by the name she had called him, he finally said, "I must live here and buy gas at his station. He'd probably shrivel up and die if he couldn't do that. You know some old people are like that."

"I know."

"Has it snowed today?"

"No, it's cold, but the sun's out. What we got on Monday hasn't melted. I suppose it's toasty warm there."

He chuckled. "Well, no, but the sun's out, too and there's no snow. It's pretty much like that day you came out to the farm to visit." He sighed, "Sweetheart, that was a terrific day, I won't soon forget it!"

ELEVEN

She smiled and he could hear it in her voice, he felt a smile curl his lips as well. She said, "You may be put through the third degree at Sandy's concert, so you'd better wear your best outfit. You don't have a three piece suit, do you? Grandma better not have to send you home to change when she gets there."

"I'm a fast learner Isabel won't have to tell me a second time! Who's going to give me the third degree?"

"Mom called last night...."

"Uh oh!"

Giggling, Raylyn said, "She said she's calling Grandma and going down for a visit. I'm sure she'll want to meet you while she's there."

"She'll come before Christmas?"

"That's what she said! She's got it on her list to meet you."

"Man! I'm glad I found my suit."

"You'd look good...." Raylyn swallowed the words that almost slipped out and said instead, "Just thought I'd warn you."

Now the laughter was in his voice, as he said, "Ah, Sweetheart, what was it you were going to say? I'd look good..."

"A Freudian slip!" she wasn't about to say what was truly on her heart.

He wouldn't push, but he'd sure like to know... "Mmm. Well, I'd better let you go. You need to be to work soon, I suspect."

She sighed, "Yes, I'm afraid so, but Roger, thanks for calling. It's great to hear your voice. Knowing your itinerary helps, too."

In a voice that didn't sound exactly like his because he was definitely sending it through cotton, he said, "You can't know how much, Love. I'll see you in about a week and a half! Say hi to Heidi for me."

"I will." She was pulling the receiver from her ear as she whispered, "I love you, Roger. I love you."

Roger still had the receiver at his ear. The words grew fainter as she pulled the mouthpiece away from her face, but Roger heard them. As he heard the click, his throat closed up and tears burned his eyes. He slowly took the receiver from his own ear to hang it on the wall, but he murmured, "Sweetheart, I love you, more than words can say. I wish I could tell you to your lovely face. I wish..."

Raylyn hung up and was mortified to realize she'd said the words out loud. Of course, they spoke what was in her heart, but wasn't it the man's place to tell his lady first that he loved her? As far as she could remember, Roger had called her some wonderful, endearing names, but he'd never told her he loved her and here she'd said those words out loud when the line was probably still open!

Heidi came running in the room and said, "Mommy, it be time to go to daycare now?"

"No, Sweety, not for a little while yet. Mr. Roger called. He asked me to say hi."

Two tears welled up immediately in Heidi's eyes, as she asked, "How come you din't call so I could talk to him?"

"He called to tell me when to pick him up at the airport."

"But I wanna talk to him! He be real special! He be my daddy."

"He'll be here soon for two days. You'll get lots of chance to talk then."

Looking at her mommy with her hands on her hips, she said, "Mommy, you *gots* to tell him he be my daddy!"

"I wish I could, Sweety, believe me, I wish I could."

Raylyn looked at the clock. "Come on, Sweety, get your things picked up and put away, it's about time for us to get our coats on and get out of here. I have to be to work in a half hour and you need to be at daycare before that. We'll barely have time to make it through the traffic."

"I hurry, Mommy," Heidi grumbled.

Saturday morning, Raylyn was barely awake when the phone rang, but she had intended to sleep late. With her eyes still shut, she groped on the nightstand and finally found the receiver. She closed her hand around it and pulled her hand back under the covers, stuck the phone on top of her ear and muttered, "Hullo?"

"My! Aren't we cheerful this morning," a wide awake, cheerful voice said.

Grumbling into the receiver, Raylyn said, "Mom, it has to be too early for normal people to be up on a Saturday morning."

Chuckling, Ruth said, "Just wanted you to know I'm about to go out the door with my suitcase, heading to Vansville, Georgia."

"Great! Have a good time."

"Got any wishes to send? I'm staying through New Year's so I'll see lots of people."

"I only know four, Mom."

"Isn't one of them named Roger?"

"Mom! Yes, say a very special hello to him and Grandma and Sandy and Ramon. Those are all the people I met while we were there."

"Okay, I'm off!"

"Drive safely, Mom. I need you back safe and sound."

"I'll be real careful, Dear. Say bye to Heidi for me, too."

"I will, Mom, thanks for calling."

Raylyn was wide awake now, so grumbling, she tossed back the covers and put her feet on the floor. She could hear the furnace running, but there was also a tree limb scratching on her window. She shivered as she left her bed. She was glad the floor had carpet she remembered how cold Isabel's floor was when she stepped off the rug beside the bed in the mornings on the way to the bathroom. She hurried into the masterbath and turned on the water for a shower.

As she washed, she thought about the conversation she'd had with her mom, glad her mom was finally leaving her house for more than a quick trip to the grocery or the church. She was so glad her mom had called and that she'd said the right words to her. God surely had been guiding her words. She was sure there'd been a time not long ago when her mom would not have listened to anything she'd say about letting go of her sadness and getting on with her life.

When she opened the door after dressing for the day, Heidi was there and said, "Mommy, is tis day when we get Mr. Roger from the airplane?"

"No, not today, but it'll be soon. You must go to bed nine times before then."

Letting out a very long sigh and her shoulders drooping, Heidi said, "Mommy, that aren't soon, that be long time!"

"I know it seems that way, Sweety, but it isn't very long. Besides, Grandma called earlier. She's going down to stay with your gamaw. She left already."

"She come by and take us?" Heidi asked, hopefully.

"No, Sweety, she's already gone. You know Mommy has a job here."

Heidi climbed onto her high stool at the table and said, fiercely, "Mommy, you needs to stop that job! You needs one close to Mr. Roger."

"Sweety, it's not that easy! There might not be a job like I can do close by where Mr. Roger lives. We need my job to buy our food and clothes and do all the things that cost money."

Heidi sighed, "Mommy, is you *lookin'* for a job near Mr. Roger? You said there be a hospital in that other place."

"Sweety, how do I look for a job there? I don't know where to look."

Shaking her head, Heidi said, "Grandma should wait for us, we go, too so you gets a job."

Raylyn still sat in her chair at the table. Her coffee mug was still full, so she scooted back from the table and said, "Heidi, come here a minute." When the child was on her lap, Raylyn said, "You may be a bit young for this, but let me tell you how it is." Raylyn took a deep breath and said, "We need to be really sure that the man I marry is the man that God wants for us. There are a lot of things we need to be sure of first. Sweety, Mr. Roger is a long ways away and maybe he can't move here. Lots of things must change for us to move down to

Vansville. We don't know if that's God's plan or if God has someone else who is from around here. Remember you asked Grandma Isabel why she didn't ask God to give us Mr. Roger?"

"Yes, she say maybe there be another man."

"That's right, maybe God has a man close by here who could be a really good daddy for you and we haven't met him yet." Even as the words left her mouth, Raylyn wanted to bite them back. She didn't want another man, she wanted Roger. She loved Roger with all her heart, but God must do something mighty.

Heidi shook her head. "Mommy, I sure it be Mr. Roger."

"We'll see, Sweety." Raylyn had no intention to commit to that statement. She knew God could do anything, but she didn't know what it was as yet.

Heidi patted Raylyn's cheek and said, "I ask Santa and God, we get Mr. Roger."

"We'll wait and see, Heidi," Raylyn said, firmly.

Later that morning, there was a knock on the door. Raylyn had warned Heidi never to answer the door by herself, so she raced to the door, but waited for Raylyn to come. Raylyn looked through her peephole and saw a young man's face, one she'd never seen before, but nothing else. He looked like a clean cut young man, but she needed to be cautious. "What is it you need?" she called through the door.

"Ma'am," the man's voice said, "my friends and I are handing out flyers in the neighborhood for some friends of ours. Actually, we are members of the local church down the block and over one."

Cautiously, Raylyn opened the door about a foot, but kept her foot behind it. Grand Rapids was a nice city, but you couldn't be too careful, she thought, remembering what had happened to Roger in the tiny hamlet of Vansville. She looked up into a pleasant face of a man who could be a professional basketball player. With a smile the man held out a piece of paper and said, "Ma'am, our pastor is leaving soon and when he does, we have an interim pastor coming who will need a place to live for probably six months until we find someone permanent to fill our pulpit. Our church is looking to sublet a house starting in February." Holding the sheet so she could see it, he said, "On the bottom here is a place for a name and address if you know anyone who'd be interested. The name of the church is also there to send this information back to." He smiled. "Thank you for your time and have a really good day, Ma'am."

"Thanks." Raylyn said, as the young man turned to leave, so Raylyn closed the door. She looked over the paper to see that the young man had told her exactly the same as what was said on the paper.

"Mommy, who was that?"

"A young man from a church close by. He handed me a piece of paper."

However, that evening, after Heidi was in bed, Raylyn sat at her desk in the little room she'd made into a home office. She looked at the flyer and read it through several times. This was something she hadn't thought about. She could lease her house almost immediately. She knew this was not a good time of year to sell a house, but if she could lease it now, perhaps the people would want to buy it later on or she could sell it in the spring when the market was better. There'd be no harm in filling out the information, if she changed her mind, she could do that and she wouldn't be out a place to live.

She laid the sheet out in front of her and bowed her head over it. "Lord, this came today. It's something I hadn't thought of, but it's a church looking for a temporary home. Is Your first step telling me I need to be ready to move to Vansville?" She smiled. "You know, Lord, I'm more than willing to be Roger's wife if You give me the go ahead and You know Heidi's more than willing to have him for her daddy. But Lord, I want only Your will, so lead me, please. In Jesus' Name, amen." She smoothed out the paper on the desk, but didn't start to fill it out. As she left the paper open on the desk, it almost felt like she was laying it on the altar. She'd sleep on it and fill it out tomorrow and mail it on Monday.

Sunday morning Roger preached another fine sermon. Instead of the numbers dwindling because the service wasn't as contemporary at it had been, the place was filling up. This surprised him a little, but as he contemplated those who came, most of them were older people. However, among the sea of faces there was no sparkling little face with auburn curls sitting beside a lovely lady also with auburn curls. Even though he knew they weren't there, his eyes still wandered to the seats where they had been last week several times. He missed them terribly it felt like half of him was missing.

After the time of music and singing, Roger stood up and said, "Don't forget, folks, next week at two thirty Sandy DeLord will be giving a concert here and there will be refreshments afterward. Ah, ladies, please remember your part to bring those refreshments." He rubbed his flat midsection. "I'm looking forward to that part. The next day I'll be flying out early for my vacation in points north. No, I'm not visiting Santa Claus, but I am visiting friends and family." Roger turned to his song leader and said, "Web, let's have one of you give us a number while we take up the offering, then we'll have another song and I'll give my message."

While the offering was being collected, the door at the back of the auditorium opened and Brad Thomas slipped in and Roger nearly fell over. Brad closed the door behind him as silently as possible, then looked for a seat in the back row, but didn't find one. Roger didn't make a move to acknowledge him, he was quite sure the man didn't want anyone to know he was there. Especially after the meeting he'd called, Roger was sure of it. Since the empty seats were all down in the front, Brad stayed in the entryway and leaned against the wall.

While the people stood to sing, Brad went around the outside aisle to find a seat three rows back from the front on the aisle and slipped into it. When everyone sat down, Brad did the same and Roger came to the lectern to speak. Since he wouldn't be at the church for Christmas, he had decided to start a two part sermon on the Child who was born two thousand years ago, but who was still changing lives today. He ended his message by saying, "Will you be like the innkeeper and tell the Lord Jesus, 'there's no room, come back later,' or will you open your heart and say 'Yes, Lord, come into my heart today and make me Your child.'?"

Almost before Roger finished speaking and before he could ask Web to bring his musicians to the platform, Brad was on his feet and rushed to the front. As he reached the platform, he fell to his knees crying. Roger immediately left the lectern and went to the man. Web brought his musicians quickly to the platform and started some music while Roger knelt beside the older man.

A few minutes later, both Roger and Brad stood, but Roger motioned to Web who stopped playing and Brad spoke immediately. "Folks, you know I haven't been to church in a long time. I ben runnin' my business seven days a week and only closed for special stuff. I never figgered Sunday was too special. I did come to that Thanksgiving meetin' here, 'cause I was closed and my wife said I had to come with her. I heard Roger here preach that day and what he said hit me between the eyes. It made me real mad! I didn't like what he said, so I determined to get him good. Folks, he ain't told you this, but I went out to his place and messed up some stuff, got his house close to burnin' down, but God was watchin' out for him."

Brad pulled in a long breath. "I was still fightin' God, but you know that don't work. I called that meetin' we had the other day and I figgered ya'll would see it my way and run him outta town, but instead ya'll voted him a raise. Today, I closed my store. If ya'll need gas I guess it'll be Monday through Saturday, 'cause it won't be on Sunday no more. I come back to the Lord today and He's gonna be in His rightful place from now on. Thanks, Roger."

"You're very welcome, Brad. I think you have a grandad who's looking down on this and is praising God about now."

"Yes, I'm sure he is."

Roger looked at Web and said, "Let's sing <u>Joy To The World</u>!"

Roger bid all his worshipers a good week, as the church emptied out. However, he went home to his lonely house after the worship service and fixed himself a double cheese burger. It wasn't like anything he'd get at a fast-food restaurant; he had to cut each mouthful with a knife. Even then he could hardly fit a tiny bite in his mouth because he'd made it so thick with lettuce and tomatoes, but while he sat at the kitchen table the events of his life since Thanksgiving came back to him.

He didn't remember that Brad had been in that service. Actually, he had to admit, that all he could remember clearly were the new lady and her little girl who came. He didn't remember the words he preached because God had made the page he'd written his notes on blank and put other words into his mouth to say. God knew Brad was there. Since then, God had been using Scripture and His Spirit to guide Roger's words and actions in and out of the pulpit. Truly, he was being blessed, but today had brought results in Vansville.

The burger was only half eaten, but Roger laid his fork down and pushed the plate away. He put his elbows on the table, then bowed his head and said, "Well, Lord, I guess I have Your answer. This little town is where You want me to be. It looks like if You want me to have a wife that she'll have to be willing to come here to live. I guess that means You'll take charge of getting her here and making us both know she's the one for me. Thank You for what You've done in my life and also what You've done in Brad's life. Make this place into something that will be pleasing to You. Thanks, in Your Son's Name, amen."

Raylyn sat in her usual seat for church Sunday morning, close to two of her single friends. Heidi was in junior church. She was surprised when none of the songs they sang were Christmas carols. It was the Christmas season and she thought they'd be singing the carols. She had to admit that this was the first year since her husband died that she was looking forward to singing carols. However, for some reason, nothing about the service was about Christmas, not even the choir number or the special music. When the pastor stood up and looked at the large number of faces almost filling the auditorium, he opened his Bible to the first book and said, "Today, folks, I'd like you to turn to Genesis chapter twelve and lets start reading in verse one.

'The Lord had said to Abram, "Leave your country, your people and your father's household and go to the land I will show you...."'

Raylyn heard nothing else of the Scripture the pastor read. 'Leave your...people and your father's household and go to the land I will show you...' Goosebumps went up and down her spine she could feel her body trembling a little at the full impact of what she'd heard. Yesterday a church group wanted to rent her house and today the pastor read the Scripture about Abram leaving his homeland for a place where God would take him. Was God showing her she needed to leave here and move to Vansville, Georgia to be the wife of the pastor there? It didn't seem to get any clearer than this! Still there was one more major hurdle that needed to change. She didn't hear much of anything else the pastor said during the rest of his sermon.

She was brought abruptly back to the service when the song leader announced the closing hymn and the piano began to play the introduction, while the audience stood up. Of course, she stood with them and sang the song, but it was only words she mouthed. This would be a message... no, a Scripture she'd remember for a while.

Monday morning, Raylyn's supervisor came to the door and Raylyn smiled at her. Right away, she said, "Maxine, you've been keeping yourself busy, I haven't seen you since I came back to work last Tuesday." Raylyn grinned at her friend and added, "Umm, you haven't been playing hooky have you?"

"You know I haven't! We're having an audit." She sighed, "You know what that means for our department and I'm in the middle of it."

"Goodness! That's because the new year is so close? I didn't think they did an audit until after the first of the year."

"Well, sometimes they do. I'm so glad you have everything on the computer so I can pull anything they ask for up in my office and print it out for these critters. They are so meticulous it's pitiful, you know."

"When will they be finished?"

Sighing, she looked at Raylyn's full desk and said, "I'm hoping by Friday. After all, they've been here a week now. It's a good thing I sleep in between the times these guys are here, I'd be ready to strangle somebody!"

"I'm sure this isn't a good time to ask, but I have a friend who's coming for two days from Georgia next Monday. I was hoping I could take some vacation time for Monday and Tuesday so Heidi and I can spend some time with them."

"Well, hmm. You did such a good job getting everything caught up from your Thanksgiving holiday, I was really amazed that you got it all done in one day, but then you are so good! I guess it won't be too much trouble to give you off those two days, it's not like you're the only one in this department. Will you need any other time other than Christmas? Oh, how stupid of me, you don't work on weekends anyway! Of course you'll have Christmas off! It's on the weekend this year."

"As far as I know now, Heidi and I'll be alone for Christmas, Mom went to Georgia. It'll only be those weekends that'll be fine, Maxine."

"Okay, consider yourself off Monday and Tuesday, but back as usual on Wednesday."

"Yes, that's right. Thanks."

After the woman left Raylyn stuck the end of her pen in her mouth and looked off into the corner of her room, wondering why she hadn't said anything about possibly moving away. Everything seemed to be pointing to that, except this job, but even that could change. She sighed, Maxine had given her a true compliment it was obvious she didn't want her to leave. Raylyn shook her head, ever since the morning service yesterday that verse in Genesis had not left her. In fact, the words seemed to be engraved on her brain. Of course, Roger hadn't asked her to move, he hadn't told her he loved her. He hadn't called since last Wednesday when he'd told her his itinerary. Something had to give!

She sighed, "Lord, it's hard to know what to do. It's a puzzle and I'm only seeing the bottom side which is all gray, while You see the top which shows the pretty picture. Can't you even make a tiny hole and give me a glimpse?"

Raylyn came back to reality with a jolt when her intercom buzzed, when she answered, the receptionist said, "Raylyn, we have another new client. This guy's mom moved to town and this is the first time she's had medical problems. The doctor wants her admitted for tests. Can you see him now?"

"Sure, show him in!"

Later that afternoon, Raylyn was putting down the garage door when Heidi said, "Mommy, the phone's ringing! Come on, hurry!"

As usual, Raylyn's silent question was, *Will it be Roger?*

The garage door touched down and she flipped the lock, then hurried to the door into the kitchen and grabbed the receiver seconds before the answering machine picked up. "Hello?" she said, breathlessly.

"Hi, Sweetheart! It's only a week!"

"I know! Oh, Roger, it so good to hear your voice! I've missed that so much. I'm counting the days." She put her hand over her mouth and the mouthpiece and whispered, "You're going to have to talk to Heidi today, she was mad as a wet hornet when you called before and didn't talk to her. She's here dancing at my feet."

Chuckling, Roger said, "Okay, put her on, but don't you go far away!"

Heidi was dancing beside Raylyn and grabbed the phone, as she handed it to her. "Mr. Roger! You be here soon?"

"It's a week, Ladybug."

"Mr. Roger, I miss you lots. A week be too long."

"I know, but I must preach next Sunday and Ms Sandy must play the piano then, too, so I can't come before next Monday."

Heidi sighed, "I know. Did Curly get all better?"

"Yes, he's fine. Linus I think misses you."

"But you 'posed to pet him. He like you then."

"He only lets me do that when he's really hungry and he's eating. You'll need to come back so you can pet him."

"Mommy gots her job, Mr. Roger, she can't come, she need her job, you know. An' you know I aren't big 'nough to drive yet. I can't see out good."

Roger chuckled. "I bet your mommy's glad of that! Say, let me talk with her now, would you?"

"'K, Mr. Roger. Come soon!"

"I'll be there as quick as I can!"

When Raylyn came back on the phone, Roger said, "So, can you be off next Monday and Tuesday or do we have to mix your work into the equation?"

"No, I asked today. I hadn't seen my boss since I came back, so today was the first I could. She said it was fine!"

"That's great! I can't wait to see you both."

Looking at the festive placemats and centerpiece on her table, she said, "We put up our Christmas tree on Saturday and decorated it, then we strung some lights on the bushes outside yesterday afternoon. We're all festive for Christmas. Of course, we were nearly the last, most everybody does their decorating on Thanksgiving."

"I never bother with anything here at my place. No one comes by to see me, at Christmas or any other time, for that matter. I'm not here for two weeks, so it's a bit silly. My animals wouldn't appreciate it anyway. Of course, I do go Christmas shopping, I have a little brother still at home and my sister and brother-in-law come for Christmas. What could I bring for Heidi?"

"She loves books. She'll have me read to her every free minute I have, so that would be great. Any kind of book with a story to read and pictures would be perfect."

"Great, I'll see what I can do."

Roger looked at the clock and knew he needed to end the call soon. He took a deep breath and decided to say what was truly on his heart. "Sweetheart, could I tell you something I've never told another person in my life?" His breath caught in his throat, what he had to say was so very important.

"I… I guess," she said, hesitantly.

Around the lump in his throat, Roger said, "Raylyn, I love you, I love you with all my heart. I don't feel complete now that you're gone."

A tear trickled down her cheek, as she blurted out, "Roger, I love you, too!"

Roger pulled in a ragged breath and said, "Love, I wish I was there to hold you, but our words will have to do for another week. Ramon's asked me to come help him with a chore and then stay for supper, so I must go, but I love you, so much, Sweetheart. I'll see you soon."

"I love you, Honey. Have fun with Ramon and Sandy. We're counting the days until you come. Bye for now."

Reluctantly, they hung up and Raylyn looked at the clock. She needed to get their supper going, but then she had something she needed to do after the dishes. She fixed Heidi's favorite, macaroni and cheese, with a hardy green vegetable and chocolate pudding for dessert.

Heidi helped put the dishes in the dishwasher, but as Raylyn put the detergent into the little pocket, Heidi said, "Mommy, did you tell Mr. Roger you love him?"

"Yes, I did and he told me he loves me."

"Good. So now we go live wif him. He can take us wif him to that place he's going and he can marry us."

Raylyn was shaking her head while Heidi spoke. "Sweety, saying we love each other is only the first step. We can't go live with him we can't go off with him to Montana. We need to plan a wedding some time soon, but he needs to ask me to marry him first. We need to decide where we'll live. I still have my job here, can he come here or do I have to quit and go there? There're lots of things to decide."

With tears in her eyes, Heidi said, "Mommy, it not be so hard! You love him, he love you. You quit that job an' we go to Mr. Roger. It all work out, you see."

"Sweety, I hope it does work out. You go play with your toys now I have something I must do in my office."

"'K!" Heidi skipped off to her room.

Raylyn went to the little room down the hall. She left the door open so she could hear if Heidi called her, but she rolled her chair up to the desk and picked up her pen. Without any hesitation she began filling out the information requested on the flyer about her house. Yes, if they wanted to rent her place starting in February, she'd gladly give them the key. She'd quit her job and follow Roger to Montana, if she needed to. She and Heidi'd live in one of Grandma Isabel's cabins until they could be married. She sighed she'd have to give Maxine her two weeks notice very soon.

It was Saturday and when Roger pulled on his barn boots, coat and hat, then opened the door with the milk pail in one hand, it was bitter cold. The wind whistled around the ends of his porch and zeroed in on his hands. Linus raced passed him into the house and Curly's tail thumped, but from inside his house. Cow stood next to the barn door where he would let her in and bawled. Quickly, Roger ran across the backyard and let himself in the barn. In the barn it was cold, but the wind wasn't blowing.

Roger got the cow feed and let the animal into her stall, found his stool, set the milk pail under the cow and started milking. "Well, old girl, tomorrow after church the farmer next door is coming over to see my layout. I'm sure going to tell him about your bad manners when the milking's done." Cow, of course, paid no attention she kept on munching her grain contentedly.

When he finished the chore and let the cow out was the first he noticed the tiny flakes sifting down to the ground. He sighed, in two days he'd leave, or he planned to leave for points north. It would not do to have snow here if there was an inch in Atlanta they'd close the airport. These southerners didn't know how to drive in the white stuff. He filled his feed pail with scratch grain, hurried down the aisle to the chicken coop and opened the door. The chickens were quiet for a change, but they scurried around as soon as he began to scatter the grain.

"Come on, girls let's get out of those nests so I can gather the eggs. I'm taking a couple of dozen along as a present." Several of the 'girls' he was talking to didn't get out of their nests. After all the grain was on the floor, he went to each nest. He gathered all the eggs he could find and shoved the reluctant hens to the floor.

After his shower and breakfast, Roger left home to drive to Blairsville. The snow was still lazily floating down, but now it was sticking on everything but the road. As he went through Vansville, he smiled as he went by the church. When he came back from his shopping he'd stop in his office for an hour or two to put the last touches on his message for tomorrow. In all the years he'd been doing readings from his book he'd never had the satisfaction he now felt from giving messages expounding on Scripture. He realized how much God was blessing him and he knew that was because he was now listening to the still, small voice speak to him.

He had definite plans for this trip to Blairsville, because he had all his Christmas shopping done except for the presents he'd take and give at his first stop. He had two stops to make in Blairsville, one at a children's bookstore, but he planned to visit a jewelry store while he was in the city. He found the children's bookstore and went in to browse, in the section for three year olds to look at the picture storybooks. He had put Heidi to bed and remembered the book he'd read to her and also the new book that Isabel had given her, so he was pretty sure of himself when he picked out two books to take to the register to pay for them.

The store was crowded, after all, it was only days before Christmas and there were many people wanting children's books to give as presents. As he stood in line he noticed a headline on the local paper that was in a slot near the checkout line. **LOCAL DOCTOR'S GROUP LOOKING FOR FINANCIAL COUNSELOR.** He grabbed up a copy and laid it on the counter along with the books to purchase. He didn't know, but he hoped that might be an incentive for the woman he loved. She was a financial counselor, he didn't know if she wanted to do it for a doctor's group.

Since he was in the mall, he left the bookstore with his parcel and went down the concourse to find a jewelry store. He hadn't yet decided whether to buy a diamond and take it with him, then ask Raylyn to marry him or to ask her on bended knee, then take her to a jeweler's in Grand Rapids and let her pick out the ring she wanted. However, he decided to at least get an idea how much of a hole he'd be in for the rest of his life. His heart sank as he looked in the window of the first jewelry store he came to. At these prices he would be in a hole for a very *very* long time. He sighed perhaps prices wouldn't be so steep in Grand Rapids. *Yeah, and pigs fly!*

True to his word, Derek Casbah had come to church last Sunday. His wife, Millie hadn't come, but there had been a significant increase in the offering. The deacons had counted the money in his office and left their report on his desk. He was glad he hadn't ever had the responsibility of handling the church's money, but he wondered if he would see an increase in his income. Obviously Brad Thomas didn't have as much clout in town as he'd once thought, but Alex Mallard had said that he should get a raise. He should get a paycheck tomorrow after the service, what would it show? Alex was a likeable man, much more personable that Brad. Was he as good as his word? Perhaps twenty-four hours would tell.

He looked in three jewelry stores and the sinking feeling didn't go away. A diamond engagement ring would take innumerable gallons of milk at two dollars a gallon to pay for it. Discouraged, he left the mall and found his Jeep. While he'd been in the mall it had continued to snow. His windshield was covered and his shoes made tracks as he walked beside his vehicle to the driver's door. The wind was still biting and he was glad to close the door then start up so he could turn on the heater. He was glad he'd invested in a hard-top Jeep those several years ago, but it still wasn't all that warm. The winter weather made him wonder what his darling was experiencing up in the truly cold country. He felt a shiver go down his back, but as the heater started spitting out warm air, his shoulders relaxed.

Sunday morning, Roger hurried through his chores and arrived at the church early. Even though Brad had confessed to the things he had done to Roger, Roger still didn't feel comfortable allowing free use of the keys to the church that were in many hands around town. He kept the front door dead-bolted and went in the church through his office. While the praise team practiced, Roger went out with a broom and swept off the steps, the walk and the ramp. He was glad that the snow had only accumulated about two inches and then stopped. He decided that was one good thing about living in the south, maybe it snowed, but never much and didn't stay around long. He could feel it in the air, if the sun came out the snow would melt.

While he preached his message, the sun came out and by the time the service was over much of the snow had turned to slush and the edges of the streets were sporting a small stream rushing toward the drains. He smiled as the people left, each lady promising to bring her prized delicacy for the afternoon refreshment time after Sandy's concert. When Roger went home, even though it was to an empty house, he was happy and excited. In less than twenty-four hours he'd be with the lady he loved and the child he wanted to make his own.

Not long after eating the last of the vegetable soup he'd made during the week, he returned to town and opened the church for the afternoon concert. He made sure that the ramp was free of any moisture. Glad that the sun had come out and dried it, he went back to his office and picked up the stack of programs he'd made up for the concert. He also put the slides in order that would go along with the numbers that Sandy would play. He was pleased to work the overhead projector, since Ramon was the MC. The words to the pieces of music added another dimension and Sandy always wanted whatever she did to be a witness for her Lord.

Only a few minutes later, Sandy and Ramon parked the van out front. They had brought Isabel and Ruth with them. Soon after he opened the doors they all walked in. Remembering what Raylyn had said about her mom being here, Roger had kept on his white shirt from the morning service. He'd loosened his tie and opened the top button of his shirt, but his suit coat waited on his chair in his office. He was still fussing with the projector as the four people came through the front door.

Sandy and Ramon immediately went around him, Sandy to the piano and Ramon to the lectern. However, Isabel and Ruth both had plates in their hands. Isabel said, "Young man, where are we to put these refreshments?"

Giving the old lady his trademark smile, he said, "Hi, Isabel, I had some men set up two tables across the back here after church this morning, so since you're the first, anywhere is fine." He looked at the middle aged lady with Isabel and asked, "Are you Raylyn's mom? Of course you must be! You have those same red curls!"

"Yes, I'm Ruth Harland, would you be Roger?"

Roger held out his hand and smiled. "Yes, I'm Roger Clemens, the pastor here at the Vansville Community Church. I'm very pleased to meet you." Nodding toward the front, he said, "I know you've met Sandy, but I'm sure you'll have a great experience this afternoon. Sandy DeLord is an awesome pianist."

"I'm pleased to meet you, too. I understand you're stopping by to see my daughter, when is it, tomorrow?"

"Yes, Ma'am. I'm excited to see her and spend some time with her and also with Heidi."

Before either Ruth or Roger said anything else, Isabel was beside them and said, with a scowl, "Young man, don't you lead that girl along. You tell her your intentions right up front!"

"Isabel, I intend to do just that!"

"Good."

Ruth looked at her mom askance. "Mom! You talk to a pastor like that?"

Isabel shrugged. "Not usually, but this one I do." She grinned at the young man. "I sent him home to change his clothes the last time there was a concert here." Chuckling, she looked Roger up and down before she added, "I see he's dressed properly this time." Intentionally, as an after-thought, she said, "You know how these young whippersnappers are."

Roger also chuckled. "I wouldn't dare do otherwise, Isabel."

After an awesome concert, when the clapping went on and on, Roger turned off the projector and said from the back of the auditorium, "I think it would be appropriate to close this wonderful concert with prayer. Let's all bow our heads. Our Father, thank You for this wonderful celebration of Your Son's birth. Sandy has done an awesome job of focusing our hearts and minds on the true reason for this season. May we continue to keep the thoughts we've had today front and center as we draw closer to Christmas Day. Bless these refreshments that we are about to enjoy and bless all those who have had a part in preparing them for us. Thank You again for Your Son and that He was willing to come as the Babe in the manger to become our Redeemer. In His Name, amen."

Ramon left the platform as soon as Roger finished praying, but hurried to Roger before he began to mingle and said, "Sandy has something she wants you to take with you to Heidi. Make sure you get it before we all get out of here and forget it. She says it's her Christmas present for her."

Roger scowled. "For Heidi?"

Ramon grinned at his friend and slapped him on the back. "Yeah, she's so sure you're going to propose while you're there that she's offering Heidi a month of free piano lessons after they move down here to live."

Roger could feel the heat on his neck and all at once his tie felt like a noose around his neck, but he said, "She does, does she? Hmm." He saw the twinkle in Ramon's eyes, so he grinned at his friend. Now that the concert was over, he shed his suit jacket and his tie and Ramon did the same, then they laid them across the back seats.

The two men couldn't move farther than the projector because of the crowd at the back where the tables were that were loaded with the refreshments and a huge punch bowl. People who had come for the concert surrounded the two tables that held all the food. Isabel had appointed herself as the official punch dipper and was putting full cups down on the table. Working as fast as she could, she was hardly keeping up with the demand. While Roger and Ramon still stood beside the projector, Alex Mallard approached and said, "Roger, do you have a minute? I need to talk to you."

Ramon turned toward Sandy and Roger said, "Sure, Alex, what is it?"

Pulling an envelope from his shirt pocket, he said, "Here's your check. I forgot it this morning, so I was glad for this concert so I could bring it. You're out of here so early tomorrow you'll be gone long before I could get it to you."

Alex gave Roger the envelope and shook his hand, but before Roger could say anything else, Alex clapped his hands and raised his voice. "Friends, could I have your attention for a few minutes?" People were still moving around the food tables, but the talking stopped, so Alex continued, "We've never done this before, but last Sunday someone made a suggestion that we needed to honor our pastor at Christmas." He pulled another envelope from his shirt pocket and handed it to Roger. "It isn't too much, we didn't have too long to gather it, but Merry Christmas, Pastor. It's to your good health."

Roger swallowed noticeably and he had to quickly blink the mist out of his eyes, before he said, "Oh, my! Thank you all for thinking of me like this. I'm overwhelmed." The mist didn't completely go away Roger pulled his hankerchief from his pocket to help.

It was obvious that Alex still wasn't finished so the people remained quiet, so he said, "We also think Ms Sandy should have something from the people of her adopted town to thank her for giving us this wonderful concert." He turned toward Sandy and looked at her, as he said, "Ms Sandy, both the last concert, but especially this one have been something we all will remember for a very long time." He pulled another envelope from his pocket and held it out to her. "Thank you for giving us your time and your talent both in September and today."

"Alex!" Sandy exclaimed. "I'm happy to do this you don't need to pay me! Really, we can't celebrate the coming of the Lord Jesus too much!"

TWELVE

Pulling his hand away, even though Sandy was trying to make him take back the envelope, he shook his head and said, "Don't think this is payment, young lady! It surely isn't anywhere close to what you should get, it's a little something to tell you how much your town loves you and how glad we are that you've made Vansville your home. Believe me you have made this town a great place to live!"

"Alex," she murmured. With eyes that sparkled with unshed tears, she looked around at everyone who stood looking at her with smiles on their faces. She swallowed and said, "I'm speechless! You're all fantastic! Thank you all so much. You're a great bunch of people!"

"I must agree," Roger added, sincerely. "You are a great bunch of folks and I thank you from the bottom of my heart."

Alex was finished, so he walked away and picked up a plate to fill with his favorite Christmas refreshments. People came to Sandy and told her how much they appreciated her concert. They turned to Roger and added their thanks that they'd had the words to so many of the pieces that Sandy had played that added meaning to the program. It was well over an hour later when people started to leave the church.

Derek Casbah came to Sandy and said, "Would there ever be a time when I could persuade you to go to Atlanta to play?"

When Sandy was finally able to speak, she looked at him, pointed to herself and said, "Me? You're asking me to play in Atlanta?"

"Yes. Ms. Sandy, you play as well or better than some of our resident musicians. I would be most happy to offer your name for a concert."

"Oh, my! Mr. Casbah, I'd have to think about it and talk with Ramon before I could ever give you an answer."

He chuckled. "I'll try to twist my step-son's arm so he'll encourage you to give me a favorable answer."

"We'll talk about it while we're away and let you know. That would be a great honor and we'll take it very seriously. Thank you."

"Have a great vacation, both of you."

"Thank you so much, we will."

Derek turned from Sandy and found Roger, who had picked up his jacket and tie and was about to go in his office. "Roger, could I speak with you for a minute?"

"Sure, out here, or in my office?"

"It doesn't matter, well, perhaps in your office would be better."

"That's fine, that's right where I was going."

He followed Roger in the room and closed the door, before he said, "I wasn't aware until that town meeting how little you made. Have you opened your salary check?" Roger still held both envelopes in his hands, so Derek said, "Go ahead and open it. I have been very remiss in not attending services. My wife has been very influential in that, before I married her, I attended regularly in the town where I lived before. I would probably have known your tiny salary if I'd been where I belonged these years, but I wasn't, I'm sorry."

Still leaving both envelopes sealed, Roger said, "Mr. Casbah, I'm very sorry to say that until Thanksgiving the messages I gave were nothing. I gave readings rather than giving a message. Sandy was the hound of heaven in my life and brought me back to the Lord. I'm glad you've started coming to service and I hope you've been blessed since you've started."

"Yes, very much. Please, open the envelope I want to make sure you have received what has been agreed on."

Roger reluctantly tore open the envelope. He pulled out the check and stared, then lifted his eyes to Derek. Tears threatened again, as he said, "Oh, my! This is too good to be true!"

Derek looked at the check over Roger's shoulder. Putting his hand on Roger's shoulder, he said, "Good; that is the amount we agreed on. Probably next year at this time you'll get another raise. I'm very sure you'll deserve that next one, too. Have I heard correctly? Are you planning to propose to a young lady soon?"

"Yes, I am. Probably tomorrow."

Derek squeezed the young man's shoulder and nodded to the other envelope still lying on the desk. "Good, that should help in that regard, too."

Roger swallowed and licked his lips. "As I said before, I'm overwhelmed!"

"Use it all in good health. Have a great trip and come back refreshed."

"Thanks, I will. You have a great Christmas."

"I'll try. Millie isn't much on the true meaning of Christmas. She puts up the lights and the trees and buys lavish gifts, but there is no celebration of Christ's birth." He took a deep breath and added, "You know, Sandy has done a remarkable thing not only for you, but also for Ramon and myself. Believe me, without her witness I wouldn't have come back to the Lord and surely Ramon wouldn't have been saved. She is an awesome lady, not only with the things she does, which are phenomenal, but also her close walk with the Lord." Derek shook Roger's hand. "Have a great Christmas."

Roger's eyes sparkling, with unshed tears, he licked his lips and whispered, "Derek, thank you, I plan to have a great Christmas. You the same. I'm hoping this concert will help."

"Yes, I believe it will."

After morning worship, when Raylyn came to junior church to collect Heidi, the teacher smiled and asked, "Who's Mr. Roger?"

Raylyn chuckled. "He's someone we met in Georgia over Thanksgiving. I presume Heidi talked about him?"

As they both stood watching the children, Lana said, "I must tell you, Heidi has been wired for who knows what today! She's been singing louder than anyone else, she's jumped out of her seat more times than she's ever done before. She claps her hands constantly as she tells everyone that her Mr. Roger is coming tomorrow."

"I'm sorry she's been such a handful, but she thinks the world of Mr. Roger."

The older lady looked at Raylyn and saw the extra color on her cheeks. "Would he be someone special in your life, too?"

"Yes, he is. I may not show it quite as much as Heidi, but I am about to crawl out of my skin with excitement that he's coming tomorrow!"

The lady patted Raylyn's hand. "I'm glad to hear that!"

Heidi ran up to them then with her coat bunched in her arms. She opened her arms and Raylyn had to hurry to grab her Sunday coat before it fell on the floor. Heidi's teacher said, "You both have a wonderful Christmas! Remember, we don't have junior church next Sunday, it'll be a special time for everyone to celebrate Jesus' birth."

Jumping up and down, hardly giving Raylyn the chance to zip up her coat, Heidi said, "'K, Ms. Lana, bye!"

Heidi put her hand in Raylyn's as they walked away toward the door closest to their car. Raylyn had her mouth open, but Heidi asked, "We go for Mr. Roger now, Mommy?"

"No, Sweety, not until tomorrow morning. We must sleep tonight and get up really early to go to the airport." She almost chuckled, would either of them sleep, knowing that Roger would be there soon after breakfast? She highly doubted that she would and she was sure Heidi would be restless in her sleep.

Heidi sighed, "Mommy, it be such a long time to see Mr. Roger."

"I know, but the wait is almost over, Pumpkin. He'll be eating lunch about the time we eat lunch today. Your grandma will meet him this afternoon when Ms. Sandy plays. After that it'll be almost time for him to get on the plane."

"I wish we could go hear Ms. Sandy play. She play so good."

"Yes, she does. Maybe we'll go back to Vansville and we'll hear her play again."

"Would she play *Twinkle, Twinkle, Little Star*?"

"She just might, Sweety, I don't know."

If she had her way, they would be headed on to Montana with Roger when he left Grand Rapids on Wednesday, but that seemed far fetched. If Roger asked her to marry him, where would they get married? Would it be here in her home church or more appropriately down at the church where he was the pastor? Still, she hadn't said anything to her boss that she was thinking of leaving. She had to give at least two weeks notice and that couldn't be until Wednesday.

Raylyn had the worst time getting her child to sleep that night. She read three storybooks, cover to cover and answered so many questions. She was sure Heidi knew the answers to most of them, but of course, it was a delaying tactic. Any parent could tell the signs. Heidi even yawned while Raylyn answered, but she still had another question and then needed a drink before she finally lay down and clutched Dollie in her arms.

Not long after Heidi was finally asleep, the phone rang and Raylyn hurried to answer so it wouldn't wake the child. As soon as she answered, Ruth said, "I met your man today and I highly recommend him!" She chuckled, "I think your grandma thinks he's pretty special too, as far as being a man is concerned, now I'm not sure she's convinced about his preaching yet, and of course, I haven't heard him preach, but he prayed after Sandy's program and it was a wonderful prayer. Say, why didn't you tell me that Sandy's in a wheelchair?"

"It never even crossed my mind, Mom! She's such a wonderful person that you totally forget that about her. Was she awesome or what?"

"I have never, and I mean never, heard anyone play like she did! She played parts of The Messiah and some other classical Christmas music, as well as some carols. She and her husband and Roger had worked out having the words displayed on the wall so everyone could read along while she played. Christmas has taken on new meaning for me. I hope this town will make a tradition of this. If they do, I'll be here!"

"Oh, Mom, that's great!"

After talking some more about the concert, Ruth changed the subject and said, "So, have you done anything about moving down here?"

Stunned, Raylyn exclaimed, "Mom, he hasn't proposed! I told you before that I must have my job until there isn't a reason to keep it. You know that!"

"Small matter, he will! Have you?"

"I received a flyer from a church close by who's looking for temporary housing for an interim pastor and I offered my house...."

"Okay, that's a start. How about your job?"

"I haven't said anything at work. In fact, I received a compliment from my boss the other day. It hardly seems fair..." She sighed, "I don't know, Mom. Actually, there are some things… but who knows?"

Ruth hardly let her finish before she said, "I think you need to, Dear. How many times have you told me your boss would need at least two weeks notice if you ever left. Well, now's the time to get that two weeks notice in. You write it up on that computer there at your house and take it with you tomorrow."

"I won't be there the next two days and things might change so that I'll feel the need by the time I go in on Wednesday."

"Okay, that sounds good. I must tell you, I'm having a great time with Mom. I love this little town. I'm going to come visit more often. Mom and I've done some shopping since I came. You know I haven't been shopping, just to shop in a very long time. I forgot how much fun it is, especially before Christmas."

"That's great, Mom! Yes, it is fun, especially when stores have Christmas songs and carols playing. Thanks for calling, I'll talk to you again."

"Yes, Dear. In case I don't get to call again for a while, have a great time with Roger and have a wonderful Christmas."

"Thanks, the same to you, Mom."

Raylyn hung up and turned on the burner under the teakettle. It was senseless to go to bed yet, if Heidi had been wired during junior church, her mommy was definitely wired now. Something would have to change for her to get any sleep tonight. After a cup of tea steeped and she added sugar, she carried the mug into the living room and curled up with her Bible and study guide. She might as well use the time productively, as sit around watching the clock hands move infinitesimally slowly. Even the second hand seemed to creep along on the clock in the kitchen! She couldn't remember – maybe when she was in labor – when time went so slowly.

At ten thirty, Raylyn closed her Bible and the book, turned off the light and went down the hall to her room. Without turning on the light, she undressed and crawled into bed, hoping that because she hadn't turned on the light and her eyes were already adjusted to the darkness, she'd fall asleep. After praying for a few minutes, she did fall asleep and much to her surprise, Heidi's cold hand was the next thing she felt. It was pitch dark, as she opened her eyes. Surely it wasn't time to get up!

Raylyn didn't even have time to open her eyes, before Heidi said, "Mommy, it be time to go for Mr. Roger now?"

Raylyn opened her eyes, but could hardly see Heidi in the dark room. Of course, it was close to the shortest day of the year, but she still looked at her bedside clock. It was not anywhere close to the time for the alarm to go off. "Sweety, we still have several hours before it's time to get up. Go back to your room and play with Dollie or read her a story if you can't sleep, but be very quiet, I'll get up when it's time. I promise. I have my alarm set for the right time to get up, so don't worry that we'll miss him, okay?"

Heidi sighed, "'K, Mommy. It be so long, I sleep good, Mommy, why it not time now?"

"I know. Look at my clock, Sweety. When the big hand is straight up and the little hand is straight down is when we need to get up. If you're still awake, you can go to the kitchen to check that clock."

The little girl heaved another sigh and went to Raylyn's door. She carefully turned the knob and walked into the hall, then closed the door behind her. Raylyn was glad for the nightlight she had in the hallway so Heidi wouldn't stumble on her way back to her room. She heard the toilet flush before the silence. She closed her eyes and willed herself back to sleep.

Roger was getting up about that time. He hurried out to the barn to milk for the last time this year. He gathered the eggs, then hurried back inside. He fed all his animals, then put Linus outside. He showered, washed his hair and shaved, then packed his razor and shampoo. When he couldn't think of anything else he'd need, he closed the suitcase and wheeled it to the back door. In the kitchen, he fixed a quick breakfast then made sure there were no dirty dishes. He loaded his backpack - that he would use as a carry-on - with presents and the eggs.

He hadn't put a very big chunk of wood in his stove last night and before he left the bed this morning, the furnace had kicked on. However, the last thing he did was check the wood stove to make sure there were no coals that would do any damage. He turned the thermostat back to sixty and hoped it didn't go out. Pipes didn't freeze very often here, but there was always the possibility. His watch beeped as he walked out into the clear, cold darkness of early morning. He put his luggage inside on the back seat, then climbed behind the wheel and started up. The stars were giving the only light, but his eyes had adjusted and he could see the shapes of his house and barn. When he came back, the last day of the old year, would there be the prospect of soon sharing his house with the woman he loved?

Just as he pulled the stick into reverse he thought about the newspaper article he'd seen the headline for and read yesterday. He jammed the stick back into park and jumped from the Jeep. He took the steps to his back porch in one leap and crashed into the door, then stopped long enough to unlock it. He knew where he'd laid the paper, so he grabbed it and ran. Only moments later he was back in the Jeep and this time he whirled around in his turn-around and headed down his driveway. When he reached the country road, he squealed around the corner, there wasn't any traffic at this early hour.

"Raylyn, my love, I'm on my way! Maybe before we even leave the airport I'll pop the question. Will you give me the answer I want so desperately to hear? Please, Love, say, 'yes.'"

Roger could make the trip to Blairsville blindfolded, but then it was some miles to Atlanta and it had been some time since he'd been there. It was still quite early as he reached the interstate, but it was busy. Before he reached the exit for the airport, he saw the lights and glanced up as a plane took off over him. He followed the signs from the exit and soon found the longterm parking garage. He took a ticket and circled the garage once before he found a place to pull in. Quickly, he pulled his things from the back seat, slung the backpack over his shoulder and pulled up the handle on the suitcase. His long strides took him quickly inside the terminal. He found the airline he needed and stepped up to the counter.

"Howdy, man," the clerk said, "You're on your way outta here for the holidays?"

"I sure am! I'm heading north."

"North! What are you, crazy?"

"Nope! I'm on my way to make a lady my fiancée then it's on to Montana for Christmas with my family."

"Montana, that's the cold country!"

"Yup, usually is!"

All during the small talk, the clerk was typing into his computer all the things he needed from the information Roger had printed from his internet ticket search. Soon, his suitcase was on the conveyor belt and Roger was on his way to the loading area for the plane that would take him to Grand Rapids. He still had some time, but as soon as he turned from the counter, his legs wouldn't walk, they took him at a jog down the corridor to the area where the signs told him he would load. He looked around, the area had several people, some of them were napping, others were reading and one mother was tending to a crying baby.

He stood at the window and looked out at all the lights. About fifteen minutes later a huge plane inched its way into position next to the building where he stood. Only a few minutes later an airline attendant came and moved the chain away from the ramp. Before she had finished setting down the post, Roger was there with his boarding pass. He handed it to the woman then hurried down the ramp and onto the plane, where another attendant met him. He found his seat, carefully hoisted his backpack into the rack above it and sank into his seat. He could smell the coffee aroma coming from the rear of the plane and hoped it was good.

Because of all the excitement from the day before and his over-the-top excitement of seeing Raylyn and Heidi soon and having to do the chores before he left, he hadn't slept too much overnight. The information he'd gotten from the internet had said there would be coffee and a Danish served on board. He'd eaten breakfast, he always did, but he knew he could easily tuck away a Danish of any size and a good cup of coffee. Soon after they were airborne, he heard noise from the galley area and soon two flight attendants came up the aisle dispensing large Styrofoam cups of coffee, cream and sugar and large, wrapped pastries. Roger accepted the offerings eagerly.

Raylyn couldn't get back to sleep after Heidi had woken her. She turned over after the child left her room and snuggled down under her blankets, but sleep wouldn't come. However, she didn't want Heidi to know she was up, so she found her book that she had started reading since coming home from Vansville and started where she'd left off. It was supposed to be a thriller, but it wasn't nearly as thrilling as what she'd experience in another few hours.

Finally, the clock radio snapped on, so Raylyn closed her book and prepared to leave the bed, but as she threw the covers off her legs the doorknob turned and a little person said, "Mommy, the big hand be straight up and the little hand be straight down, but what about the other hand that keeps going around so fast?"

"We don't worry about that one, Sweety. It doesn't help us tell time much it just keeps going around and around. You need to go brush your teeth and get dressed in the clothes I laid out for you. Now run along while I get ready and then we'll eat breakfast."

"Mommy," Heidi said, wistfully, "I wish we had some of Gamaw's buns."

"Yes, they were good, weren't they? I'll have to make some one day soon, but it won't be today, we're in a hurry to get to the airport."

"I know. Can I gets the Ojuice and milk out?"

"Sure, you can, after you get dressed. That'll be a big help, Sweety. You can get out the glasses and cereal bowls, too, but please don't try to pour the juice, okay?"

"'K, Mommy. Hurry!"

"Oh, yes, I'll be along."

After church last evening, Raylyn had pulled out several outfits she thought would be good to wear to the airport. She hurried with her shower, but didn't wash her hair, since she'd done that only yesterday. When she came back and looked at the outfit she'd finally decided on last night, she changed her mind and took it back to the closet. What should she wear? What would Roger have on, would he be dressed up or casual? She sighed and pulled out one of her better work outfits and pulled on the slacks, but she couldn't bring herself to put on the top she usually wore with it for work. She wanted to look nice, but she didn't want to even think about work.

After finding the top she wanted, she took her brush to her hair and stroked through it until it shone. Attaching her watch to her wrist, she took one last look in the mirror and headed for the kitchen. *What you see is what you get.*

Heidi was kneeling in her seat when Raylyn reached the kitchen. All the cereal boxes were on the table, the bowls, glasses and spoons were in their places and the jugs of juice and milk sat on the very edge of the table. Raylyn looked at the clock and decided she'd wait on making coffee until they were back home from the airport. She pushed the milk jug back from the edge, filled two glasses with the orange juice then put that jug away. After filling Heidi's other glass with milk, she and Heidi held hands while Raylyn said the blessing.

Raylyn dumped the usual amount of cereal into Heidi's bowl and poured milk over it, then filled her own bowl. However, Heidi did more wiggling in her seat than she did putting cereal in her mouth. "Sweety, come on, we can't leave until you're done."

"Mommy, we can so!" Heidi said, indignantly.

Sternly, Raylyn said, "Well, we're not, so you'd better get eating, young lady. We got up when we did so we could eat breakfast."

Several mouthfuls later, Raylyn looked at Heidi. Her mouth was so full her cheeks were puffed out as far as they could go, but she was hardly chewing or swallowing. Sternly, Raylyn said, "Heidi, that is not eating your cereal! Now chew and swallow what's in your mouth. You can't drink your orange juice or your milk with a mouthful like that and we are not leaving this table until your whole breakfast is gone."

The child couldn't say anything, but tears welled up in her eyes and slid down her cheeks. She looked up at the clock, as if she knew they would miss reaching the plane on time. Hiding her exasperation as best she could, Raylyn said, "Heidi, we will not be late, unless you fool around like you are now. We have time to finish our breakfast and still get to the airport before Mr. Roger's plane lands. Now empty your mouth. Remember, I said we would not be leaving this house before we finished breakfast!"

Finally, the mouthful was gone. There was still a full glass of orange juice and half a glass of milk in front of Heidi, when she said, "Mommy, please, can't we go now? It be time!"

Shaking her head, Raylyn said, "It'll be time when your juice and milk disappear. I'll probably finish mine before you get yours gone, though."

Heidi picked up her orange juice and chugged down half the glassful, but she had to stop for breath. As she grabbed a breath, she said, "Mommy, you cheat! You gots a bigger mouth!"

"Well, hurry, I'll rinse the dishes while you finish up."

"'K, Mommy," Heidi said, resigned.

At last, all the dishes were in the dishwasher, the milk was away and so was the cereal. Raylyn zipped up Heidi's coat, buttoned several buttons on her own coat and grabbed her purse and keys. The two of them hurried into the garage and Raylyn opened Heidi's door. While she settled into her seat, Raylyn unlocked and opened the garage door, then came back and fastened Heidi's seatbelt. According to Raylyn's watch they had over an hour to get to the airport to meet Roger's plane. That was plenty of time.

The sky wasn't black, but there was a hint that the sun would be up when they came back home. It hadn't snowed in several days and Raylyn was happy about that. There was some snow on the ground, but the roads were clear and dry, so she backed out onto the street and turned toward the airport. After they had made several turns, Raylyn looked in the rearview mirror to see why Heidi was so quiet and couldn't believe that she had fallen asleep. She must not have slept very much last night.

It struck her as she started across the city that the last time she'd been to the airport was three years ago to take Dan there when he was being deployed. She and her in-laws had both been there. She swallowed and quickly pulled one of her favorite CD's from the visor and slid it into the player. She didn't care if it woke Heidi, she didn't want to think about that sad time, not when she was meeting Roger.

Of course, the music did wake Heidi and she said, "Mommy, are we there yet?"

Keeping her eyes on the road with all the traffic, Raylyn said, "No, Sweety, we're not there yet. It'll be another fifteen minutes, at least. I think lots of people want to get to the airport this morning. Didn't you sleep last night?"

"I sleep good! Dollie be awake a lot, though."

Looking away from the mirror, to keep her smile from showing, Raylyn said, "I see. Will you help me watch for the place where we turn off? The word should start with a big 'A'. I'll have to watch the traffic. I guess there are a lot of people going to the airport. Since it's the week of Christmas lots of people are traveling."

"We isn't trabling, right?"

"No, Sweety, we're staying home. I have to work the three days after Mr. Roger leaves and then we get three days off with Christmas in the middle."

"Free Saturdays?"

"Well, Sweety, only one of them's a Saturday, just like at Thanksgiving. The first day is Saturday, the next is Sunday and then Monday. We'll go to church on Sunday, but there won't be any junior church, just like Ms. Lana said."

"I 'member, Mommy. There be a sign wif an 'A' first!"

"That's it, Sweety! You were good to see that."

Raylyn found a parking place close to the airline Roger had told her he would be on. She locked the car, took Heidi's hand and they hurried into the terminal. They were glad to get inside it was cold even in the parking garage. Raylyn found the arrival's board and Roger's plane was scheduled to arrive on time. They hurried to the waiting area, which was as far as they could go, but not where the plane docked. Raylyn found two seats and they sat down.

"Mommy, where be Mr. Roger?"

"We have a few minutes, Sweety. His plane is on time, though."

Twenty minutes later people started walking toward them. Heidi climbed up and stood on her seat and Raylyn didn't stop her. She felt like climbing up on the seat too. Why did kids have all the advantages? However, Raylyn stood up and went up on her tiptoes. She hoped to see a tall, blond man very soon.

Only minutes later, Heidi exclaimed, "Mommy, Mommy, he be comin' right now! There he is! Oh, Mommy, it be Mr. Roger!"

"Yes, I see him, I see him, Sweety!"

Of course, with Heidi jumping up and down on a chair, Roger saw her easily, but he also saw the sparkling eyes of the lady standing close to her and his love for them made his heart turn over in his chest. He could hardly wait to get to them. The instant he saw them, he broke into a fast jog, his backpack bumping against his back, but he didn't even notice. He had to wend his way around people to get to them, but he didn't waste a minute of precious time. Raylyn wanted to start running to him, but with Heidi in tow, it would be better for them to stand still and Roger come to them, so she put her hand on Heidi when she would have jumped down from the chair.

"Oh, Mommy! He almost here!"

Never taking her eyes from the man she loved, she said, "Sweety, let Mr. Roger come to us, it'll be better that way."

"'K, Mommy, he come fast!"

Breathless, Raylyn said, "Yes, he's getting around people pretty quick!" She felt like jumping up and down herself.

Heidi stayed on the chair jumping up and down and clapping her hands, as Roger moved quickly toward them. Of course, Raylyn's smile was radiant. He was so excited to see them, his heart was going faster by the second and it wasn't all because he was running. He was nearly out of breath when he reached them, but Raylyn didn't care, she threw herself into his arms and of course, his arms went tightly around her immediately.

"Honey!" she exclaimed.

"Sweetheart, I have missed you so much!" he murmured, into her hair, then their lips met and they shared a welcome kiss. "Mmm, so good!"

Of course, Heidi didn't want to be left out, so since her mommy stood beside the chair she stood on, she stayed on it and wormed her arms underneath Roger's and Raylyn's to his chest and hugged him fiercely. Looking up at him, even though he and Raylyn were kissing, Heidi exclaimed, "Daddy Roger, I so glad you be here! I missed you heaps and gobs! You finally be here, Daddy Roger!"

That brought Roger and Raylyn's lips apart and they both looked at Heidi. Both Raylyn and Roger wondered if Heidi even knew what she had called him in her excitement. Keeping one arm around Raylyn, Roger bent his legs and scooped Heidi up in his other arm. Her arms went tightly around his neck and she delivered one of her big, slobbery kisses to his cheek, then pulled her hand from his neck and rubbed it in. As soon as Heidi moved her head away, Roger planted a kiss on Heidi's cheek. He'd felt so alone for these weeks, now he was complete. Both the ladies he was holding had smiles on their faces powerful enough to light a hundred watt bulb.

Still in his arm, Raylyn asked, "You do have luggage, don't you?"

"Yes, I'm sure it's coming through on the luggage belt, wherever that is."

"It's on the lower level; we'd better go down now."

"Yes, I guess so. I could stand here and kiss you all day," he sighed.

Still carrying Heidi against him and holding Raylyn close to his other side, he turned toward where she had pointed and they all started for the escalator. As they began walking, Raylyn slid her arm around Roger's waist. Her arm around him sent goosebumps up and down his spine. It felt so right. When they reached the moving stairs, Heidi wanted down, she loved to ride the escalator whenever they went to a department store and the airport was no different. Grasping the handrail, she stepped on ahead of the two adults. Raylyn didn't want to be that far from Roger, so they stepped on together, still with their arms around each other.

The luggage flopped onto the belt, so there were many people crowded around it, but Roger was in no hurry, he stayed back, content to hold his lovely lady. Heidi, of course, stayed close, but didn't want to hold Roger's hand, she was too used to being on the go all the time, but with so many people around them, she did stay close.

After they collected Roger's suitcase and went back to the main level where they needed to be to reach Raylyn's car, she looked at Roger's jacket and said, "I hope you're warm enough in your coat, it's really cold today, not like Georgia."

Hugging her again, he smiled and said, "I'll be fine, Sweetheart. With you beside me, how could I be cold?"

She grinned. "I've been told that Southerners have thin blood."

Roger chuckled. "Mmm, I've heard that, too, but so far, living in the south hasn't done that to me. Maybe it's because I go to Montana each year. Still, some year, but I don't plan to let you get too far away, so I should be fine."

She smiled and her eyes sparkled, he wanted to kiss her right there on the spot, but she said, "That's fine with me, I don't want you far away, either."

"Come on, Mr. Roger, our car be over there!"

He held the door and the cold blasted through the opening, but Heidi took his free hand before they even went through the doorway. That left Raylyn walking beside him with the suitcase between them. Even before they crossed the sidewalk, he looked at the suitcase, then at Raylyn and said, "Here, Love, will you pull this with your other hand so I can hold you?"

Without hesitation, she grinned and grabbed the handle, then stepped into his arm. "Of course, Honey, I've been waiting to be in your arm."

The three of them crossed the three busy lanes as a unit with the suitcase trailing along behind. They kept walking and making the turns until both Raylyn and Roger spotted her car and headed for it. Raylyn hit the remote, the lights winked and as she hit the little gizmo again, the trunk went up.

"Sweety," Raylyn said to Heidi, "the door's unlocked, I think you can pull it open and get in. I'll buckle you in in a second."

"'K. Mommy, hurry, it be cold, you know."

"I know, the wind really whips through this parking garage," she said, pushing her hair, that the wind in the garage insisted belonged in her eyes away.

With the trunk lid up, there was a spot where Heidi couldn't see them, so Roger again wrapped his arms around Raylyn and she immediately let go of the suitcase and put her arms around him. They savored a longer kiss. When they came up for air, Roger's voice was ragged, as he said, "Sweetheart, I love you so much! My arms have been so empty and just now are finally feeling right again." He took one hand away and touched her chin so that she looked into his eyes, because what he wanted to say was so important he had to see her face. Just above a whisper, he asked, "Love, will you marry me?"

"Honey," she murmured, "I want to say yes, but is there any way?"

"I think so, Sweetheart, we'll talk and work on it while I'm here."

Heidi knew they weren't getting the suitcase into the trunk. She hadn't heard anything bumping into the back, so she jumped out and came to the back of the car. Putting her hands on her hips, she exclaimed, "Mommy, Mr. Roger, it be cold. The door be still open. Come on! We gots to get home, you know!"

"We're coming, Munchkin, give me a minute to get this suitcase in here."

"'K, but hurry!"

Roger threw his suitcase into the trunk, then shed the backpack and laid it beside it, then pushed the trunk lid down. He followed Raylyn up along side the car, but Heidi was shaking her head at her mommy. She had the seatbelt in her hand but she held her other hand out to Roger. He smiled at the child, knowing what she wanted and bent his head into the back seat. He took the seatbelt from her and clicked it in place, then kissed the top of her head. He straightened up and closed Heidi's door, then reached around Raylyn and opened her door for her, of course, snagging another kiss while he did.

Before she bent to get in, he said, "There you go, Sweetheart."

Raylyn sighed, "Now to fight all the traffic again."

"Yes, there is that, Love."

She watched the signs and safely maneuvered her way on one way lanes through the congested, busy airport onto the road leading back into the city. Finally, when they were away from the buildings they could see that the sun was shining brightly and the sky was a deep blue, no clouds or haze covered it. It was a beautiful December day. But all Roger wanted to see was the lovely lady beside him.

When they finally reached a city street, Roger said, "Whew! You did good Sweetheart! So what's on for today?"

"We're going home to get you settled into the guest room and I'm making coffee. After that, we'll think of something," Raylyn said, emphatically.

"Ah, that sounds like a good plan, especially the coffee. The smell on the plane was great when I first walked on and I looked forward to a good cup, but the coffee they served didn't measure up. I think they sent the aroma through the air ducts, but then at the last minute added two or three quarts more water before they served it."

"Why they do that, Mr. Roger?"

Laying his hand along the back of the seat and therefore being able to play with a strand of Raylyn's hair, he turned his head and said, "What they served looked like muddy river water. What a river or lake looks like after a big rain."

"Ugh! Did they make you drink that?"

Shrugging, Roger said, "The Danish was good and I needed something to wash it down, so I had a few sips of it, but no more than that."

"Mommy make good coffee."

"I'll be glad for some, believe me."

"I don't know, but people say it be good."

"It has to be better than that stuff on the plane!"

Raylyn pulled onto her driveway and Roger looked at the house. From the road the house didn't look big, especially since the garage was attached. There was beige vinyl siding and black shutters beside the front windows and a small porch that went across what he assumed was the front of the house. There was a picture window on one side of the door and a regular window on the other, then on the side of the house was another window before the one car garage started. It did look comfortable and Roger could see the remains of a flowerbed on either side of the walk. Of course he saw the lights twinkling on the bushes. Raylyn pulled up to the garage door, put the stick in park and reached for her door handle.

Roger scowled and asked, "What are you doing?"

"I have to raise the garage door."

"You don't have a garage door opener?" when Raylyn shook her head, he asked, "Is it unlocked, can I go open it for you?"

"Yes, it's unlocked, just turn the handle and pull up."

"Okay, it's as good as done!"

He quickly opened his door and stepped out, slamming his door behind him. Raylyn watched him as he made his way to the handle of her garage door. She hadn't forgotten, but she watched the handsome man move confidently away from the car. Her heart flipped over as she watched. He'd asked her to marry him! He said they could work it out somehow. Would he give up his church to come live here or did he expect her to give up her job without any prospect of a job there? Did he make enough salary at a community church to support them? She didn't know any of the answers at this point. She sighed, right now, she must be patient, God had it all taken care of already everything would work out.

Roger turned the handle and gave the door a hefty pull. It started up then he gave another push under the bottom edge which sent it the rest of the way. As soon as she could clear it, she drove the car inside. Roger waited inside until the car was in place, then as she put the stick in park, he pulled the door and it started down, groaning and grumbling. It reached the ground, as Roger opened Heidi's door and Raylyn's for them. Raylyn popped the trunk lid and stepped out while Roger went to retrieve his luggage. Heidi, of course, didn't need help getting out of her seatbelt, so she was out of her seat in a flash, even before the belt retracted completely and headed for the door into the kitchen before Roger had his backpack slung over his shoulder.

"Come on, Mr. Roger, I show you the room you have."

"I'll be along in a minute, Munchkin."

With a grin, she leaned back and said, "Mr. Roger, I aren't no munchkin! I be Heidi! I don't even know what a munchkin is!"

"Well, I'll be, so you are!"

She disappeared through the doorway, expecting Roger to follow, but Raylyn stood beside the trunk and waited for him to pull out his suitcase. When he had it out, even before he pulled up the handle, he leaned forward and planted a kiss on Raylyn's lips, glad to be in the same building as she was, even if it was only for two days. Realizing again she had this house to get rid of if his desires were to come true.

As he pushed the trunk lid down, he looked at her and said, "Love, you can't know how glad I am to be with you again."

"Mmm, well, I think I know a little about it myself. These past days have crept by."

"I can't say they've crept by for me, there've been some interesting happenings since you left, but I've been very lonely, especially when I was home alone. That big house.....Curly and Linus don't provide much companionship, when they're both outside animals. So is there any hope for us, Sweetheart?" he asked and pulled up the handle on his suitcase.

She voiced what her heart felt, when she said, "I hope so!"

He pulled her close with one hand and said, "Me too, Love."

He put his free hand on her back then walked with her to the back door that Heidi had left open. Two steps and they were in the cheery kitchen. Raylyn sighed and closed the door behind Roger. "Heidi is good at leaving doors open, thinking you're right on her heels. She forgets that most people don't move in overdrive most of the time."

Roger chuckled. "I understand."

Heidi stood in the archway between the kitchen and the living room and said, "Mr. Roger, you be so long! Come on, I show you the room, so Mommy can make you guys coffee and me some hot choclate."

Roger dropped his hand from Raylyn and said, "Okay, fearless leader, lead the way."

Heidi giggled. "Mr. Roger, you be funny!"

Seeing the pack slung over Roger's shoulder, she asked, "What be in your backpack?"

"I brought some things for some people in it," he said, mysteriously.

"Can I see?"

"Uh uh, not yet."

Heidi sighed, "Mommy say that a lot at Christmas."

THIRTEEN

Heidi took Roger to a small room that appeared to be an office, a small desk had a state-of-the-art computer set up on it, but she skipped around the desk and stood beside a loveseat that sat against the back wall and said, "This be our spare bed. Mommy know how it open, I forgot."

"We'll let her show us after a while. After all, it's morning and there's plenty of daytime left to do stuff before we go to bed. Where's your room?"

"It be next, in the corner, I gots two windows in mine, this only gots one. Sometime, Mommy do work in here and I falls asleep on this seat."

Smiling at the pretty little girl, that he would love to call his daughter, he asked, "So is Dollie in your room now and all your books?"

"Oh, yes, Dollie not want to get cold. I lef her home when we comed for you. Gamaw's book be on the couch. My others be in my room. Mommy don't let me bring so many out. She say it look messy."

"Ah, I understand. I guess she wants all your toys in one place." Roger could smell the rich aroma of brewing coffee coming down the hall from the kitchen. Appreciatively, he raised his nose and sniffed. He took his hand from his suitcase and said, "Mmm, smells like Mommy has that coffee just about ready. Shall we go see if your hot chocolate's ready, too?"

"Yup, I get Dollie first."

"Okay, I'm heading back, Munchkin."

Roger left his suitcase, but lifted the strap of his backpack and left the little room. He followed his nose back to the kitchen and Raylyn had three mugs sitting beside the stove. However, on the table were spoons on three placemats, a matching cream and sugar set in the center of the table and a large plate full of homemade Christmas cookies that looked good enough to make Roger's mouth water. Never mind that he'd had breakfast – a Danish on the plane – but coffee and cookies would hit the spot.

Roger walked immediately to Raylyn's side and wrapped his arm around her waist. She smiled up at him and said, "I guess you can figure out where you'll sit, since Heidi's chair has her booster seat in it."

"Gotcha!" Instead of sitting down, he kissed her, then placed his backpack on the counter and opened it. "I brought you something from the farm, Love. Do you like fresh eggs?"

"You mean brown eggs?"

"Yup. Here's two dozen that I collected over the last few days."

"Oh, super!" As he pulled them from his pack, she said, "You brought them in that backpack on the plane? Weren't you afraid they'd break?"

"My backpack went with me every step. I didn't trust another soul with handling it, so I know all the eggs are whole." He set the cartons on the counter and then said, "I brought Heidi's Christmas present, when should I give it to her?"

Raylyn whispered, "If it's books, you'd better save it for after supper, she'll want you to read everything all the way through as soon as she opens it. Surely you remember how she is with her books!"

Roger grinned and zipped his backpack closed again. He set it beside the chair that was his and said, "We'll wait, then."

Nodding, she said, "That's probably wise."

She set a child's mug in front of the chair with the booster seat, then brought the two coffee mugs to the table and slid into her seat; pushing Roger's the few inches to his place. He laid his hand on her shoulder and squeezed it, then leaned over and grabbed a cookie from the plate and popped it into his mouth, then put his hand over hers before she could pull it back.

As he settled into his chair, he said, "I have something I need to purchase here, when's a good time to go find a mall, Love?"

She shrugged. "We could go any time you want, Honey. I haven't made any plans that are cast in stone."

"There's no Isabel to care for Heidi either evening, is there."

"No, not even my mom. You did meet her, she called to tell me."

"Yes, we met at Sandy's concert, they all came together. She's a very nice lady, takes after her daughter a little."

Raylyn giggled. "Not hardly!" She looked at Roger's backpack and asked, "So what else is in your bag of tricks?"

Reaching in, he pulled out the paper and said, "When I went to Blairsville for Heidi's present, I saw this article. I didn't know if you'd be interested in working for a medical group or if it must be a hospital setting." He sighed and said, "It doesn't appear that I can leave Vansville at all. I got a substantial raise yesterday and also a very nice Christmas present from the church. The church attendance is up and getting better each Sunday." His voice took on an awed sound, as he continued, "Only God could have done what's happened in that town. It's truly amazing!"

Eyes sparkling, Raylyn took the paper and started reading the article about the need for a financial counselor for a doctors group immediately. She read a few lines, then looked at the date and looked up at Roger. She asked, "Is this position still open? This was last week."

"I called on Saturday and they said it was. They gave me a website address to get in touch with them quickly."

"Yes, let's do that!" She raised her voice because Heidi hadn't appeared in the kitchen yet. "Heidi, are you coming for your hot chocolate?"

"Mommy, Dollie gots wet pants, so I had to change her," she said from the archway. Clutching the doll, she went to her chair and climbed up.

Looking at her child sternly, she said, "One cookie, Sweety. It'll be lunch time before you know it. This is only a snack."

"Yes, Mommy, I know. I only take one."

Heidi leaned over the table as far as she could to inspect the cookies. However, only moments later, she kneeled in her booster seat then pulled the plate closer to look at them all. Roger had a huge grin on his face as he watched her, but he didn't laugh or say anything and neither did Raylyn. Finally, she picked out one of the largest cookies that she thought had the most icing and sprinkles on it. Roger expected her to take a big bite instead, she nibbled off an elbow from the angel. It took her a long time to eat her cookie and drink her hot chocolate.

When Heidi had finished her cookie and hot chocolate, she said, "I go play?"

"Yes, that's fine. Mr. Roger and I need to use my computer for a few minutes."

"'K. Dollie and me read a book," she said and scampered off to the living room.

Raylyn led Roger back down the hall to the middle room. As they entered the little room where Roger's suitcase was, he said, "I was told you'd have to show me how to open this loveseat. The helpful little person said she forgot how." He grinned. "I told her it was no big deal I wasn't planning on sleeping just yet, so it could wait."

"It's not hard. Of course, you take off the cushions, then put your hand down between the back and the seat and pull up. It unfolds two times and opens out into a three quarter size bed. It doesn't fold well made up, so I'll have to get the sheets and blankets after a bit." Looking him up and down, she chuckled and said, "You may be a little cramped, but Heidi's bed is only a single and way too frilly for you."

"Thanks, Love, I'm sure this'll be fine. When we grew up I was so glad I didn't have to share a room with my older sister. Talk about frilly!" He rolled his eyes. "You have no idea and it didn't get better as she got older, either. The dolls gave way to posters of the most current male star of the day and I mean that sincerely, the posters could change almost daily. It was a room I stayed as far from as I could."

Raylyn laughed. "My room wasn't too bad. Since Dad was a cop, it was mostly the young, good looking ones that played on the cop programs on TV. I did have a fancy doll collection that went by the boards when I went to college."

After booting up her machine, she logged on to the internet and typed in the address that Roger gave her. Soon the name of the medical group came on the screen and pictures of four men appeared. Roger put his hands on her shoulders then watched as the names of the four men appeared and said, "Hmm, I wonder if you can speak the language. Look at those names! I thought people with those kinds of names only worked in big cities." He shook his head. "You'll even have trouble calling them by a first name!"

"Probably they all trained here in the states. They probably all speak English, with an accent." She chuckled. "At the teaching hospital where I trained there was a doctor with a last name about a mile long. He had a thick accent. I was leaving a patient's room after talking about her finances, when he walked in with a pair of latex gloves and some lubricating jelly. He wanted to do a pre-op exam and as he looked at the woman, he said, 'Meesus, Boolgar, I have glubs and grrrape jaellee here. I do eekxam now beeforre youur suugeary tomorrow.'"

Roger chuckled. "He knew it was grape?"

"I don't know, I left."

Raylyn scanned the entire web page, then went back and clicked on a page specifically about the opening they had. She placed her name, address, E-mail address and phone number in the appropriate slots and sent off the information. She sighed, "I guess we might as well go to the mall, I doubt they'd answer for a while."

As she closed out the internet, leaving the machine running, Roger took her hand and asked, "What about your house, Sweetheart, your job here, your aunt you said lives here, your mom who lives close?"

"Some guy came to my door a week ago and gave me a flyer that said his church was looking for temporary housing for an interim pastor. I sent some information about my house to the address on the flyer. I haven't heard from the church, but if I could rent it for a while until spring when the market's better, it would be good. My job? Well, I got a compliment the other day from my boss, but I can give two weeks notice without any qualms on Wednesday."

"Two weeks is long enough?"

"That's all my job description asks for."

Roger bent over and kissed her. "That would be awesome, Sweetheart! I was afraid it would be much harder than that."

She shrugged and said, "My aunt is so senile she just smiles and is happy to see anyone, but knows no one. Heidi and I'll probably go see her and take her maybe a tiny box of chocolates for Christmas, but I sure don't feel tied here because of her. Mom's… I don't know we had a long talk when I first came back. She called me and we talked, but she was still stuck on Daddy's death, as I told you, but I told her about my long talk with Grandma Isabel and she listened. I told her Grandma missed her, so that's why she went down. She told me when she called last night that she wants to visit down there more often. If we move there, I guarantee she'll visit more often, she's told me several times that she wants to see Heidi grow and be a part of her life."

"So that's pretty much it?"

Raylyn nodded. "Dan's parents send Heidi money for her birthday and Christmas, but all they expect is a picture once in a while and a thank you for the money. I tried to keep in touch for a while after Dan died, but it seems I foster bad memories for them. They made excuses about coming to anything I asked them to and we're never invited there since he was deployed."

"That's sad!"

"Yes, Heidi missed them for a while, but she hasn't said anything lately, just looked at her birthday card and put it down. Money means nothing, so she handed it to me. I expect a check in the mail this week to spend on her, then when I write I tell them what the present was."

As she finished speaking her computer came alive and notified her that she had a new E-mail message. She clicked on the I-con and the machine automatically began the steps to get on the web. Only minutes later the voice through the machine said, "You've got mail!" Both Raylyn and Roger watched as Raylyn clicked on the mailbox.

The mail was from the doctor's group in Blairsville and Raylyn exclaimed, "Wow! They're writing back already!"

Free Saturdays

There was a list of things Raylyn needed to submit as well as questions they wanted her to answer. As soon as she printed the list, she started answering the questions. About a half hour later she sent her answers back, including where they could get information about her current job. There were still some things she must fax to them, but she had answered their questions.

She looked up from the computer screen and saw Roger hanging a suit in the closet. He caught her eye and said, "I hope you didn't mind my hanging this in the closet. It's my only suit and Mom'll want me to wear it for church. I just happened to think about it and didn't want it to be too wrinkled when I need it."

"Honey, I know Heidi wouldn't have told you, but while you're here, this room is yours. Feel free to use anything in here. I'm sorry I can't move the computer out so you can feel more comfortable. This thing takes up a lot of room."

He came to her and bent over to kiss her. "Sweetheart, I am comfortable, I'm with you and that's perfectly wonderful!"

"Great! Shall we round up Heidi and go to the mall now?"

"That'll be perfect. We'll do the shopping I have in mind then get some lunch at the food court, if that's okay."

"Oh, sure."

This time, Raylyn shut down the computer and as the screen was turning black, Heidi came to the door and asked, "Is we gonna do sompin?"

"Yes, Sweety, we're going to the mall so put your dollie in your room. You don't want to leave her at the mall."

"'K. Mr. Roger go too?"

"Yes, it's his idea."

"Super!" Heidi's grin stretched from ear to ear, as she clapped her hands and ran. Roger was surprised to see Heidi holding her dollie by one leg.

As Raylyn stood up from the desk chair, she sighed and said, "She loves to go to the mall. Believe me she can do more window shopping than you can believe. Wow! I forgot, Santa is there, I'm sure she'll want to talk to him."

Grinning as they went through the doorway, Roger looked down at her, his eyes twinkling and asked, "What'll she ask for?"

"She already sent him a letter. She wrote it herself, so you can imagine what it looked like, but I had to address the envelope, put a stamp on it and put it out for the mailman. She told me what she'd asked him for."

"And that was?" Roger prompted.

"A daddy for Christmas," Raylyn murmured.

In all seriousness, he pulled her tightly to his side and said, "Darling, it's fine with me, the sooner the better."

Before Raylyn could figure out what to say, Heidi was beside them and said, "You guys be so slow! Come on, we long time."

"Heidi, get your coat and mittens on now!" Raylyn said, glad for the reprieve.

Roger helped Raylyn and Heidi both into the car, then raised the garage door so Raylyn could back out. The wind was brisk and as he waited for Raylyn to back out, it whipped through his jacket and he shivered. He wondered what he would do when he arrived in Montana, he wouldn't have a lady to snuggle close to his side. He quickly pulled the garage door down, then climbed into the passenger seat and slammed the door.

Raylyn went a different way to the mall than the return from the airport. Roger realized that he was used to the village of Vansville, with its one grocery store, one gas station, one post office and one church. Blairsville wasn't that far away, but it was probably much farther than what Raylyn traveled to her work here in Grand Rapids. She'd said she was willing to move, but roads could get icy and sometimes they could be really hazardous early in the morning. He gave an inner sigh, '*In all things God works for the good of those who love him.*' (Rom. 8:28)

Raylyn pulled onto the parking area for the mall from the street, but continued on around the building, going by several entrances. As she finally pulled into a space, she said, "I don't know what you need, but I usually park close to this entrance because there's a Christian bookstore with a play place where Heidi loves to go. It has an attendant that the store employs for that area, so people can leave their kids there and go shop. Unless you need her?"

His eyes sparkling so much that Raylyn was sure she'd lose herself in them, Roger said, "At least for a little while, that'd be great!"

Before Roger finished speaking, they heard Heidi's seatbelt click and she said, "We be here! Come on, Mommy, Mr. Roger, we get out!"

"Yes, Heidi, we'll let you play at Murphy's for a while. Remember, stay with us, no running ahead. This time of year there are so many cars, it'd be easy for someone to miss you."

"I hold Mr. Roger's hand."

"Okay, Munchkin, but you wait until I come over there to open your door."

Heidi sighed, "'K, Mr. Roger but you forgot already. I not Munchkin, I Heidi."

Roger snapped his fingers. "Did I forget that already? Well, Heidi it is."

Roger hurried around the car, opened Raylyn's door then reached back for Heidi's. Both of them stepped from the car, but Roger's hand was there for Heidi and his arm snagged Raylyn before she could step away from her door to close it. As soon as the car was locked and they were walking as their unit, they hurried toward the door into the mall. The wind blew across the wide open area and stirred up some loose papers. There was music in the air. Christmas music was playing from speakers mounted on the walls of the building.

Heidi skipped beside Roger, her hand securely held in his. With both hands holding these two precious ladies, he wondered for the first time what his mom would have to say. She'd been suggesting in recent letters and phone calls that he wasn't getting any younger and didn't he think it was about time he found a nice young lady and deliver some grandchildren. Of course, he'd agreed with her, but only at Thanksgiving had things seemed to become favorable. He wasn't sure what her reaction would be to a grandchild as part of the package.

He realized Raylyn hadn't answered him about Heidi's wish for a daddy for Christmas. Yes, the day was only six days away, she had to give two weeks notice at work and he'd planned to leave for Montana on Wednesday. Any girl wanted her mom at her wedding and Raylyn's was in Georgia. There were a few complications to having Heidi a daddy for Christmas. But she had offered her house to sublet and she had submitted information for a job in Georgia.

They pushed open the doors and at once the warmer air from the mall enfolded them. They looked through the next set of doors and saw streams of people walking around. "Just what we get for coming to the mall only days before Christmas!" Roger exclaimed, as he pushed open the second door for Raylyn and Heidi to go in.

"That's the truth!" Raylyn exclaimed.

Raylyn looked down at Heidi, who for the moment, stood between them and said, "Sweety, you must stay with us until we get inside Murphy's. After we get over there, you must stay in the play area until we come back for you. It's too crowded to do anything else, so don't even ask whichever lady is there."

Heidi sighed, "I know, Mommy, I not ask."

Roger holding both ladies, they soon made it across all the waves of shoppers and into the much more quiet Murphy's. Heidi pulled on Roger's hand anxious to reach the play place, but Roger looked at some of the racks as they went by and said, "Hmm, I'd like to look around here for a bit. This is a much bigger store than the Christian bookstore in Blairsville."

"Sure! It's fine, we came for you, you know," Raylyn said.

Roger smiled and looked into the happy face of the lady beside him. "I think we'll do that after I make the purchase I have in mind. Heidi, is this where you're supposed to go?"

"Yes, Mr. Roger." She grinned at him and clapped her hands, "Oh, Ms. Allison be here, she be my favorite."

Raylyn chuckled as Heidi let go of Roger's hand and ran to the lady sitting at the desk. "I don't know one lady who works in this play area who isn't Heidi's favorite. They're all super nice ladies and this place can keep a child entertained for hours."

"Great! Let's get on our way, Love!"

They left the store and she looked at him and asked, "Where did you want to go, Honey?"

"To a jewelers for your Christmas present, of course."

"Honey, really?"

He put a kiss on her smiling face and pulled her close. "Yes, really. Do you have one especially picked out?"

"No, but if it's okay, I'd like something with emeralds. I don't wear much jewelry, but two of my great aunts have given me their diamond rings. I've taken the rings off that Dan gave me, but that was a diamond, too. I love emeralds, but I never had one, would that be alright?"

The man looked down at the lovely lady and said, "Sweetheart, whatever is your heart's desire is what I want to get you."

In the middle of the stream of shoppers, Raylyn turned in front of Roger and slid her other arm around his waist. She stood on tiptoe and reached her lips to his. Pulling her tightly against him, he quickly matched his lips to hers and kissed her. "Honey, God has been so good in giving me you! I love you!"

Groaning, Roger said, "Darling, I love you so much!"

People jostled them all around, but for a few seconds, they didn't notice. Finally, one older lady made sure they knew she was beside them. She bumped into Raylyn, almost unbalancing her against Roger. When she knew she had their attention, she grumbled, "What is wrong with this younger generation, for goodness sake? They can't even keep their show of affection out of the public eye."

Still holding Raylyn against him, Roger said, "Yes, well, it's Christmas and I've been gone for some time."

"Sonny, Christmas or no, that kind of behavior belongs in the parlor."

Raylyn pulled away then turned to walk beside him again. Looking at the older woman, she said, "My man's getting me an engagement ring for Christmas! Don't you think that's a good enough reason to leave the parlor for a trip to the mall?"

Disgusted, the old lady said, "Not so much that you can't stick a piece of paper between the two of your bodies!"

Raylyn sighed and looked at the old lady's left hand, it had no rings on it. Nothing like an old spinster to spout her views and put a wet blanket on their happiness! "Thanks for your advice, Ma'am," Roger said, as they left the lady behind.

"Honey, it seems like a dream to have you here with me! Christmas is such a romantic time and here you are! The jewelers is down a few more stores, at least one of them is. I think there are at least four in this mall and I know that one of the department stores has a jewelry section that has lovely rings."

Roger began walking, happy to hold his love so close after so long and said, "Lead on, lovely lady, I'm right beside you."

Raylyn sighed, "It's great with your arm around me."

They found the first store and started looking in the windows. Inside were three couples and three salesmen, so the couple outside knew they had some time to look at the rings in the windows. They walked slowly from the edge of the window toward the doorway. There were many diamonds on display, but they didn't see one emerald ring. Raylyn looked up as one of the salesmen straightened up and looked out at them.

Raylyn saw him watching them and dropped her head. "Honey, let's go on to another store, please. I know that salesman; he's not my favorite person. He's tried to ask me for a date a couple of times and I'd rather not talk to him about an engagement ring, if it's okay with you."

"Sweetheart, of course! You shouldn't feel uncomfortable when you pick out your ring."

They walked on and found a much smaller jewelry store. There were a few diamond rings in the window, but there were also other rings on display, there were opals, rubies and even a few emeralds. As soon as Roger saw the variety, he steered her toward the entrance. There was a couple with a salesman, but another man came immediately to the counter as they entered.

"May I help you?" he asked.

Roger nodded. "My lady wants an emerald and we saw a few in your window. Could you give us a better look?"

"Sure! I even have some in the back." The man led them to a small table with two chairs and indicated that they should sit in them. He brought several rings from different places in the store, then said, "I'll go to the back and bring out several I have back there. Be right back!"

"Thanks," Roger said.

Raylyn looked at each ring. They were all beautiful, of course, but none of them reached out to grab her like the diamond that Dan had given her did. A few minutes later the salesman returned carrying a small tray and on it were several more rings nestled on a velvet cloth. Roger saw the one he liked the best immediately and picked it up.

As he turned it for Raylyn to see, he said, "What do you think of this one, Love?"

She gasped, "Yes! Yes, that's the one! It's beautiful!"

Smiling at the salesman, Roger said, "I guess the lady's made her choice."

A big man, not just in height, but in girth sat in his huge office, behind his large oak desk and slammed down the receiver so hard it made the cradle vibrate. His cup of cold coffee sloshed a puddle on his papers. It was the third time he'd tried that number and each time after four rings the voicemail clicked in and had said, 'You have reached the voicemail box of financial counselor, Raylyn Keys. I'm sorry I'm not here right now, but leave your name and number and I'll get back with you as soon as I can.'

He swore colorfully as he pushed his chair back with enough force to put a dent in the wall. Rounding his desk, he stormed from his office and down the hall into another part of the executive suite to another group of offices, to the office of the head of financial services. He barged in without knocking, looked ominously at Maxine and said, "Come here!" The man turned on his heal, stomped out of her office, expecting her to follow and stomped furiously to a closed door a few doors down and across the hall. Scowling, the man turned to her, pointed to the door and demanded, "Why is this door closed?"

Knowing that she had done nothing wrong giving Raylyn off, Maxine said, in her most reasonable voice, "Chet, Raylyn asked for these two days off because she has out-of-town company here today and tomorrow."

The big, imposing man turned from the door, took a step and faced Maxine directly, then rammed his fists on his overly padded hips and getting right in her face, bellowed, "Didn't you give her off an extra day and a half over Thanksgiving? Why'd you give her off again so soon? This is a business we run here, not a... a resort! Woman, this place needs that woman here and I mean here, NOW!"

The lady knew how to stand up to the man, so she said, "Chet, she was going a long ways over Thanksgiving, so I gave her extra time. She had everything caught up the very day she was back. She's always very conscientious and I've always been pleased with her work. The other day she asked for vacation days for today and tomorrow. She'll have her work all caught up and any work that comes in these two days, she'll have finished on Wednesday. I guarantee it!"

The man's face was red and he was wheezing, but he grumbled something under his breath that Maxine couldn't understand - maybe she didn't want to understand. His eyes became slits and he kept one hand fisted on his hip, but he shook his finger in her face and said, "I don't care, she's the boss of the three financial counselors and she should be here whenever they're here! You call her and get her in here tomorrow, no, better yet, this afternoon, I won't have this place short staffed!"

Maxine took a long breath and blew it out slowly, before she felt she could say anything in a normal voice. With her own eyes looking like steel, she looked first at the man's finger crowding her space, then up to his eyes and said, "Chet, I will *not* call her to get her in here now. She asked for two days off, I gave them to her. She's planning not to take any extra days off for Christmas or New Year's, so she deserves this time off. You know we always give every employee an extra day or two at this time of year. Besides, don't you take time off when you have out-of-town friends come?"

Narrowing his eyes at his subordinate, he said, "I'm the Administrator!"

"Chet, I'm well aware of that! What is really the problem?"

"Nothing," he grumbled, he wasn't about to tell her his real reason. "Just have her here!"

"No, Chet, I won't!"

"Then fire her!"

Shaking her head, Maxine said, "I won't do that, either! Especially over Christmas we don't have to have full staff. The hospital's never to capacity this time of year, you know and I give each one of the counselors time off over the holidays, they know that and so do you."

Bending over, putting his face right into Maxine's, the man roared, "When she waltzes in here on Wednesday I'll be waiting with her pink slip!"

Glaring at the man, Maxine stood her ground and didn't back up. She wanted to take his beefy finger and twist, but didn't move. The man was an incompetent oaf, she wished she knew how to get rid of him. Instead she put her hands on her hips, narrowed her eyes to barely slits and drew herself up to her tallest height and said, "Oh, Chet, that's just peachy!" sarcasm dripping from her voice. "You'd fire her three days before Christmas. She's the best we've ever had in this department, but you'd fire a widow, a single mom, with no family here in Grand Rapids and three days before Christmas you'll hand her a pink slip without warning and for no good reason, am I reading it right?"

"Yes!" he hissed. "Be advised, your job's in jeopardy too!"

"What, cut off your nose to spite your face, Chet? That's exactly the way to handle your own frustrations, of course." Before she said anything else, Maxine spun on her heel, held her head high and marched to her own office and shut the door firmly. She would not grace the man with another word.

Still more than angry, Chet blew out his breath and stormed back to his office.

On the way home from the mall, Heidi was noticeably quiet. She sat buckled in, her hands still in her lap and she stared out the window at the barren trees. Roger sat in the passenger seat, his hand resting on the back of Raylyn's seat, playing with a curl close to his hand. He loved the feel of Raylyn's hair it felt like silk as it slid through his fingers. After several minutes of quietness from the back seat, Roger glanced back and noticed how solemn she was. Since he knew her well enough, he wondered what she was unhappy about, since she'd played at her favorite place for well over an hour, he couldn't imagine the problem.

"What's going on, Munchkin?" he asked.

"Nuthin," Heidi grumbled. "I not munchkin!"

"I think there is something. What's up?" he insisted.

Heidi's shoulders heaved, as she took in, then let out a big sigh. She finally looked at him and said, "Mr. Roger, you gived Mommy her Christmas present already!"

"Ah, I get it!"

"Get what?" Heidi grumbled.

Chuckling, Roger said, "Munchkin, I needed your mommy's finger to buy her present. I didn't need yours."

Brightening a little, Heidi said, "Did you get me one?"

Purposely misunderstanding, Roger said, "What, a finger? No I didn't get you a finger, you don't need another one. Four fingers and a thumb on each hand is plenty, you know. You think I should have?"

Completely ignoring Roger's talk about fingers, Heidi, said, "Mr. Roger, it be Christmas! Big people alays give children presents."

"Are you serious? They do?"

With another big sigh, Heidi said, "Of course!"

"Oh, wow!" was all Roger said. Heidi gave another big sigh and looked back out the window at the scenery she saw every day.

Raylyn was quiet, too and she was driving two handed. Her left hand was on the steering wheel in a way that she could take a quick glance away from traffic to look at the beautiful ring that sat on her left ring finger. That ring and what it meant, only a month ago were inconceivable to her mind. Today they were a reality. After looking at her ring several times, she left that hand on the wheel, but put her right hand down on the gear stick between the two seats. Only seconds later, Roger's hand left her curl and covered her hand with his much larger one. Only a few seconds later, they twined their fingers together and let them hang down between the bucket seats. Having him touch her always sent her heart into flutters.

When they reached the house, Roger jumped out to open the garage door so that Raylyn could drive in. As soon as she cleared the door, he pulled it back down the wind was cold and penetrating. As he'd done before, he opened their doors and they all went inside together. When they were all inside, with their coats hung up, Heidi took Roger's hand and led him into the living room. Raylyn followed them closely, but Heidi said, "Mommy, come light the lights. It be dark soon. Asides, it be Christmas an' I saw lots and lots a lights on people's houses when we come from the mall."

Moving around the pair, Raylyn laughed and said, "Heidi, it's only a couple of hours after lunch, it won't be dark for a while yet, but since it's so close to Christmas and Roger's here, I'll turn on the lights. We can enjoy them the rest of the day, I can't think of a reason to go back out today anyway."

Heidi spun around the room, watching as Raylyn turned on the tree lights first the tiny lights wound into the greenery on the mantel that made it sparkle and also through the nativity scene nestled among the evergreen bows. Last of all she lighted the candle lights in the windows. Heidi's grin grew as each group of lights came on and her blue eyes sparkled, of course, she clapped her hands. Finally, she said, "Mr. Roger, Mommy and me gots you sompin for Christmas."

"Really, you did?"

Nodding vigorously and jumping up and down in her excitement, she exclaimed, "Uh huh. We did, really!"

"Can I see it now?"

Solemnly shaking her head, Heidi said, "Not now, affer supper."

Looking at his watch, Roger said, "Oh, man, that's so long!"

Patting his hand, Heidi said, "It not long, Mr. Roger, it be soon. Mommy got stuff to do, could you read me and Dollie a story?"

Roger sighed, trying to imitate Heidi, "Well, I guess, since you won't let me have my Christmas present yet."

Giggling, Heidi said, "Mr. Roger, you big, you can wait lots better'n me. Sit there. I get Dollie and my book."

Roger sat in the big recliner as Heidi told him, but only moments later, Heidi was back holding Dollie in one arm and three books in the other hand. She put the books down next to Roger and laid her dollie on top of them, but then without any hesitation or an invitation, Heidi climbed up on Roger's lap and snuggled close to his chest. Loving the feel of the little body against his chest, Roger hugged her close, enjoying the clean scent of her baby shampoo then kissed the top of her head.

Only a minute later, Heidi leaned back a little and looked up into the man's face. "Mr. Roger, since you gived Mommy that ring, can I call you Daddy?"

Roger felt the love for this child swell in his chest and move into his throat. It clogged it completely it felt huge, like the rock of Gibraltar. He cleared his throat twice before anything came out. Even then it wasn't his normal voice, as he whispered, "Munchkin, I would be so happy for you to call me Daddy."

Throwing her arms around him and hugging him as tightly as she could, she whispered, back, "Oh, Daddy, I love you!" With Roger's arms around her, she pulled back again and called at the top of her lungs, "Mommy, come here!"

Raylyn had gone to the kitchen after turning on the Christmas lights. She would take advantage of Roger being here and let him entertain Heidi for a few minutes. She pulled a head of cauliflower from the crisper and started cutting it up for the salad she had in mind for their light supper. Of course, each time she could, she turned her hand and looked at the absolutely beautiful ring that sat on the third finger of her left hand. It made her heart beat heavily in her chest each time she thought about the man who had given it to her. She loved him so much and he'd asked her to marry him!

Heidi's call roused her from her thoughts. The knife clattered into the sink and the cauliflower she was cutting up for supper followed it with a thud. Her hands dripping and the water still running, Raylyn ran to the living room. Breathlessly, she asked, "What is it, Sweety?" Looking at Roger's face and seeing his expression, she wondered what had been going on since she'd left them alone in the living room.

"Mommy! I got my daddy for Christmas!"

Still looking from Heidi to Roger, she asked, "What do you mean?"

Hugging Roger tightly again, she said, "Mr. Roger say I call him Daddy now, 'cause you gots your ring!"

Raylyn came up beside the big chair and crouched down in front of Heidi. Taking her hand, she said, "Sweety, Mr. Roger gave me a beautiful ring this morning, but it wasn't a wedding." She held up her left hand so that she and Heidi could see it. "Sweety, this is an engagement ring, this is Mr. Roger's pledge to me and my pledge to him that we love each other and we will get married soon."

Earnestly, Heidi looked at her mommy and said, "But Mommy, I love Mr. Roger, can't we pretend so I can call him Daddy?"

"If Mr. Roger told you it was okay with him for you to call him Daddy now it's okay, but I wanted you to know we aren't married yet."

"I know, Mommy, I know."

Raylyn was crouched beside the big recliner when the phone rang. She scowled, then pushed against the floor to stand up and said, "Wonder who that could be?"

She hurried to answer and a man's voice she didn't know said, "Mrs. Keys?"

"Yes?" she said, tentatively.

"Ma'am, this is Art Lankaster, the pastor from the neighborhood church. I believe you sent us information about your house when we made inquiry about finding a place for an interim pastor who will be coming in February. Is that correct?"

Her heart started beating double time. Was this the first answer to their prayers? "Yes, I did, Reverend. Is your church interested in my house?"

"Yes, we are. Since you put your address on your letter, I took the liberty to drive by yesterday afternoon. How many bedrooms does it have?"

"There are three. One is much smaller than the others, but it can accommodate a single bed, a dresser and a desk comfortably. Would someone want to come see it this afternoon? I'll be here the rest of the day."

"Yes, that would be very good. How about in an hour?"

"That'll be fine. See you soon."

Roger was reading to Heidi in the living room, but Raylyn hurried back to them after she hung up. "Guess what?" she asked, excitedly.

Both Roger and Heidi looked up at her, but Heidi was the first to ask, "What, Mommy? Who called?"

"That was the pastor from that church. They're interested in renting our house for their interim pastor who's coming in February. Someone's coming in an hour to look the place over." Looking at Roger, she continued, "If they take it, that'll be one more thing to cross off the list. That'll be super!"

"It sure will, Sweetheart! That'll be great!"

Much to the adults' surprise, Heidi asked in a frightened voice, "But where do we live?"

"Munchkin," Roger said, "no one would move in here for over a month. That gives Mommy and me a lot of time to get married and then you both will come live with me in Georgia. What do you say? Wouldn't that work just fine for you?"

Her expression changed miraculously. She bounced on Roger's legs and clapped her hands. "Oh, that be super!"

Nodding, Roger said, "I thought so, too."

"So do I," Raylyn murmured.

It was almost an hour later when the doorbell rang. Raylyn had finished making her salad and it was cooling in the refrigerator. Roger was right behind Raylyn when she went to the door and let in five men. In front was a man with his hand out. "Hello, I'm Art Lankaster from the church a few blocks away. These are some of the deacons from my church. You must be Mrs. Keys. Is this Mr. Keys?"

Raylyn had her mouth open to answer, but Heidi's voice came out first. "Uh uh, this be my new daddy, Mr. Roger."

Roger took the man's hand and said, "No, I'm not Mr. Keys, I'm Roger Clemens, visiting for a few days. Raylyn and I are engaged. We're getting married soon and then Raylyn and Heidi are relocating to join me in my pastorate. Come in and look around."

"So will the house be available for an indefinite period of time?"

"Yes, as soon as we move," Raylyn confirmed.

Looking past them into the living room, the pastor said, "That would be good. We're wondering if six months will be long enough."

"Come look around," Raylyn said.

Twenty minutes later, Raylyn led everyone to her kitchen table and brought all her chairs to place around it so that they could all talk and work through any problems. About an hour later, the men followed their pastor out the front door with the promise that he would return in a little while with photocopies of all the papers they had written up and signed.

FOURTEEN

As things stood after their meeting, Raylyn and Heidi could live in the house until February first, but the church would take over paying the mortgage payments starting in January. Not only would the house become the home of the new interim pastor, but if the man worked out for the church, he would remain as the youth pastor and would need a home. The church would buy the house as a parsonage. The man was as good as his word he returned shortly with a large envelope and handed it to Raylyn at the door. Both Roger and Raylyn couldn't be happier.

After supper, Heidi took Roger's hand and also Raylyn's and pulled them into the living room, her face glowing with happiness. She did her backward hop and landed on the center cushion of the couch, before she said, "Daddy, Mommy and me gots you your Christmas present. It be under the Christmas tree!"

"Before I open it, I must get something from my carry-on bag."

Heidi sighed, "Well, hurry, Daddy!"

When Roger came back from his room, Heidi still sat on the couch, but she had a box in her lap. There was a space beside her then Raylyn sat next. Of course, Roger didn't hesitate he sat between them, holding his brightly wrapped package in one hand. "Here you go, Munchkin, here's your present!" he exclaimed.

"Daddy, why you call me Munchin?"

Roger tilted his head and looked at Heidi. "You just look like a Munchkin."

"I do not! I look like Heidi!"

"You don't think Heidi can look like a special Munchkin?"

Heidi sighed, "I suppose. Here, I got your present so you don't have to crawl on the floor to find it."

"Okay, but here's yours. Why don't you open it first, before I open mine?"

Her eyes sparkling, Heidi nearly pushed Roger's present onto the floor, as she grabbed his present and tore the paper immediately. Roger still had his hands out, but released Heidi's present quickly and grabbed the other one. "I loves presents!" Heidi exclaimed. Moments later she pulled out the top book. The other two were still in the wrapper and fell to her lap, but she hugged the first book to her chest. "Daddy! I wanted this book real bad for long time. You read it afore bed tonight!"

"But you didn't even look at the others, Heidi." Raylyn reminded her.

"That's okay. I do now." She took the other two books from the wrapping paper, but didn't make as much over them as she had the first one. Raylyn looked at the book title and realized it was one of the newer ones in a series she'd thought about getting.

After Heidi had looked at all three books, she put them behind her on the seat and looked up at Roger. "Daddy, it be your turn now."

Roger nodded then picked up the card that was secured under the ribbon around the present. He opened it first. It was a card like he'd never had before, Heidi had drawn a lopsided Christmas tree on the front, but inside she had drawn a blond daddy a shorter red headed mommy and a child with red hair and curls. All three were inside a much deformed red heart, but Roger was sure he got the message. At that moment, he couldn't have said a word, if either Raylyn or Heidi had looked closely they'd have seen a tear in his eye. Life had really turned wonderful in only a few short weeks!

"I done that, Daddy. That be my present. Mommy's present be in the box."

"I think you got it just right! I know that's you and Mommy and me and we're right inside a heart. That's perfect!" Shaking the silent box, Roger scowled. "What's in here? I don't hear anything, maybe it's empty."

"Uh uh, Daddy, it not empty! Open it!" Heidi could hardly sit still, but her hands were clapping as she bounced on the cushion.

Roger pulled off the ribbon, released the tape holding the wrapping paper that covered the dress-shirt sized box and opened the lid. Inside was a bill hat with the words 'University of Michigan' on it in the school colors. However the scarf under it was the colors of Montana State University. Grinning, Roger said, "What's this hat thing? Can I wear it to the barn?"

"Daddy! That be from Mommy's school! It not a barn hat!"

Roger set the hat on Heidi's head and picked up the scarf. "But these colors are for my school. How can I wear both of them?" With a puzzled look on his face, he picked the hat from Heidi's head and held the scarf in the other hand.

"Daddy, you marry Mommy, she be one school, you be the other."

"Ah, I get it, clear as mud."

"Of course! Now you read my new book. Mommy gets hot choklate afore I goes to bed and we say my prayers."

"We'll do that, Miss Heidi, but first I must thank Mommy for the present."

Acting quite put-upon, Heidi sighed, "Daddy, you kiss Mommy lots!"

Roger set the box on the other side of Raylyn, but as he did, his arms came around her and he pulled her tightly to him. He looked into her sparkling eyes before he matched his lips to hers and they savored a kiss. "Thanks, Love," he whispered.

After their kiss, she said, giggling, "You don't mind the hat?"

"Why, of course not! I needed a new one to wear to the barn."

Heidi exclaimed, "Daddy!" while Raylyn's sound came out, "Humph!"

Heidi's eyes finally went closed on a very happy, exciting day and Roger took Raylyn back to the living room. Instead of the couch, he took her back to the big recliner. He sat down and pulled her onto his lap. When he had her where he wanted her, he matched his lips to hers and gave her a super kiss. When he finally pulled his lips away, he picked up her left hand and rubbed across the new ring. After kissing her hand, he said, "Love, when can we have the ceremony and put the two other rings on the fingers where they belong?"

"I've been wondering that all day, Honey."

"Let's see. Your house is taken care of. On Wednesday you'll hand in your two weeks notice. We can hope that the doctors group will write back tomorrow and offer you the job. Your mom should be back after New Year's, but Isabel is in Georgia. How do we work that? She should be at the wedding, too."

Not hesitating an instant, Raylyn answered, "All that's true, Honey. I have vacation time built up so that after New Year's I could take vacation days and not have to go back in at all. I can call Mom and tell her to stay down there and also ask Sandy when they come back to play the wedding music for us. I could stay in one of Grandma Isabel's cabins for a few days until the next Saturday. What do you think?"

Scowling, Roger said, "You don't want to get married here in your home church? You want to get married in my church? But who would we get to do that?" He chuckled. "I'm not about to perform my own wedding!"

She put her hands on Roger's cheeks, then after looking in each other's eyes for several seconds, she leaned in and kissed him. "Honey, I want Sandy to play for our wedding. I don't have feelings for anyone 'specially in this church. I don't want Grandma Isabel to make the long trip, but I want her at my wedding. Now, you find a good minister to marry us and we're set."

He snuggled her tightly to his chest and captured her lips again. Sometime later, after a very long kiss, Roger pulled his lips away from hers and in a very ragged voice, said, "As you wish, Darling. As you wish."

After another kiss, Roger looked around the living room, noting there were some things he'd want to keep if this was his home, so he said, "I guess it's a good thing that church wants to buy the house furnished, but surely there are some things you'll want to bring along with you to Georgia, aren't there? Surely, some things here have sentimental value? Actually, I can see a few things I'd want to keep."

Also looking around and of course, seeing the things she couldn't part with, she said, "There are a few things, but really not many. I'll bring Heidi's furniture and a few things I feel attached to, but there's nothing much that I can't fit into a small pull-behind trailer. Of course we'd have the trunk of my car, I'm glad they wanted the house furnished! Where in the world would we have put all my furniture in your house? I didn't see much of it, but you surely have it mostly furnished, don't you?"

"I don't have much in the two bedrooms. Heidi's furniture would go in that smaller corner room. If you'd want to bring what's in the room I'm sleeping in, we could put those things in my little bedroom. I have a family room downstairs that's somewhat furnished, but we can work on that together."

Raylyn scowled. "Wait, I just thought of something, Honey! You're going to be in Montana until the day before New Year's. If we get married the next Saturday who would be available on such short notice?"

He shrugged. "Tomorrow when you call your mom and tell her to stay there ask Isabel to ask her pastor if he'll do the honors." She impulsively put her hands on Roger's cheeks.

Before she touched her lips to his, she exclaimed, "Yes! Yes!"

The chime clock on the wall started the Westminster chime and Raylyn looked at the clock. She snuggled into Roger's arms, but she said, "Since Heidi gets up at dawn, maybe we'd better get to bed, Honey."

"Yup, you're right. This day started pretty early."

All good things come to an end and Wednesday morning, Roger had to be at the airport by seven thirty to board his flight for Billings that left at eight thirty. Of course, airport regulations were that anyone bringing passengers to the airport could only go to a certain point. No one could go as far as the boarding area, so Roger checked his suitcase at the ticket counter, received his boarding pass and stuffed it in his pocket.

He slung his backpack over his shoulder, then took Heidi's hand and put his arm around Raylyn and the three of them went down the concourse. There were shops lining the wide concourse and only a few doors down, on one side was a coffee shop sending out inviting aromas and neither Roger nor Raylyn was immune. Without even asking, Roger veered his little family inside, since all they'd had at home was coffee. They found an empty table and soon had made their orders for breakfast.

As soon as they finished eating, they left and walked on to the area where passengers were checked through. Before he went through the sensor, Roger dropped his carry-on bag and turned to the two people he loved the most in all the world. Heidi hugged his leg, but he took Raylyn in his arms and kissed her. He groaned as she eagerly accepted his kiss and slid her arms around him to hug him tightly.

Into her hair, he murmured, "Darling, I love you so much. I wish I could be taking you along with me! What I'll have to do is make sure they all come down for the wedding. I'm sure that'll be the first they'll know my lovely Raylyn."

Raylyn could hardly speak. Her throat was clogged and her eyes glistened with tears she didn't want to shed. She nodded, but the voice over the wall speakers announced Roger's plane. She snuggled into his arms and pressed her cheek against his chest, holding him as tightly as she could. She felt him place a kiss on her head.

Roger felt a tug on his leg, so he took one hand from Raylyn's back and reached down for Heidi. He held her close and kissed her on the cheek, but as soon as he had, she gave him one of her trademark kisses then rubbed it into his cheek. "Daddy, you be good for your mommy, like I be good for Mommy."

"Okay, it's a deal, Munchkin."

He turned his head and kissed Raylyn on the lips, then whispered, "I must go, Love." Loud enough for both Raylyn and Heidi, he added, "Have a great Christmas. I'll see you soon."

"Have a safe trip, Honey," Raylyn whispered, no louder sound came from her mouth, as he pulled away from them.

"I'll try, Love."

Roger put his carry-on on the belt and walked through the detector. Nothing went off, so he picked up his bag, waved at the two still standing where he'd left them, then ran down the rest of the concourse toward his loading area. Before he turned toward the gate he looked back and waved at the two still standing where he'd left them. Right then, he was sure he could feel his heart rip from his chest and wing its way back to the two people who stood waving to him.

When he was out of sight, Raylyn took Heidi's hand and said, "Come on, Sweety, we must hurry. We only have a little time to get you to daycare and me to my office."

"'K, Mommy. I wish we could go wif Daddy."

"It won't happen this year, Sweety, but probably next year it will."

"'K, Mommy, I ready to go."

Roger boarded the plane, found his seat and stowed his carry-on bag over it, he didn't have to be so careful with it now, there were no eggs, then sat down in the aisle seat. He didn't buckle up, he knew that at this time of year, this close to Christmas the plane would probably be full and he'd have to let at least one other person into the seats beside him. Only minutes later, a mother and her daughter came up to him and looked expectantly at him, so he stood up to let them in. As he watched them scoot into the seats, he was glad that neither of them had red hair nor curls and the child was almost a teenager. He was glad he still had the memory of his two lovely ladies as they waved to him.

When they arrived at the airport the sun had been shining, not brightly, but still there was only a haze across the sky, but while they'd eaten breakfast and said their goodbyes, the clouds had become thicker and as Roger looked at them out the window, he realized they could very easily start sending down snow. He was glad he'd soon be above them, but he hoped when he arrived in Billings the airport would be open. They hadn't thought to look at any weather reports on the TV before they'd left the house.

The big plane taxied away from the terminal, then made several turns before it reached the runway where it was to take off. As they waited their turn, the pilot came on and said, "Folks, I need to inform you that you need to keep your seatbelts fastened until you hear an announcement otherwise. We will be going through cloud cover, but most of the way to Billings we will be flying above the clouds and there may be some turbulence. At this point, we are clear to land in Billings and we are expecting to make our destination on time."

The intercom went silent and the plane started moving. Soon the signs and lights began flashing by, the nose went up and the roar of the engines told Roger they were airborne. The girl next to the window was glued to it watching, but her mother and Roger both were also looking out at the bank of clouds as they went through. The clouds were thick, but finally they broke out into sunlight.

They flew for quite a while and Roger pulled out the magazine that was in the pocket on the chair in front of him, because mother and daughter beside him didn't seem eager to talk to him. They were self-contained in their own little world. The lady nearly turned her back to Roger and concentrated on her daughter. Roger didn't turn the pages very fast he was concentrating on the mental picture of his lovely fiancée and her child as he'd last seen them before boarding the plane. His foremost wish, he could have brought them with him.

The cloud cover was below them during the entire flight. When he was sure it was close to the time to descend, the pilot came on the intercom again and said, "Folks, we'll be descending through the clouds again. We've been informed by the airport in Billings that we still have a window for a good landing. To the west, over the Rockies, there's a storm brewing, but it hasn't started snowing in Billings as yet. We hope you've enjoyed your flight with us and we hope you don't have too far to go from here."

Roger was also glad of that, but he made sure his seatbelt was fastened and slid the magazine he hadn't read into the pocket. He turned to the woman beside him and asked, "Do you have family here in Billings?"

"I have a sister we're visiting for the holidays and you?"

"My folks should be meeting me."

When they touched down, Roger looked out the window and saw that the runways were the only things that weren't white. Obviously it had snowed recently and quite a lot because even the buildings had snow on them. The sky was overcast and hovering quite low. If the snow didn't start before they reached the ranch, he'd be surprised.

After the plane was secure, he stood up and retrieved his backpack, then headed down the aisle toward the door. The flight attendant smiled at the handsome man and said, "Thanks for flying with us, hope you have a fun holiday."

"Thanks, I'm looking forward to a wonderful Christmas with my family."

"Ah, good for you."

He left the plane and headed into the building. He looked around, getting his bearings, then headed for the signs to reach the luggage claim. He and his folks had decided they'd meet him when he picked up his suitcase. Soon, he found the escalator that had a sign pointing down to the luggage claim. It all reminded him of a few days ago in the city he'd just left.

As he reached the bottom, he heard a deep voice that started coming closer. "Roger Clemens, Roger, my boy!"

He looked up in time to catch his mother as she hurled herself into his arms. "Roger! It's so good to see you! Welcome home!"

He kissed her on the cheek and said, "Hi, Mom, it's good to see you and Dad."

The lady leaned back in her son's arms and asked, "Why didn't you come on Monday like you usually do?"

"I needed to stop off someplace else first."

Roger's dad saw his suitcase, so he grabbed it from the belt and asked, "Why? Where was this place you needed to go?"

Taking his mom's elbow and moving beside his dad, Roger grinned and light-heartedly said, "Mom, Dad, I've met a lovely lady. It was Thanksgiving Day when she was in Vansville visiting her grandmother. Her home is in Grand Rapids, so I went to visit for two days and we became engaged. I'm hoping you'll get plane tickets to join us for the happy occasion the first Saturday in January."

John Clemens chuckled. "You don't waste any time, do you?"

"I try not, Dad."

"It's about time," Mattie said. "After all, you aren't getting any younger and I've been hoping for some grandchildren for some time now. It doesn't seem like your sister is going to oblige me any time soon."

It seemed that at that moment no voices were blaring over the terminal-wide intercom and no backup beepers from luggage jitneys were going off, no mothers with disappearing small children were calling them, so Roger said, "Well, Mom, this lady that I've asked to marry me comes with a three and a half year old little girl."

Both of his parents stopped suddenly. Roger still had his mom's elbow, so when she stopped it swung him in front of her. "What did you say?"

"It's not noisy, Mom, I think you heard me."

She scowled at him and said, sternly, "Roger Clemens, we're a Christian family. You're a pastor of a church. I should hope you've remembered your roots and your upbringing. What do you mean this woman comes with a three and a half year old girl?"

Looking perplexed, Roger asked, "What do you mean?"

John looked at his wife, then at his son and said, in his booming voice, "Son, what your mother means is that we don't cotton to divorce and we certainly don't tolerate our son marrying a divorced woman!"

Roger let go of his mom's elbow and whirled around to look his dad in the eye. John was a big man, but Roger didn't have to look up to look into his eyes. Angry for Raylyn's sake, Roger spoke with force, "Dad, I never said she was divorced! She is not! Her husband was killed in Iraq two years ago. She is a fine lady, raising her child in the ways of the Lord. I have known her grandmother in Vansville ever since I moved there and she is an outstanding Christian lady."

Mattie slid her hand around Roger's elbow and said, "I'm sorry, Son, I'm sorry I assumed and spoke hastily."

"Thanks, Mom, I accept your apology." John didn't say anything even though it had been his voice everyone could hear. Did he really expect his dad to apologize? After all he was a big Swede, a life-long Montana rancher.

Swallowing, Roger said, "Thanks, Mom."

"Of course!"

They left the airport, going through the proper aisles to reach the short term parking area. When they came out in the open, Roger realized that his prediction was more than accurate, it was snowing already. Two rows away from the road that led out of the airport compound sat his parents' Jeep. John unlocked the hatch and he put in the suitcase, while Roger put in his backpack. Mattie climbed in the back seat before John closed the hatch. Roger didn't say anything, he'd expected as much.

The two men opened the front doors and Mattie asked, "So what's this lovely lady like, Son? I want to know all about her!"

"She's maybe a year or two younger than me, but she's been to college and is a financial counselor in a hospital in Grand Rapids. She's the most beautiful woman I've ever known with auburn curls around her face and a few freckles across her nose. She is probably watching herself grow up in her daughter, who also has auburn curls. The child is so happy that we became engaged she's already asked if she can call me 'Daddy.'"

"And their names are...?" Mattie prompted.

"Raylyn and Heidi Keys." Roger swallowed and then said, "I wish I could have brought them with me, but she has yet to hand in her two weeks notice. She's pretty sure she can take vacation days starting the first of the year so she can pack up and come down. She'll stay in a cabin her grandma owns until our wedding."

"So it'll be the week after you go back from here?"

"Yes, if all things work out. I'll need to use your phone, but I'll be glad to pay the bill."

"That's no problem, Son," his mom said.

John started up and backed out of the parking space, but all he would say was, "My, my! You met the girl on Thanksgiving Day and you're getting married the Saturday after New Year's. It must have been love at first sight."

"Pretty close, Dad, pretty close. She came to my church for the Thanksgiving service and I could hardly take my eyes off her, then she, her daughter and grandmother joined me at a mutual friend's house for dinner that afternoon."

The lady that was being described in far off Billings helped her unhappy child into the backseat of her car and buckled her in. Raylyn wasn't too happy herself, after watching the man she loved leave and knowing she wouldn't see him for two weeks. She started up and let the heater take off the chill while she searched her wallet for the change she needed to pay at the gate. They left the covered parking garage after paying the fee. Cars going by on the street had their windshield wipers going and Raylyn's heart sank. Roger had barely left and it was raining. She hoped his plane didn't run into bad weather. Cautiously, Raylyn looked both ways, making sure there was no traffic and pulled out onto the street and turned toward Heidi's daycare.

Raylyn pulled to the curb in front of the building, but as she lifted the handle on the door, a car whizzed by them and sprayed icy crystals on the side of the car. They sounded like BB pellets from inside. Raylyn waited a heartbeat until hers settled down into its normal rhythm. She was very glad that Heidi had learned the lesson she'd taught her: 'Don't open your door onto the street until I'm there to open it for you.' Cautiously, Raylyn looked behind the car to see if any other cars were coming.

Heidi's voice sounded scared, as she said, "Mommy, that stuff from that car went all over our car! It be real loud, too!"

"Yes, I know, Sweety. I'm so glad you didn't open your door. He went so close, he could have done some damage to our car and you could have been hurt." Raylyn knew he didn't need to go that close, but she left that unsaid.

"Yes, Mommy. I 'member what you said."

"I'm really glad!"

Raylyn left Heidi at the daycare, knowing that in only a few days she wouldn't have to leave her there ever again. It wasn't a bad place Heidi had a good time and had friends. The food they served for lunch was usually nourishing and wholesome, but the reason why she was happy about not leaving her was the same bottom line, she and Heidi were moving in about two weeks to gain a husband and a daddy.

All the way from the daycare to the hospital, Raylyn was formulating the words for her resignation. She parked in the employee lot, locked her car and hurried toward the employee entrance. She wasn't late, but she'd be barely on time after she reached the time clock. She punched her card then turned to the elevators. Before it came, two more people joined her.

Moments later, they joined three others in the car. Two of them she knew, so she smiled and they all greeted each other. Two of the women worked on Raylyn's floor, but the others were nurses and went higher in the building. When the door opened on their floor, the three parted, waved and went to their respective offices. Raylyn still wished Roger was with her, she'd felt like her heart went with him.

Raylyn turned the corner and from there saw the administrator standing with his back against her doorjam. Her heart climbed into her throat, wondering what the man wanted. He had never been one of Raylyn's favorite people and he had never given her any reason to start liking him. Today, the look on his face didn't give her much confidence that he liked her, either. However, she continued to walk toward her office.

When she was still a yard or so away, the man straightened from the wall and in a voice everyone on the hallway could hear, demanded, "Why were you gone Monday and Tuesday? You'd already been gone extra time over Thanksgiving!"

"Chet, Maxine gave me the extra time over Thanksgiving, I didn't ask for it. I asked for vacation time for these two days because I had out-of-town company coming. It's hard to entertain someone from so far when you have to work. Since I had the vacation hours coming, she gave them to me. Besides, it's close to Christmas I'm not taking any extra time off for Christmas or New Year's, so she gave it to me."

"You're supposed to be here!" he bellowed, pointing to the floor.

"Not when my boss gives me vacation days that I ask for!" she shot back.

Being the bully that he was, he stepped into her space, glared at her and demanded, "Come to my office immediately!"

Not allowing him to bully her in any way, she answered, "Shortly, Chet, I need to take off my coat, then I'll be right with you."

Raylyn stepped around him and Chet turned to watch her every move. She inserted her key into the lock on the doorknob, but didn't look at the man as she turned the knob and stepped inside, then closed the door behind her. Chester Manifold glared at her back as he heard the door catch then continued to glare at the closed door. This woman always pulled his string the wrong way. When she didn't come out immediately, he whirled around again and stormed back to his office, muttering things under his breath.

It wasn't hard Raylyn could see the hand writing on the wall. She quickly hit the buttons to start up her computer and while it booted up, she shed her coat and hung it on the hook behind the door. She only had to wait a minute before the display of her I-cons was on the screen. She clicked on the one she needed then opened a clean page. Only a few minutes later she had completed her letter of resignation. As soon as it printed out, she pulled it from the box and signed it, then went back out to the hall, hoping that Chet had returned to his office without waiting for her. She let out a sigh of relief when he wasn't still standing in the hall.

When she reached his office suite, she walked right into the secretary's office without knocking. The older lady had been raised on protocol, but today Raylyn didn't care one whit about that. Instead of stopping at her desk, she marched around it and turned the knob to Chet's door, her paper held tightly in her hand.

Glaring at her, the older woman said, "You can't do that! I must announce you!"

Raylyn pushed on the door and over her shoulder said, "Watch me!"

Chet's massive desk was straight ahead, but he stood by his window. However, there was a pink half sheet of paper on his blotter and Raylyn knew it was supposed to be for her. Without looking behind her, she gave the door a hard shove, not knowing that the secretary had followed her and now stood only inches from it. It almost smacked her in the face. Raylyn never knew, but the woman gasped and quickly took a step back before the door engaged.

Standing in front of the desk, holding her own piece of paper, Raylyn asked, "What's the meaning of the pink slip on your desk, Chet?"

He whirled away from the window and thundered, "It's yours!"

"And that's because…?" she shot back at him, barely containing her anger.

Facing her, but looking anywhere but at her, he said, "You weren't here!"

Glaring at him, she swallowed, so that she could control her voice, as she said, "I wasn't supposed to be! I asked for the days off. I already explained that to you. Just now when I walked inside, there is no mail on my floor or in my box, from these past two days. I'm not behind. Anything entered into my computer in the last two days will be dealt with by five o'clock this afternoon."

"Not by you, it won't!"

Willing her hands not to shake, she laid her own paper down on top of the pink slip and said, "Fine, my resignation takes effect immediately. Since I have resigned, I am entitled to all my sick time, my personal days that haven't been used and all my vacation days. They will begin today, as soon as I walk out this door." She looked at him then and said, "I have no idea why you wish to fire me. My reports have always been on time and my work has always been correct. None of my evaluations have been negative, but for some reason, you have never liked me. I can say the feeling has always been mutual. Could it be, Mr. Manifold, that it's because I'm competent and you are not? That question deserves a review by the hospital board, I think. Good day, Mr. Manifold, I will not miss your condescending attitude or your degrading words!" She turned and took one step toward the door.

Chet was a big man and his long legs brought him to her in two strides. He grabbed her arm and hissed, "What do you mean degrading attitude!" His hand felt like a vice on her arm, she couldn't shake it off. His beefy face was red, showing how high his blood pressure was.

His face was only inches from Raylyn's, but instead of cowering, she lifted one foot then lowered it only inches in front of her and ground the sturdy tip of her heel into the top of his foot. Instantly, she knew she'd hit her mark, his hand dropped from her arm and he jumped away from her, pulling his foot from under hers as quickly as he could. Hopping on one foot several feet from her, he threw his head back and let out a high keening sound. With his exorbitant excess weight he could hardly stay on his one foot.

His secretary heard the noise and came barging into the office. Looking at Raylyn standing calmly in front of Chet's desk, then at Chet hopping around with his head thrown back with the noise coming from him, she scowled and asked, "What is going on in here? Mr. Manifold, what is it?"

"Get her out of here!" he bellowed.

Folding her hands across her chest, Raylyn looked at the woman and said, "On second thought, I think I'd like to know the reasons Mr. Manifold has on his pink slip for firing me. Mr. Manifold, would you care to explain?" Disdainfully, Raylyn continued to watch the fat man jump around the room.

"NO! JUST GET OUT OF HERE!"

As the woman advanced on Raylyn and Chet continued to hop around, Raylyn whirled around, picked up her own paper and grabbed the pink slip under it. She started reading at the top looking closely at each item on the list. The man had four things listed, each entry on the list made her more furious. She began to tremble, her anger was so intense. She stood holding the paper in her trembling hands.

"What do you mean by all this!" she demanded.

Finally, the big man put his foot down on the floor and with a very obvious limp came toward Raylyn, but stopped several feet from her, mindful of his throbbing foot. The man swallowed. "It's all true," he said, in a voice not like his at all. He picked up his foot and put it down gingerly, but didn't leave it on the floor for long.

With eyes firing darts, she pinned him to the spot. "It's not true! None of it! You know it isn't! Every word on this paper is false! I'm never late for work, especially not consistently, as you allege. I've never been insubordinate, not to you or Maxine, and she's the only one who matters. I never slough off, my work is done each day when I leave and I have never talked about anyone behind their back. You, Mr. Manifold, have made slanderous, libelous statements in writing about me which could be taken to court and upheld, because I know of several people who would stand up for me against you! Furthermore, if my next place of employment asks for a reference from this place," she shook the paper in his face, "this sheet of paper, or a photocopy had better not be in my file or get passed on to them. **Do you understand?!**"

Chet reached out and tried to take it from her, but she was too quick and whipped it behind her back, where she folded it twice, also making sure the secretary couldn't take it from her. "No, you will not take this from me, I'm keeping it." Quickly she pushed it in her pocket and said, "Miss Butterfield, I will see myself out of this office. I will be taking a few minutes to empty my office of my things and then I will leave." Looking at the woman with eyes like steel, she continued, "You make sure your boss doesn't leave this office! If he so much as sets foot in my office before I leave, I'll call the hospital security. That's not a threat it will happen if he shows up at my door. If he goes to Maxine's office, I'll know, but while I pack up, I'll call her and tell her what this man's done to me!"

"Maxine already knows." Chet muttered.

"Oh, she does! She knows I was to get fired today."

"Yes, I told her on Monday."

"I see."

The man licked his lips, hating to admit what he was about to say. He turned away, not wanting to face her, as he admitted, "No, you don't. She was on your side. She came in early, planning on standing up for you, but I made sure she was called away before you came."

Barely containing her fury at the treacherous man, she said, "Very interesting, Mr. Manifold. I'm certainly glad I intended to hand in my resignation today even before I arrived. Good day to both of you."

With her head held high, she moved around the big man, who didn't try to stop her and skirted by the woman, who also didn't make a move to keep her in the office. She yanked open the office door, walked through the door way, then pulled the door shut deliberately behind her and left the suite. Her anger and therefore her adrenalin hadn't simmered down very much. She moved as quickly as she could down the hallway to her own office. Her heels clicked with each step, showing how angry she was. She had never been falsely accused before and it wasn't something she could tolerate. She couldn't remember ever in her life being so furious. Chet Manifold could do that to a lesser person!

She turned the corner onto the hallway where her office was and standing beside her door was her boss, Maxine. They both registered the expressions on the other's face as Raylyn moved closer to her office. Neither was smiling, but Maxine reached out to her and was the first to speak. "He fired you, didn't he?"

Raylyn pulled the pink slip from her pocket. "He intended to, but when he was here at my door when I arrived, I knew what was coming down, so I took my resignation with me. It is effective immediately, Maxine. I'm here now to remove my things from this room. I'm sorry for you, I hope you can find my replacement, but I will not stay with that man in the position that he is in! Maxine, if I weren't planning to move away, I'd take this pink slip to the hospital board and demand his removal from his position just from what he has written on this paper."

"Do it, Raylyn, do it!" Maxine exclaimed. "He tried to force me to call you in on Monday and then, since I wouldn't, he demanded that I fire you. Then he threatened my position, too. I don't know what his accusations are, but none of them have foundation."

"No, they don't! I'm sorry, Maxine, I'm packing my belongings and moving as soon as I can, so I won't be able to go to the hospital board. However, I told him that what he has written on this paper better not find its way into my file or be sent in any form to my new employer."

"It won't, Raylyn, it won't. I'll make sure of it!"

Raylyn turned the knob on her door and as she went through the doorway, she gave Maxine a smile and said, "Thanks, I knew all along that you are a true friend."

"He tried to make out that I wasn't, didn't he?"

"Yes, his conscience pricked him he said he found a reason to detain you before I came."

"That louse!" Maxine hissed and followed Raylyn into her office. "Since you resigned, you'll want to be paid for your sick time, personal days and vacation days, won't you?"

"Yes, I will. I told him I was entitled to that and he didn't deny it."

While Raylyn gathered her things, Maxine worked the computer on her desk and even sent the information to Raylyn's bank for her final paycheck. It only took ten minutes to get everything including Raylyn's pictures and her framed degree into a box that Maxine found in a nearby storage closet. Raylyn had one small plant, but she knew she didn't want it as a reminder of her time here and there would be no good place for it while she was planning her move.

As Maxine picked it up to help her leave the room, Raylyn said, "Maxine, keep that plant. I don't want it, I won't have room for it and I know you love plants."

"Why, thanks, Raylyn! I'll remember you with this." After Raylyn walked out of her office with her purse over her shoulder and the box in her arms, Maxine pulled the door closed and said, "Best of everything to you, Raylyn. I see you're new ring and I know you're getting married soon. May everything go well for you in the future."

"Thanks, Maxine. I'm sure it will. The same for you."

With a light step, Raylyn left the hospital and drove back to the daycare. Heidi saw her and ran over. "Mommy, how comed you be here so soon? It not even lunch time."

She smiled at the child. Not wanting to upset Heidi, she said, "I don't work there at the hospital any more, Sweety. We'll go home and start packing up. The day after Christmas we'll take down all our decorations and pack them and leave. We'll probably beat your new daddy back to Georgia."

Her eyes as big as saucers, Heidi asked, "Will he know where to find us?"

"Of course, Sweety, I'll tell him tonight when he calls."

"Oh, 'K! I get my coat now?"

"Yes, pumpkin, while I tell Teacher you won't be back."

Not long after supper, Raylyn called Isabel's house. When she answered, Raylyn said, "Hi, Grandma, could I talk to Mom? Oh, wait, I need to ask you something first."

"What is it, child?"

"Could you ask your pastor if he'll officiate at our wedding the Saturday after New Year's? We want to get married in Roger's church, but of course, he can't perform his own wedding. Would you ask him?"

Isabel chuckled. "Of course I'll ask him, Child! He'll do it, I guarantee it! There won't be that first problem!"

"Grandma Isabel! Will you twist the man's arm?"

Chuckling, Isabel said, "We old ladies don't call it that, but we do have a sure-fire method in our 'gentle persuasion' you know."

Raylyn laughed. "Thanks, Grandma. Now can I talk to Mom?"

Ruth must have been standing at Isabel's elbow, because she said immediately, "I'm here, dear, what is it?"

"The hospital administrator tried to fire me this morning, but I beat him to it and resigned immediately. Heidi and I've spent most of the day packing what we plan to bring. I promised her we'd spend Christmas here then pack up our decorations and leave, but if we do that, we'll be in limbo for the next five days."

"If you're all packed, load up and come now! Mom's got an empty cabin and the little town's all decorated for Christmas. It's lovely, really."

"We'll talk, Mom, we'll see. Mom, I wanted to ask you a favor, though."

"Yes?"

"Roger and I want to get married there in Vansville on the Saturday after New Year's. Would you please stay down there until then?"

"Aaahmm, really, that won't be a problem, dear. I'm thinking about staying down for the winter as it is."

"Great! When we do get there, I want us, you and me, to go shopping for my wedding dress and Mom, I want you to walk me down the aisle."

Raylyn heard the sniff and Ruth's voice changed. There were obviously tears in Ruth's voice, as she said, "Dear, that will be my highest honor. We'll be waiting anxiously to see you. Remember, do drive safely, those roads can get so slippery!"

"Oh, I know that, Mom!"

FIFTEEN

Heidi was in bed and Raylyn sat in her living room reading her Bible and study guide. She couldn't get much enthused about her reading, because she had the cordless phone on the arm of the couch. They had agreed that Roger would call at ten o'clock and as her watch beeped, the phone rang. Raylyn jerked it from the arm and punched the key to activate it.

"Hi, Love, how's everything?"

"Considering that as of nine ten this morning I'm unemployed, I guess you could say everything's peachy," she answered with a bit of sarcasm.

Raylyn had to yank the phone from her ear, as Roger screeched, "WHAT!"

"Old Chet, the incompetent administrator, was waiting for me at my door when I arrived this morning. He demanded I come to his office, but before I went, I typed up my resignation. He had a pink slip all made out, but I never let him fire me, I grabbed the slip and laid my resignation on his desk. Heidi and I've been packing up all day."

"You didn't have that much to pack, Sweetheart."

"I know, I told Heidi we'd wait until after Christmas and take down the decorations and then leave for Georgia, but we packed up stuff all today."

"Sweetheart, would there be any way that you could come out here?"

"It'd take more than a day to drive, wouldn't it?"

Gaining more enthusiasm by the minute, Roger said, "Fly, Sweetheart! Find out all the particulars and I'll meet you in Billings. We'll spend Christmas here with the family and then we'll fly back to Grand Rapids, rent the trailer and I'll help you drive the whole kit and caboodle down! What do you say, Love?"

The excitement swelling in her own voice, Raylyn said, "Sounds like a better way to spend Christmas than you out there and Heidi and me here. I'll see what I can do. If we don't do something, Heidi will have us climbing the walls!"

"Man! I sure hope it can be done! I've missed you beyond belief today, Love. I'll be waiting to hear from you. I love you, Sweetheart."

"You know I love you!"

At breakfast, Heidi grumbled, "It be time to leave, Mommy."

"What do you mean, Sweety? I told you we'd leave after Christmas and you know it's not Christmas yet."

"Mommy, we gots to do sompin! It be boring!"

"Roger called last night...."

"I know, Mommy! Could we go see him?"

"Hmm, I suppose we could," Raylyn said, as if it was a new idea.

Heidi jumped from her chair and said, "Mommy, come on! Get our coats, we go see Daddy now!"

"Hold on, Sweety, it's too far to drive. I need to call the airlines and get us a flight. Then I'd have to call Roger for him to come meet us out there."

Letting out a huge sigh, Heidi said, "Well, do it, Mommy! We go see Daddy!"

Raylyn had already packed up her computer, so she couldn't go on line to find an airline, so she found her phonebook, turned to the yellow pages and made a list of all the airlines listed. Surely it would be almost impossible to find an airline that wouldn't be booked solid between now and Christmas Day. When she had them all on her paper, she started calling each one.

She was glad that Maxine had run her time worked and all the time she had saved up through the computer and gotten a lump sum for all the money she had coming to her and had the authority to direct deposit it. Now she had some money to get a ticket and to rent a trailer for the trip to Georgia. She knew they would both be major expenditures on her credit card.

Much to her surprise, she found a place for both her and Heidi on a flight that afternoon. When she hung up, she looked at her watch. After she called Roger, she'd have just enough time to pack quickly, make a quick sandwich for them both and head to the airport. They could be at the airport in Billings later that afternoon.

At breakfast, Roger said, "Mom, how about two more for Christmas dinner?"

Mattie scowled. "Stop talking in riddles, Roger. Lonnie and Abigail are getting here this afternoon of course there'll be two more for Christmas dinner."

"I'm talking about two *more*."

"Roger...."

"Raylyn lost her job yesterday...."

Mattie's face lit up. "They're coming!"

Nodding, Roger said, "If they can get a flight."

"They'll get one!"

The phone rang.

Roger lunged for the phone on the wall. "Hello?"

"We're leaving for the airport now, Honey. We'll be there long before supper."

"I'll be there, Love!"

John walked in as Roger hung up the phone. "I need some help out on the range. Some cattle are missing and it's supposed to storm tonight."

Roger swallowed hard and looked at his shoes, he wasn't sure he thought his heart fell at the same time. Normally, his dad had plenty of help with the ranch hands under him, but one of them had left to spend time with family over Christmas and another had taken his wife to the hospital because she was in labor. If the beasts were hiding behind the barn he could get them rounded up and be on the road to Billings to the airport, but he knew cattle didn't hide like kids did. They were probably in the farthest wadi from the barn. Go figure.

Mattie looked at the clock. "Say, Lonnie and Abigail should be coming in about the same time. What if I go to the airport and pick everybody up?"

Through strangled vocal cords, Roger said, "I guess that could work, Mom."

John scowled. "What's the deal?"

"Roger just got a call that his fiancée found a flight for them to come out. He was about ready to leave for the airport."

John shrugged. "That's life on the ranch. Never a dull moment. Take the Jeep, Momma, that way you'll have room for everyone's luggage and all the people and you'll have four wheel drive in case the weather moves in early."

Mattie nodded. "Sounds like a plan."

His shoulders slumped Roger never said a word, just left the kitchen for his room to change. How he wanted to pick up his dear ones, he'd even wait for his sister and brother-in-law, but his dad needed his help now and his mom could do the honors at the airport. He couldn't give her a picture of Raylyn and Heidi, but surely he'd described them well enough she'd recognize them. Of course, they'd look for him, not her, but surely it would work out.

After he dressed, he joined his dad at the back door. He pulled on the insulated boots that came up his legs to his calves to keep the snow from going down inside, then hunched into his old winter coat that had hung on the hook since the last time he'd been home. He pulled the warm scarf that Raylyn had made for him around his neck and pulled on the fleece-lined hat with the flaps that covered his ears. He jammed his hands in the thick woolen gloves that he'd worn for the long walks to the school bus in high school and wished he could be going to the airport.

In the cold mudroom, John asked, "What gives? Why's she coming out?"

"Her administrator tried to fire her yesterday, instead she resigned. She's not taking much from her house, since mine's furnished and the church that's buying hers wants any furniture she'll leave. She's all packed up with nothing to do, so I invited her to come. She'd just called when you came in to say she and Heidi were on their way to the airport. We'll fly back to Grand Rapids together and I'll help her drive her rig down to Georgia next week."

"I'm sorry, but I'm sure you understand how it is, Son. Life on the ranch is never predictable, especially in the winter."

"I know," he sighed. It surprised him his dad had said he was sorry.

Mattie hurried into her bedroom and changed clothes. She and Roger had expected him to meet his sister and brother-in-law at the airport, but now the happy task fell on her shoulders. She turned on the radio beside the bed as she changed. The forecaster said, "We expect the winter storm that's building in the Rockies to be with us late this evening. We should expect snow to start around eight and continue through the night. Snowfall is expected to be heavy at times. Travelers should plan to be at their destinations early due to expected snow buildup."

"Great!" Mattie muttered.

On the way to the airport Mattie had a thought. For the first time in a very long time they would have a child in residence on Christmas Day! She swallowed, what did she have for a present for under the tree? She shook her head, there had to be *something* under the tree for a child. There were a few things of both Roger's and Abigail's she and John had stored in the attic, but she couldn't remember what all they'd saved and what they'd given or thrown away. Would there be time between now and Sunday to go up and rummage through the trunks? She surely hoped so. Actually, she would *make* time! No child she knew who would be in residence at her home would be without a present on Christmas Day!

Raylyn was excited and of course, Heidi was almost over the moon. Their seatbelts were fastened the plane was getting into its landing pattern. They hadn't been assigned window seats, but when two men saw Heidi and her mommy, they'd given up their seats so that Heidi could sit by the window and Raylyn next to her. She'd been grateful those men would never know what a lifesaver they'd been.

The plane touched down and moved slowly through the maze of roads toward the terminal. When it reached the building it inched along and eased into place. Only moments later the flight attendants opened the door and attached the ramp. It was so cold outside that the warmth inside the plane quickly evaporated and the people gladly left and hurried up the ramp. This was winter in sight of the Rockies.

Raylyn grabbed the carry-on bag she had, helped Heidi into her small backpack, took her hand and joined the group getting off. Heidi tried to pull Raylyn even faster, but there were people right in front of her that she couldn't scoot around, so Heidi had to be content to skip slowly at her side. They went through the detectors and stood looking around. As the crowds thinned out, both Raylyn and Heidi realized that Roger wasn't there.

Tears hanging in her eyes, Heidi looked at Raylyn and said, "Mommy, where's Daddy? He not here!"

Choking back her own disappointment, she murmured, "I don't know, Sweety."

For a minute Raylyn wondered what to do. Should she go to the luggage claim for her suitcases or wait? Had he been delayed in leaving? She had no idea how far he'd have to come from the ranch to the airport and it hadn't been too long since she'd called. She couldn't have called any sooner, but that could have made a difference. There was a chair close by, so she dropped her carry-on in it and decided to wait. Perhaps it took longer to get from the ranch to the airport than it did to fly from Grand Rapids to Billings.

Mattie couldn't find a parking space close to the arrivals for the airline Roger had told her to meet. She'd had to drive around a bit to find a place. When she rushed in the terminal, she looked at the arrivals board and her heart sank to see that the plane she was to meet had already landed. Moving as fast as she could, she headed for the area listed on the screen. As soon as she arrived in the area she knew she had it right. There stood a lovely young woman with a little girl and as Roger said, she was the image of her mommy. Mattie breathed a sigh, the lady was everything she'd ever wanted for her son she was beautiful. The little girl had to be a bonus, a precious bonus, to be sure.

Breathless, she came up to them and said, "Hi, I'm Mattie Clemens, Roger's mom. From how he described you, you must be Raylyn and Heidi."

Swallowing a sigh, Raylyn said, "Yes, you've found us."

Heidi wasn't as diplomatic. "Where's my new daddy?" she demanded.

Mattie hunched down and looked Heidi in the eyes. "His dad needed his help very badly. We found that out a minute after your mommy called. He was very sad that he couldn't come for you. I'm his mom, though, will you come with me?"

"I guess," Heidi grumbled. "We see Daddy at your house? We miss him lots so we comed real fast on that plane."

"I'm hoping they'll be back by the time we get there, yes." She stood up and looked at Raylyn and said, "I hope you're not too tired from your flight. My daughter and her husband are arriving in about two hours. I wouldn't get you home with time enough to get back for them. It is alright that we wait, isn't it?"

"As long as we can entertain Heidi. Our suitcases are at the luggage claim."

"It's on the lower level we'll go down now and get them. If we load them, that'll take up a few minutes anyway." Mattie smiled.

By the time they had retrieved Raylyn's luggage and taken them to Mattie's Jeep all of twenty minutes of the two hours had gone by. Heidi spotted an ice cream shop, so the three went in and had an ice cream cone. One can only eat an ice cream cone so slowly before it starts to melt, especially in a building that has some warmth in it. Mattie looked at her watch as they threw away their napkins and swallowed a sigh. They still had an hour and ten minutes to wait for the other plane to arrive.

Some time later, Mattie and Raylyn sat in the receiving area of the airline that Lonnie and Abigail were to arrive on. Heidi was playing with her dollie close by, showing her everything new in the huge airport. Mattie looked at Raylyn and said, "You know, you'll be a total surprise to my daughter. Neither of my far off children are very good at corresponding with their parents. You were a surprise to us until yesterday."

"I was afraid you'd say that. Roger's told me about you and his sister, but I was sure he hadn't told you folks about me… about us."

Mattie gave the lovely young woman a breath-taking smile. "Believe me I'm so happy for you to become part of our family! Roger told us you'd resigned yesterday from your job in Grand Rapids. What did you do?"

"I was head of the financial counseling office in the hospital where I worked. The reason I was able to come today was that yesterday, after we put Roger on the plane, I went to work and the administrator, who has never liked me, tried to fire me unjustly. I had intended to hand in my resignation yesterday giving two weeks notice, but he made it very easy to resign on the spot. A similar position has opened for me in Blairsville, Georgia and I'll be starting there in January."

Looking at Heidi playing, Mattie whispered, "Your child is adorable, so well behaved."

"Mmm, well, sometimes that's up for debate."

Sometime later, the arrivals screen flashed that the flight number for Lonnie and Abigail's plane was about to land. "Oh," Mattie said, "Our wait's about over! Their flight's been added to the screen. If that can be believed, they should be on time. I am so glad! It's only once a year we're all together."

"What's Roger doing that he couldn't come for us?"

"According to the forecast, another winter storm is coming off the Rockies tonight. John, my husband, is the ranch manager and he discovered when he went out earlier that quite a few head of cattle have gone missing. He felt he needed to bring them closer to the buildings and two of his hands are unavailable. He never asks Roger for help unless he has no other choice."

Just then, the screen changed. The words, 'flight 2106 is experiencing some difficulty with its landing gear. There will be an emergency landing.' appeared.

Mattie looked at Raylyn. Tears sprang to her eyes. "No!" fell from her lips.

Raylyn didn't know what to do, so she reached for the older woman. "Come, let's pray that everything will be okay."

"Yes, you pray, will you?" She pulled Raylyn into her arms.

Raylyn said, "Father, God, we've just learned that Mattie's daughter and son-in-law are on a plane having trouble. Lord, You can make the landing mechanism work, or You can bring them in without it. Father, keep them safe and all those on the plane with them safe. We know 'that in all things God works for the good of those who love him.' We trust in that verse in Romans and know that You will see them safely in Mattie's arms. In Jesus Name, amen."

Mattie hugged Raylyn fiercely and whispered, "Thank you!"

They looked up at the screen again and this time, it said, 'Flight 2106 is on the ground. All passengers are fine and will be leaving the plane immediately.'

"Praise God!" Mattie said, fervently.

It was only a few minutes later that people started coming down the concourse toward them. There were many and Raylyn called Heidi. The little girl looked up and saw the stream of people, quickly picked up her dollie and ran to Raylyn. Mattie stood up where she was and only moments later began to wave.

The young man and woman came quickly to Mattie, who had her arms open. Abigail stepped into them and hugged her mom fiercely. Mattie, of course, held on for several minutes, she was so glad to see her daughter. The young man said, "We'd better get on the move, freezing rain is falling, that's why our landing gear locked up. I know we have over an hour's drive and it'll be right into it."

"We must hurry, but first, I must introduce you both to our soon-to-be daughter-in-law and our new grand-daughter. Abigail, Lonnie, this is Raylyn and Heidi Keys. Raylyn, my daughter and son-in-law, Abigail and Lonnie Webster."

Abby's mouth was hanging open, but Lonnie swallowed and held out his hand. "You're quite a shock! But welcome to the family."

"Thanks, I'm pleased to meet you."

Heidi looked at the adults and said, "Her's takin' us to see my new daddy. We go now?"

"Yes, we'll go now," Mattie said.

Back on the ranch, Roger and John were joined by several other men. They all saddled up and headed away from the main compound toward the hills. The cattle could be anywhere, they could be all together, but more than likely, there were small pockets of them scattered over miles of rolling hills that were covered with a foot of snow. The sun was out, but all the men were aware that things could change in only minutes. After all, this was winter in Montana. If you didn't like the weather, wait just a minute, it would probably change, maybe for the worse.

As afternoon came on, John stopped, so the others reigned in and dismounted. John had brought lunch for himself and Roger and the other cowboys had brought their own. Roger ate his and swilled down his coffee, he wanted to get back in the saddle and get the critters home. He was cold, but not chilled to the bone. Even so, being in the warm house, with his arms around his lovely Raylyn was uppermost in his mind.

It was two o'clock when John said, "Ah, I hear them!"

One of the men rode ahead to an edge overlooking a small valley and said, "Yep, I'd say they're all there. It's just a matter of getting them out of there and headed back."

"Let me take a gander," John said, "see if I can come up with a plan."

John looked out over the valley and surveyed the situation. He sat for a while taking in all the angles and finally came up with a plan. Roger's heart sank, as he listened to his dad tell them what needed to be done and how they would do it. They would be lucky to get back to the main barn by dark. Just as they split up to implement the plan, Roger felt the first icy sting on his cheek and knew the storm was upon them. It was quite a few hours ahead of what the forecasters had predicted, but this was Montana after all.

Lonnie lifted their luggage from the belt and everyone fell in close to him. They headed outside to the parking lot to look for Mattie's Jeep. Heidi was quiet, she held her dollie tightly, but she held Raylyn's hand in a grip so tight Raylyn wondered if she'd have any feeling in her hand when they reached the Jeep.

When Mattie saw her car, she hit the remote and unlocked the doors and the hatch. As Lonnie put the suitcases in the back, she said, "Lonnie, I'll let you drive, if you don't mind. I'll feel more comfortable if you do."

"Okay, Mattie, I'll do my best to get us to your house safely."

Mattie smiled. "I know you will."

It was slow going. Roads were full of travelers, since it was so close to Christmas. In Billings, trucks were out with sand and the roads were in good shape, but Mattie knew that before they reached the ranch not only would the sand stop, but they would probably be the only vehicle on the road and by the time they reached the ranch there could be a thick buildup of ice. She was glad John had insisted she take the Jeep. She wondered how the men were doing, but she kept her thoughts to herself.

A trip that normally took over an hour, from the airport to the ranch, took well over two hours, almost three. The icy conditions kept them at a slow speed. By the time Lonnie turned from the two lane road under the arch that read 'Harland Ranch' the icy rain was bending all the trees and the wires were coated over with a heavy blanket of ice. The sky was leaden and even after they bumped over the cattle crossing they couldn't see anything but more snow and ice. Raylyn was very glad she hadn't had to drive.

Lonnie followed the plowed road and after several turns they finally saw up ahead some dark objects that as they traveled closer turned into a house, a barn, several outbuildings and a bunkhouse. Heidi was glued to the window she had never seen anything like this place before in her life. Dogs came bounding toward the Jeep from the barn, obviously happy to finally see someone come around. However, there weren't any people to be seen.

Lonnie pulled up beside the dark house and shut off the vehicle. Heidi took one long look at the dark building and turned eyes filled with tears to her mommy. "Mommy," she whispered, "it be dark in that house, Daddy not here! Where is he? Where could he be? I want to see Daddy, Mommy!"

Around a lump, Raylyn took Heidi's hand and said, "Yes, I know, Sweety. I'm sure he'll be here soon, though."

When the five from the airport arrived, Lonnie unloaded the hatch immediately, setting all the luggage on the ground. The others piled out of the car quickly glad to finally be at their destination. Lonnie pulled up the handles on his and Abby's suitcases, while Raylyn did the same with hers and Heidi's and Abby staggered under the weight of the two carry-on bags. Mattie took Heidi's hand

and hurried ahead to open the front door and turn on some lights, especially the porch light. It cut through the nasty, icy rain. It also helped those coming not to slip and fall on the treacherous ice.

It was only five o'clock in Montana, but as soon as she helped Raylyn and Heidi find their room for their stay, Mattie hurried back to the kitchen to heat water for some hot drinks and to start dinner. Since she had no idea when the men would get in, she found some beef chunks in the freezer and put them in her largest pot with water and started it cooking, then as she fixed the vegetables, she added them to the pot until she had a hearty stew that would warm up anyone on a cold, nasty winter night.

Heidi was especially quiet. Raylyn had gotten her to hang up her Sunday dress and help her a little by taking a few things into the bathroom, but after only fifteen minutes, she appeared in the kitchen. Looking up at Mattie, she asked, "Where I watch for my new daddy?"

Mattie was setting out five mugs, getting ready to put herbal tea bags in three of them when Heidi asked her question. Mattie looked at the solemn child and bent down immediately. She could see the tears hanging on her eyelashes, so she pulled her into her arms. "Heidi, honey, I'm sure the men will be here soon, but they'll go to the barn first to take care of their horses and then come to the house. But you can see the barn the best through that window right there." Mattie pointed to the large window behind the table.

Heidi nodded and wiggled from Mattie's arms. "I watch for Daddy out that window. I see him when he come."

Raylyn came into the kitchen on the last of Heidi's words, so she said, "But you'll only stay at the window, Sweety, it's much too cold to go outside. Your daddy will come in and that's soon enough to greet him. Okay?"

Heidi sighed, "Yes, Mommy. Dollie and me watch from here until he come inside." She went to the window, tucked her dollie into the crook of her arm, then put her hands around her eyes and stared through the glass. "It be dark! I can't see nothing but white out there!"

Raylyn came up behind Heidi and stared out through the upper glass. What Heidi said was true it was only a vast whiteness outside. There was little light in the sky and even the snow looked gray.

Raylyn turned away from the window it was too depressing to watch as the light faded, since she couldn't see even the barn that wasn't too far from the back of the house.

Soon, Lonnie and Abby joined the others in the kitchen. The beef stew filled the room with a tantalizing aroma and the adults sat around the large kitchen table with their mugs of hot drinks. Mattie had made Heidi some hot chocolate, but Heidi refused to leave the window to come to the table, so it was cooling and untouched in front of the chair where Mattie had put it.

The adults were talking, getting to know Raylyn when Mattie heard a little tummy complaining from the window. She glanced up at the kitchen clock and exclaimed, "Oh, my, look at the time! It's nearly seven o'clock, we must eat."

Abby set the table and Mattie filled bowls with the stew while Raylyn went to the window to look out, but also to urge Heidi to leave her post and come to the table. Heidi looked up at her mommy and shook her head. "I not eat now. When Daddy come I eat wif him. He be hungry and I eat wif him."

Raylyn put her arm around the child and said, "Sweety, it may be a while and we all heard your tummy growl. I know you're hungry."

"Daddy be very hungry. He be cold, too. I wait for him."

Raylyn looked at Mattie and said, "I guess we'll wait for Roger."

Unable to speak louder, Mattie whispered, "That's okay, Raylyn."

The dark, dismal, miserable afternoon faded into an even more dismal night. Roger had forgotten how slowly cattle moved when they were being herded. One or two could break out of the pack at any given time and try to race away into the vast nothingness and that made one of the cowboys break away from the slow moving herd to round them up and bring them back.

The tiny chips of ice continued to fall until darkness then it changed to snow, cold and fine. Now, instead of the soft plinking of the ice pellets, as they fell against each other, there was no sound at all as the snow fell. There was plenty of noise from the cattle, they bellowed conversationally to each other as they plodded along. As Roger rode beside his dad he wondered how any of them knew that they were headed for the ranch buildings. He'd lost track of where he was long ago. He was glad he'd never had to go after any of the strays that insisted on following their own leads and had to be brought back to the herd over and over again.

The men were wet. At first, the ice melted when it hit them and soaked into their jeans, but as the temperature dropped, the ice didn't melt, but became imbedded in the fibers of their clothes. Roger had never really thought about becoming accustomed to the warmer weather in Georgia. Vansville was nestled in the mountains and they had snow several times in any given winter, but as dusk gave way to full darkness, he realized that his body was beginning to shiver and he couldn't control it.

He tried to reach back to his saddlebag for his thermos, but his fingers couldn't work the clasp open, so he gave up and straightened back into the saddle. It had been hours since he'd looked at his watch, he had no idea what time it was, but there wasn't any light around them, and he knew he would only get more discouraged if he knew. He hoped and prayed that all those who had flown had arrived before the storm moved in. The drive from the airport could be long and perhaps a bit treacherous in this weather, but if a plane went down, usually that was the end of the line. A huge shudder went down his back. He wouldn't think of that, not in regard to his beloved Raylyn and Heidi.

His muddled mind had just turned to Raylyn when one of the cowboys exclaimed, "I see the porch light on your house, Sir!"

"Ah, good!" John returned, "Mattie's back from the airport, that's good news. We're nearly finished."

"Yes, sir, that we are!"

John had been concerned for his son for the last forty-five minutes. As the light came closer, he came up beside Roger and took the reigns from his hands and said, "Before we turn toward the barn, you slide off and get up to the house."

Roger tried to nod, but he felt frozen into the shape he was. When he tried to speak his words were slurred. "Ieee won't-t-t commmp-p-plain, D-d-dad."

The cowboys kept on with the herd, but John reigned in and also stopped Roger's horse. Roger's hands finally molded to the saddle horn and he leaned forward as much as his cold body and his stiff clothes would let him. He had to think hard to will his leg to move from the stirrup and move over the horse's back, but then he only crumpled to the ground. John was out of the saddle in a flash and bent over his son who was struggling to get up. With some help from his dad, he did get back on his feet.

When he was back on his feet, he stuttered, "I-I-I'mmm, ok-k-kay, I-I-I'lllll mmmmake it." He moved out of his dad's grasp and staggered toward the light.

The clock on the wall said it was eight thirty. Back in Michigan Heidi would have been in bed two hours ago, but Raylyn couldn't peal her away from the window, not for supper and certainly not to put her to bed. Dollie had fallen, unnoticed to the floor and most of the time Heidi had her hands around her eyes and they were leaning on the cold window glass as Heidi looked out into the darkness.

All at once she started dancing, still keeping her head glued to the window, but her muffled voice exclaimed, "Daddy be coming!" Only seconds later she turned from the window and Raylyn, who had stood up, saw the tears sliding down Heidi's cheeks, as she said, "He fall off that horse. He not good! Mommy, Daddy hurt! Mommy, that big man, he pick him out of the snow just now! Mommy!" Tears streamed down Heidi's cheeks. Mournfully, Heidi looked back out the window, saying, "Daddy Roger, oh, Daddy!"

Mattie was on her feet and turned on the fire under the teakettle and turned up the heat under the kettle of stew. Lonnie jumped from his chair and raced to the hall for his coat then as he shrugged into it, he flung open the door and ran out into the night. He reached Roger as he was about to go down again, but he grabbed his arm and held him up, then put his arm around him and supported him as most of Roger's weight sagged onto him. He could feel Roger's body totally consumed with shivering. Only moments later they struggled up the steps to the porch.

The three women and Heidi waited inside the front door as Lonnie brought Roger slowly across the porch and into the warm house. Abby closed the door behind them. Raylyn and Heidi both had tears chasing each other down their cheeks, but Mattie was the first to speak. "Lonnie, take him to the spare bedroom off the kitchen and get all those wet clothes off him. Put him to bed then and toss more covers over him. We need to get him warmed up before we feed him. I'll go to his room and get dry clothes."

"Will do, Mattie."

Lonnie never broke stride, he continued their slow progress across the entryway and down the hallway to the room Mattie had directed him to. Raylyn and Heidi watched helplessly as the man they loved moved passed them, with his head bobbing against his chest as he shuffled on. Raylyn wasn't sure he was even aware of being inside or of his surroundings.

Abby ran around the pair and threw open the door to the room that Mattie indicated. Lonnie took Roger into the room and Abby closed the door behind them. That left Raylyn and Heidi alone in the entryway and as Raylyn looked down at her child; Heidi threw herself at her mommy's legs. Great sobs racked her little body as she cried. Tears slid down Raylyn's cheeks, but she bent over and picked up her child and held her tightly to her chest. Right now, they had to console each other.

In the bedroom, Lonnie pealed off Roger's hat and threw it toward the chair. He wasn't sure how long Roger would remain standing before he collapsed, so he went for the zipper on the coat. It was frozen. Before he could get anything else off, the ice on his clothes began to melt and started dripping on the rag rug where they were standing.

Mattie came in the room with dry clothes. She immediately saw the dilemma, so she grabbed a chair and brought it up behind Roger. Only seconds later, Roger collapsed, but the chair was there and caught him. Lonnie went for his boots, while Mattie worked with the zipper on the coat that didn't want to budge. Finally, it thawed enough that she could work it down.

Lonnie found that Roger's socks were dry, so he left them on, but helped Mattie remove the rest of his clothes. Between the two of them, they pulled a warm sweatsuit on him then moved him to the bed. When he felt the soft mattress beneath him, Roger turned on his side and pulled his legs into a fetal position. He tucked his hands under his arms, but his whole body began to shake so hard that the bed shook. Lonnie pulled up the blankets that were on the bed, but Mattie went to the closet and pulled out several more. When she brought them to the bed, they took turns throwing them over him, making a huge pile.

Abby came back to the entryway and found Raylyn and Heidi still there crying. She wasn't as tall as Raylyn, but she put her arm around her and said, "He'll be all right in about a half hour. Mom knows what to do, she'll be out in a minute and I'm sure she'll pour a cup of coffee and have you take it to him."

With a great hiccup, Heidi raised her head from Raylyn's shoulder and said, "He be my new daddy. He *gotta* be okay!"

Abby patted Heidi's back and said, "He will be real soon, Heidi. I know it, you'll see."

In a few minutes they heard the door down the hall open and Mattie did come out. She scurried into the kitchen and only minutes later, she called, "Raylyn, I have some coffee here. Do you want to take it in for him?"

She set Heidi on the floor and they both ran to the kitchen. Eagerly, she said, "Yes, I'll be glad to take him the coffee. Can Heidi go in, too?"

Mattie looked down at the little girl as she handed the mug to Raylyn and said, "Of course, she can go in! You may have to look for a minute, Roger's buried under a pile of blankets, but he's there."

Raylyn walked down the hall holding the mug carefully, but Heidi held nothing, so she reached the door first. She turned the knob and pushed the door open, while Lonnie came and held it open from inside. Heidi didn't even notice him she only saw the huge lump of shaking blankets on the bed and ran to it.

She flung herself at the lump and cried, "Daddy! Daddy Roger!"

Roger's thought processes had just started to operate when he felt something hit him and heard noise in his ear. His body continued to shake, but he couldn't seem to stop. His eyes opened to slits, but the vision he saw made him blink, he wasn't sure if he was still in Montana or if he was seeing an angel. Raylyn's tear-stained, smiling face was all that he could see. Heidi had climbed up on the bed and now sprawled on top of him.

"Honey," the soft voice said, as she came to the bed, "your mom made you some coffee, want to drink it now?"

Lonnie saw that things were under control, so he slipped out and pulled the door behind him. The room was warm, the furnace was putting out plenty of heat, so he was sure Roger would warm up soon. Just before the door closed, he looked back and saw the child on top of the shivering lump and his heart turned over. When would Abby be ready to be the mother of his child? Maybe since they would spend some time with this lovely child, she'd help his cause.

Finally, Roger's shivering slowed and then stopped. He felt the weight on his body and thought it was all the blankets, but then he heard, "Daddy, you be warm now?"

Still stuttering a little, Roger said, "Almost, Munchkin."

"I watch for you. I tell everybody when you fall from the horse."

"I'm glad. I don't remember much after someone said they saw the porch light."

Lonnie and Abby were in the kitchen with Mattie when the back door flew open and John came in breathless. "Is he all right?"

"Heidi saw him fall from his horse and Lonnie reached him before he fell again. We have him warming up in the spare room now. Raylyn took a cup of coffee in a few minutes ago, I'm sure he'll be right as rain real soon, Dear."

John fell into his chair at the table and said, "I was really worried about him for the last hour or so, but there wasn't much I could do except watch him. I swear, I'm going to fence these critters in so that next winter they won't wander so far."

"It would be a good idea if there was food enough."

"We'll bale the grasslands! Anything so they can't go so far out."

Finally, Roger pulled his hands from his armpits and Heidi slid from his back. Slowly, he stretched his legs out, then pushed the mountain of covers off and worked his way to a sitting position. Eagerly he reached for the mug that Raylyn held out to him. He knew his mom had made it with regular coffee and perhaps it was strong enough to walk. Right now he needed the stimulation of the caffeine and the warmth that would spread inside his body.

Heidi stood at his leg and put her arms around his free arm. She laid her head on his shoulder and said, "Daddy, I so glad you be okay now."

After drinking down almost half of the mugful, Roger raised his face and sniffed. "Do I smell Mom's beef stew?"

"Yes, she has a big pot, Honey."

Heidi's tummy growled and Roger scowled then asked Raylyn, "Didn't you guys eat?"

Shaking her head, she smiled at her fiancé. "Your mom served the others but we decided to wait for you."

Roger drained the mug, hung it on his finger and said, "Well, come on! Let's get out there and eat some! I'm famished."

Testing his feet and legs, Roger stood up carefully, but Raylyn was beside him and put her arm around him immediately. Heidi grasped his hand, so they made their way from the room into the hallway together. John's chair faced the hall, so he was the first to see the little group come from the bedroom.

He took a sip of his own coffee and said, "Son, I'm glad to see you're back with us! There at the last I wasn't sure."

"When I woke up I wasn't sure whether I was in Montana or heaven, but then the angel spoke and I knew my own beautiful darling was the one smiling at me." He looked at the others at the table and said, "Thanks for rescuing me, everybody."

Lonnie waved his hand and said, "Think nothing of it, southern boy. So you're marrying a wife soon! I'll be dipped!"

"Yes, we've set the date for the first Saturday of the new year, can you guys come? It'll be in Vansville."

Lonnie looked at his wife, but said, "We haven't talked with all the excitement, but we aren't tied up too much. After all, you're my brother-in-law and her brother."

"I guess you've all been introduced except Dad, so Dad, meet my lovely fiancée, Raylyn Keys and her precious daughter, who will soon be my daughter, Heidi."

Nodding, Heidi said, "I call him Daddy, now!"

John stood up and reached for Raylyn's hand. He grasped it warmly and smiled, as he said, "I'm pleased to meet you, young lady. Sorry he couldn't come for you, but I really did need him this afternoon. In winter time cattle can be truly ornery." John looked at Heidi and scowled. He reached toward her ear and said, "What's that behind your ear, young lady? It's shiny, did you know that?"

Heidi scowled, but before she could reach for her own ear, John produced a quarter and held it out to her. Grinning at the little girl, he said, "Well, would you look at that! Did you folks see that? She had a quarter stuck behind her ear."

Heidi's hand brushed a curl behind her ear, looked up at the big man and said, "I did not! I not got a quarter behind my ear!"

"Well, no, it's right here in my hand."

"Mr….." Heidi looked up at the big man at a loss.

John sat back down in his chair, so that he was more on Heidi's level and looked up at his son. Roger had no idea what the man wanted to say, so he sat down in an empty chair and waited for John to speak. "Miss Heidi," John said, "since you're calling my son daddy, would you like to call me grampa?"

A smile burst across her face as she looked from Raylyn to Roger and then at the older man. "Could I? Would it be okay?"

A tear clogged John's throat and he croaked out, "I'd be honored."

Heidi whirled around and looked at Mattie. "Can I call her gramma?"

Mattie dropped the ladle into the stew and squatted down instantly. Heidi took the few steps and let Mattie's arms circle her. Tears were hanging in her eyes as she said, "Heidi, I'd love for you to call me gramma!"

"'K, you be Gramma and he be Grampa. Is we gonna eat now? Daddy be hungry, you know and I be hungry, too."

Mattie stood up and grabbed the ladle. "Of course, supper coming right up!"

Finally, Roger took his little family upstairs and deposited them in the room Mattie had prepared for them, then went on to his own childhood room. Soon, he'd be able to enter his room with his wife. Lonnie and Abby went to her old room and John and Mattie closed the door to the master suite. The old house grew quiet, but the furnace kept on putting out warm air as the snow continued to fall outside.

SIXTEEN

Christmas Day at the base of the Rockies was a beautiful, sunny day. Everything sparkled in the sunlight. The snow had stopped on Friday, but it was still very cold. Walking outside in the clear weather, one could hear twigs snapping. Walking was treacherous, because the ice still covered the ground, but on top was a thick layer of snow. Because of the ice, it was hard to clear the foot paths from the house to the barn.

John had gotten up before sunrise and had met his foreman at the barn. They made sure there was plenty of water for the cattle and the foreman had brought in several round bales to the lot so that there was plenty of food for the animals. By the time he came back inside, Mattie had the kitchen table groaning with lots of good food.

The Clemens' lived too far from the closest town to try and brave the roads to go to church, but they had a minister in residence, didn't they? They sat down at the large table and John said the blessing. Raylyn saw how excited Heidi was and wondered at the wisdom of putting much food on her plate, but she did. Heidi took a few mouthfuls, but her fork clattered to her plate and she didn't eat anything else.

Since Friday, several packages had appeared under the Christmas tree that stood in the corner of the living room. Heidi looked around at the adults still eating and said, "Is we gonna open packages?"

"Yep," John drawled. "How 'bout after church?"

Scowling at him, Heidi said, sternly, "Grampa, we isn't goin' to church!"

"But your daddy's a preacher!"

With a loud sigh, she said, "So? He not alays preach, he eat, he open presents."

"Really? He did?"

"Uh huh. I seen him, he open stuff at my house afore."

"He did? What'd he get?"

"I made him a card wif our family, but Mommy make him a pretty thing for his neck and gived him a hat from her school."

With a straight face, Roger said, "It's my new barn hat."

Heidi turned to him and said, "Daddy! It not a barn hat! It be from Mommy's school. Cow would get it dirty!"

Lonnie scowled and asked, "Why would you make a new hat a barn hat, Bro?"

"The colors and the words are 'University of Michigan'."

John and Lonnie both laughed and Raylyn's eyes were twinkling. "Well, now, Son, you can't let Cow get your new hat dirty."

Finally, all the adults were down to sipping their coffee, so Heidi said, "Come on, ever'body, it be time to open presents!"

Roger stood up and took Heidi's hand. He put his other arm around Raylyn and said, "Well, then, since it's time, let's go where the presents are!"

Heidi punched her free hand into the air. "Yes!"

As the adults sat around the living room and carols were playing softly from the entertainment center, Heidi flopped down between Raylyn and Roger's feet. Mattie looked up and said, "Heidi could you be our Santa Claus?"

The little girl looked at Mattie and scowled. "Me? I not got white hair and whiskers! Or a big belly or a red suit."

"How about one of his elves, then. You can pass out the presents."

"But I not read."

"No, but your daddy can, show him the name and he'll tell you."

She jumped up and ran to the tree. "'K, I be Santa's elf!" She took her job very seriously and carefully took each package to Roger, then to the right person. It was a long process, traditionally they all waited until everyone had a present.

Of course, there was no present for Roger from Raylyn or a present for Raylyn from Roger, but there were a few things for Raylyn and Heidi that had been hiding in trunks in the attic for many years. Much to Raylyn's surprise, Heidi received a doll that looked suspiciously like her dollie and immediately she named her Dollie Two.

Both Mattie and Abby tried to give her a real name, but Heidi shook her head. "Uh uh, she be Dollie Two. They be twins, so you gotta name 'em 'like."

"Is that so," John said. "I wondered how they named twins, since we never had any."

"Grampa, you name twin babies girls names or boys names, but if you already gots a dollie named Dollie you gotta name her twin Dollie Two."

Sagely, John nodded. "I understand. Yes, that would be proper."

"Of course!"

The others sitting around the room tried not to snicker, but it was hard.

Monday morning, the sun came up and brightly shone down on the frozen ranch. After breakfast, Roger took Raylyn into the living room and asked, "When do you want to leave for Grand Rapids, Love?"

"Can we get out? Would there be a flight today?"

"I don't know, but we can sure find out."

Roger called the airline that they both had used to come to Billings. When Raylyn had secured her ticket, she had left the return open, so that all she had to do for her and Heidi was to find out when there was place available. However, Roger's ticket was for the Saturday still to come and it was to return to Atlanta. The agent for the airline informed him that he didn't have any space on any flight for three people to return to Grand Rapids until Wednesday. Roger was able to exchange his ticket over the phone, so he booked them for the flight on Wednesday. Going back to Grand Rapids however would make their arrival time well into the evening.

Heidi and her new grandparents had fallen in love with each other, so they were not the least bit unhappy to learn that they would stay two more days. When Lonnie called to confirm their flight back to St. Louis, he found that because of the storm last week and Christmas, their flight had been cancelled. They had to wait an extra day, so they would also be leaving on Wednesday. Mattie was in heaven having both her children and their chosen mate staying. Abby and Roger found themselves doing some of the traditional things they'd done as children.

However, all good things must come to an end. Wednesday came and with it a dreary day, but no snow or forecast of any at least for twenty-four hours. This time, to go to the airport, John drove his big six seater diesel truck so that they could all go together and still have room for all the luggage. They arrived at the airport in time to wave Abby and Lonnie through their check point, then the five that were left had lunch in one of the sandwich shops on the concourse before Mattie and John waved Roger, Raylyn and Heidi through their check point. The diesel felt mighty big and empty on the long drive back to the ranch later that afternoon.

On the flight back to Grand Rapids they watched the sun set and by the time they landed at the airport, it was dark, but the stars were out. Because their flight was during the dinner hour, they had served a light meal, but when they left the plane, Roger felt like he hadn't eaten since before breakfast. Now as they left the flight area, Roger was intent on finding another place to eat. They were able to find a fast food restaurant and bought some food to go then they went to the lower level to claim their luggage.

Now that Heidi had two dolls just alike, she had a hard time carrying them, especially when an adult was holding one hand. At the luggage claim, they had three suitcases and two carry-on bags, so Roger found a luggage trolley and put everything on it. There was still a bit of room, so before they went outside, Roger picked Heidi up and set her in front of him on the trolley. When he started to push it, Heidi clapped her hands and both dolls fell to the floor.

As Roger skidded to a stop, Heidi said, "Daddy, bof dollies fall down."

"I see that, Munchkin. I'll pick them up, but you must hold onto them very tightly because on the other side of that door we must cross a three lane street and Mommy and I must watch out for all the cars, so we can't be watching your dollies."

"I know, I hold 'em real tight."

"Okay, here we go!"

In the morning, Raylyn gave Roger directions to the place where he had called to rent a trailer for the one way trip to Vansville, Georgia. He left with the car and while he was gone, she and Heidi took down their Christmas decorations and put them in boxes. About an hour later Roger came back with the trailer hooked on behind. They immediately began loading the things that were to go south. Heidi's bedroom furniture went in first, along with several boxes of toys and books. Next, they loaded the things from the little bedroom, the loveseat that converted into a bed, Raylyn's computer and computer table and chair.

That was all the furniture they would take from the house, but there were boxes of clothes, books, knickknacks and dishes that Raylyn didn't want to part with. Last of all, they loaded their suitcases into the trunk. Raylyn breathed a sigh of relief when Roger pushed the trunk lid down and everything was in. She hadn't wanted to have to put anything on the back seat with Heidi except for her toys, dollies and books.

It was two o'clock when they pulled away from the house and they still had to make one stop before they could start on the trip south. Roger drove to the church that was purchasing the house and left the keys with the secretary. They hadn't taken time to eat lunch and as he went back to the car, his stomach growled. He remembered what Raylyn said about take out food with a three and a half year old, so he knew they wouldn't get on the road, out of town, until probably three o'clock. He sighed, that meant they would be making an overnight stop somewhere down the road. Not only that, driving with a trailer hitched on the back made going slower than just driving a car.

After stopping for lunch, Roger buckled Heidi in and slid behind the wheel. Raylyn looked at her watch and said, "At Thanksgiving I left at two o'clock and got to Grandma Isabel's at three. I napped for twenty minutes between Blairsville and Vansville. I don't think we can do that this time, though. You can't go as fast with that trailer on the back and we'll have to stop more often for gas. I guess that means we'll have to stop and get a motel."

"Yes, I think you're right, Love. It's Thursday, which isn't a heavy travel day, but it is between Christmas and New Year's so we still may have some trouble with finding a place. Should we go for as long as we can or decide to stop soon after supper?"

Her eyes twinkled as she said, "Honey, maybe you'd better decide, because as far as I'm concerned, I'd just as soon you did all the driving with that thing hanging on behind. It almost looks like it's sailing in the breeze."

Chuckling, Roger said, "Now you tell me! Let's see how I feel when it's suppertime."

Raylyn smiled, her eyes twinkling. "Okay, we're ready!"

Heidi looked at the two adults. She clapped her hands and said, "I ready, Daddy! We're gonna see Grandma and Gamaw!"

They made it to Knoxville and stopped for supper and gas. The restaurant was right next to the gas station, which made it easy. As Roger paid for the gas, a man in line behind him said, "You with that trailer out there?"

"Yes."

"You got a flat on it. You got a spare?"

Shaking his head, Roger said, "Not that I'm aware of. Guess I'll have to find a dealer or a service station that can fix it."

"You're in luck with the service station, there's one across on the other side of the interstate. I'm pretty sure they can fix little tires like that."

Shrugging, Roger said, "Thanks, I hadn't noticed any change, I thought it was the wind making the trailer sway like it was. I guess this little set back determines that we won't be driving straight through to Georgia."

The man smiled. "Guess you'd better find a place for the night, then."

Roger sighed, "Guess so."

It was almost noon when the travelers pulled onto Isabel's parking lot. Raylyn had called earlier and they had decided to eat lunch with Isabel and Ruth, then leave Heidi with them, while they took the trailer on to Roger's house and empty it there. When they returned it to Blairsville, Isabel insisted that they must come back to her house, she would treat for supper.

Roger pulled in, but made a big circle so he wouldn't have to back up with the trailer on. Raylyn looked at the cars in the lot and scowled. "Who does that third car belong to? I know Mom's and Grandma's, but whose is that other one?"

"That's Duncan Roads' car. He must have come back from his visit with his relatives. I thought he planned to stay until after New Year's. He's a big, strong fella, maybe I'll ask him to come help us empty this trailer. Taking that two-seater down the stairs to the family room doesn't sound like a fun thing for you and me."

"Yeah, it was a bit hard for us to carry back home."

The three of them went to Isabel's door and much to Roger's surprise, Duncan pulled the door open before Raylyn could knock. "Hi!" he said, in a booming voice. Heidi took one look at him and grabbed Roger's hand and held tightly.

"Hi, Duncan, you're back early, aren't you? Glad to see you!"

"Yeah, a day or two, come on in. I guess we're all guests of Isabel's for lunch, since you're here now."

"Yeah, we'll stop for lunch then head out to my place."

Duncan nodded, but he turned to Raylyn and said, "I guess you're Isabel's grand-daughter?" he said, holding out his hand to Raylyn. "I'm Isabel's tenant in her second cabin, Duncan Roads. Pleased to meet you."

"Yes, I'm Raylyn and this is Heidi, my daughter," Raylyn said, looking up at the huge man. "We're happy to meet you."

Ruth came into the living room when she heard talking. "Hi, everyone!"

Heidi saw her grandma, letting go of Roger's hand and spreading her arms, she ran and barreled into the lady's legs. "Grandma! I glad to see you!"

"Hi, Precious! It's good to see you! Are you ready for lunch?"

"Uh huh, Daddy be ready, too. He be hungry real bad, his tummy growl."

"We'd better feed him, hadn't we?"

Raylyn also went to her mom and hugged her. The three ladies wandered off to the kitchen, but Duncan turned and looked from Roger back to Raylyn and Heidi. Scowling, he said to Roger, "Did I miss something while I was gone? Did that child call you daddy just now?"

Roger chuckled and also watched the disappearing back of his fiancee'. "Yup, you missed it while you were gone. Over Thanksgiving, I snagged me the most beautiful lady in all the world and got the added bonus of her little girl thrown in. We're getting married a week from tomorrow at my church. You're invited."

Duncan shook his head. "Not me! I don't do church or any other kind of worship. I'm a confirmed atheist."

"Let me get this right. You're working with Ramon and Sandy's the receptionist for the both of you and you're a confirmed atheist?"

"Absolutely!"

Mysteriously, Roger said, "We'll see."

* * * * * * * * *

Sandy sat at the piano in the little church on the corner in Vansville. Lovely music came from her hands, as she played a long prelude for people to walk into the church. Outside it was cold, but the sun was out and there was no snow on the ground. The church was filling up, after all, the townspeople wanted to see their pastor get married. Of course, by two o'clock, the post office was officially closed, but because of such a special day, both the hardware store and Alex's grocery store were closed.

At two o'clock, Sandy stopped playing the music she had in front of her and began an introduction, then lifted her hands from the keys and sang, without any accompaniment, a lovely song to the bride and groom. After her song, she started playing again and a young man escorted Isabel to her seat and sat down beside her. Another young man followed them and also sat with them. Roger had never met Raylyn's brothers until they drove into town from the airport in a rental car the day before.

John brought Mattie down the aisle and Lonnie followed them. When the family members were seated, Sandy began playing the wedding march. The pastor from Isabel's church opened Roger's office door and led Roger, Ramon and Duncan to the front of the church. At the same time, Abby, who had become fast friends with Raylyn during their visit to Billings, started down the aisle. Heidi, in a lovely blue gown, followed her new auntie down the aisle. Roger had never seen her walk so slowly and carefully since he'd known her. She was sprinkling petals, but she was also Raylyn's Maid of Honor. Last of all, Ruth appeared at the back door and soon, Raylyn moved beside her and took her arm. As soon as Heidi reached the front of the church, she looked up and looked at the handsome man close by. Her new daddy smiled at her. Of course, Heidi smiled back. Sandy stopped playing the march, but then started over, playing the piece more loudly. Everyone stood as Ruth brought Raylyn down the aisle.

"Oh, my!" Roger murmured, under his breath. His breath stalled in his chest. He had never seen his lovely lady look so exquisite.

Ruth, Raylyn and Heidi had gone shopping during the week and Roger hadn't been welcome to go along. The dress Raylyn wore was lovely, it covered everything, but hinted at everything a redblooded American man could imagine. Ruth and Raylyn reached the front and Ruth took Roger's hand and placed Raylyn's in it.

"Who gives this woman to be married to this man?" the pastor asked.

"I do!" Ruth said, fervently.

Heidi stood quietly just as she was supposed to until the pastor said, "Roger, you may kiss your bride."

Heidi's hands erupted as she threw both her basket with the petals and Raylyn's bouquet at the front seat and rushed up beside Raylyn. "Daddy! You gots to kiss me, too! Mommy and me be a package, you know."

Roger never missed a beat. He kept his eyes on his lovely bride and put the short veil over her hat, then drew her into his arms and kissed her. After their lips separated, he moved a fraction and keeping Raylyn in one arm he scooped Heidi up with his other and placed a kiss on her cheek. Heidi, of course, moved from his kiss and placed her own, big slobbery smack on Roger's cheek, then rubbed it in. There wasn't a dry eye in the house after that.

The little family turned as a unit to face the gathering. The pastor swallowed and said, "Friends, I'd like to introduce to you your pastor, Reverend and Mrs. Roger Clemens and Heidi. May they have many happy years together as pastor of this church."

As the pastor finished speaking, the entire assembly stood up, clapping loudly.

www.ingramcontent.com/pod-product-compliance
Lightning Source LLC
Chambersburg PA
CBHW030316100526
44592CB00010B/463